By Patience and Perseverance, and a Bottle of Sweet Oil

Grandpa`s War Volume 1

BY PATIENCE AND PERSEVERANCE, AND A BOTTLE OF SWEET OIL

Grandpa`s War Volume 1

George West

Transcribed and edited by Effie Cadwallader

YOUCAXTON PUBLICATIONS
OXFORD & SHREWSBURY

Copyright © George West 2020
The Author asserts the moral right to be identified as the author of this work.
ISBN 978-1-913425-36-4
Published by YouCaxton Publications 2020
YCBN: 01

YouCaxton Publications
enquiries@youcaxton.co.uk

Contents

INTRODUCTION 1

ONE – Patriotism or Expediency 5

TWO – A "Terrier" 9

THREE – Camp 12

FOUR – Convoy 17

FIVE – Called to the Colours 23

SIX – In Limbo 28

SEVEN – The First Move, to Yarm 33

EIGHT – The Battle of Danby`s Yard 41

NINE – The Second Move and We`re On Our Way to War 44

TEN – Vive La France 50

ELEVEN – War Zone: The Somme 1914-18 55

TWELVE – Bombed! 61

THIRTEEN – The Rot Sets In 70

FOURTEEN – Leaving Bécourt 80

FIFTEEN – Retreat 86

SIXTEEN – Dunkirk 94

SEVENTEEN – Home Again 102

THE INTERVAL 109

EIGHTEEN – Life on the South Coast and some Nasty Doings 111

NINETEEN – Not Quite the Dunkirk Spirit 121

TWENTY – The Stately Home and Clerk i/c 128

TWENTY ONE – Local Relations 135

TWENTY TWO – Bristol Bombed 141

TWENTY THREE – Promotion 146

TWENTY FOUR – An Unpleasant Incident 150

TWENTY FIVE – Leave, and the Last Few Months in Blighty 155

TWENTY SIX – Farewell Britain 162

TWENTY SEVEN – Finally We Arrive 169

TWENTY EIGHT – First Port of Call, and On 174

TWENTY NINE – Civilisation Again, Of Sorts 181

THIRTY—Cape Town 189

APPENDIX – Dad`s Box 199

INTRODUCTION

The Second World War finished many years ago. During the first ten to fifteen years after 1945 a lot of war books were written "hot off the press" by men whose memories were very vivid. Some wanted to tell the world all about it; cathartic, perhaps. Others wanted to put the facts straight while their readers could still remember what it was all about, and, human nature being what it is, not a few wanted to cash in on a very popular story line.

I read all the war books I could find. Most of them suited my taste and I enjoyed them. The writers in the first category were impressive if not a little fanciful at times, but I forgave them that: they'd survived to tell the tale. Those in the second category I found particularly interesting because they produced facts, well backed up by cross references to war diaries and Imperial War Museum papers, or an interview with General This, Air Marshall That, or Admiral The Other. Having been a small cog in the very big wheel of wartime forces, I found their information solved several puzzles and, I suppose, my chief reaction to all this group had to say was something like, "Well, fancy that," or "So that's why!"

The authors in the third category sometimes annoyed me, although I continued to read their books. I couldn't help wondering if they had actually been where they said they had because our paths crossed occasionally and, comparing the events in their version, I could only imagine that I had spent the time in a deep coma. Perhaps I'm eating sour grapes: maybe I should have written my story earlier instead of being certified to teach little boys and girls.

"Why, then, are you doing it now?" you may ask.

Why, indeed, after all these years and retired from the world of education? I haven't a conclusive answer, nor even a sensible one. Simply, I would like to string together a chronicle of memories for the interest and enjoyment of anyone who wants to read a narrative not of substantiated facts, nor of the movements of troops and warlike hardware, nor even a story which tells the tale of my Division, Brigade, Company or Unit. It is simply a series of episodes which happened to me between 1939-1946. Some of these events gave me great pleasure, some hurt me, some puzzled me, and an awful lot terrified me.

The account unfolding in these pages makes no reference to official documents of any kind or even to personal diaries. It is a story from memory. Whilst I have not been deliberately untruthful, inaccuracies of fact are sure to be detected should anyone check an official record. I make no apologies for such mistakes: it is my story as I remember it.

I conclude my Introduction by saying, as I`ve often said to those who have asked me about my wartime experiences, "I would have enjoyed myself a lot more if I`d known I was going to survive." Taking into account that I was one of fourteen out of the original two hundred and forty men in my Company who were not taken prisoner, or wounded, or transferred, or killed, or who fell by the wayside, you will see that my observation has added significance.

George West 1980

"By Patience and Perseverance, and a Bottle of Sweet Oil"

Grandpa`s War

Part 1

Dress Uniform Royal Engineers.

CHAPTER ONE – Patriotism or Expediency

I turned nineteen on 2nd January 1939, having lived a closeted and narrow upbringing with my elderly parents, lifelong and staunch Methodists. I am grateful to the army, in some respects, for having given me an understanding of people and situations which I might never otherwise have met. I am not critical of Methodism, any more than I would be of any other form of worship, but maturity and my subsequently widened experience of life did cause me some wry smiles when I considered the vehement rantings of Ministers and Lay Preachers against the evils of drink, gambling, swearing and riotous living, not to mention that subject darkly hinted at but never referred to, the awful three lettered word "sex." My rude awakening was still to come, however, because in January 1939 I still thought that "Pygmalion" should be banned because of its bad language. What a laugh!

On this birthday I was working for a local coal company and, not being unintelligent, had risen to the dizzy heights of Junior Clerk in the Accounts Department. My future seemed rosy, too, because I'd been accepted by the Institute of Company Accountants as a student member, confirmed by a beautiful certificate adorned with the official seal. My sights and efforts were set on the Intermediate Examination, but all this was being put in jeopardy by a chap called Hitler.

Accounts Clerk, Harton Coal Company, South Shields. 1939.

His antics on the continent had prompted our Government to announce that by the end of March 1939 anyone not enrolled in one of the Auxiliary Forces would be called up for a six months period of National Service, or go down the pit. The former proposition didn't appeal to me at all: I wanted to work, to study and pass my exams, and National Service for six months was certainly going to delay that ambition. The second option horrified me as an employee of a coal company. I knew the working conditions of miners in those days, not to mention their pay, or lack of it.

There was only one answer: join the Auxiliary Forces double quick. I pondered the possibilities of this during the next Sunday service and as the sermon concerned one of Paul's journeys by sea to Macedonia, I felt this to be a suitable omen. Navy blue was a sober Methodist colour and the gold stripes wouldn't be too gaudy, not to begin with anyway, so I made my way along to H.M.S. Satellite.

H.M.S. Satellite looked like a warship and was run like one by the very efficient R.N.V.R. The fact that she had no engines was not a deterrent to me. I presented myself to the officer in charge of recruitment. He was all I would have expected of the Senior Service: charming, polite, and every inch an insurance agent in sub lieutenant's clothing. I think he really meant it when he told me their complement was complete: in fact, they had more crews in reserve than there were ships afloat, even those without engines.

I was disappointed but navy blue would have accentuated my pallid complexion anyway. Perhaps a paler shade of blue would be better.

A bus carried me the rather round about journey to Woolsington, a Royal Air Force base, to try my luck. I found my way without difficulty, chiefly by following others with a similar objective to my own. On the base, the uniform looked grand and those in it young and busily active.

The Recruitment Officer was quite emphatic about my possible enlistment. "An Observer if your maths is good enough, possibly with a commission, or a tail gunner."

My maths wasn't bad but I was reluctant to trust other people's lives with it, not to mention my own. As for a tail gunner ... no, I wasn't going to war backwards. If I had to go up, or down, I preferred to see where I was going.

I declined the light blue uniform and became one of the first of the few to be brought down before ever going up.

And what was there left? I'd read so many war stories of the "P.B.I." and "Cannon Fodder," and somehow khaki wasn't at all the colour I'd visualised myself wearing, but time was passing. What about the cavalry? After all, Churchill had ridden on horseback somewhere or other, and there was a drill room located in my home town, with stables. Not only that, but I had learned to ride during one "Holidays At Home" fortnight.

At the Territorial Drill Hall everything smelled very antiseptic and not a hoof mark in sight. The cavalry turned out to be the Artillery and the pawing chargers in the stables were "ugly bloody great towing vehicles called Quads, mate, wot took the place of the cuddies," said the Sergeant in charge of recruits.

It was quite disheartening: nothing was working out. I didn`t want the Quads of the Artillery: they were ugly, noisy and smelly. Little did I know, when I walked out of the drill hall in disgust, that one of those very Quads would save my life in the not so distant future!

Nine days of March passed by and on the morning of the 10th one of the younger members of the Goods Department at the coal company came to work in his army uniform. That was unusual but it seemed he had to go straight to the Territorial Hall at the end of the day to carry out his weekly "drill." He was the centre of attraction, however, because his uniform was different. It was new and it was battledress, something not seen at first hand by many of the old sweats, nor anyone else in the office for that matter.

It was Stan who remarked, as I fingered the ghastly rough material and shuddered at the cut, "Didn`t you want to get in somewhere? There`s a vacancy in the Royal Engineers at Jarrow for a clerk."

The Royal Engineers …I`d never thought of them. They weren`t P.B.I. or cannon fodder: they were specialists. They dug wells, built bridges and carried out drainage for ablutions well behind the lines; safe, comfortable, no bangs or horrible things to do in the night, and a clerk, my own job. What could be better? I arranged to meet Stan outside the drill hall in Jarrow that night.

He was there waiting for me in that appalling ill-fitting battledress, but by then I wasn`t choosy: I couldn`t afford to be. We went in. Groups of other battledress were standing around the large arena. Along one side were doors marked with strange script like "2 i/c" or "QMS" or "Mess", and two doors next to each other labelled "O/ranks" and "Officers Only," both for identical use, even to stance, but it was a crime to pass through the wrong portal no matter how desperate the urgency.

We entered the room marked "Coy Off." Inside not an occupant could be said to be coy. Their language, in fact, was most forthright and to me at that time, quite unintelligible.

Stan introduced me to the "Sa`arnt Major," or rather he announced me as the "silly sod who wants to be a clerk."

The Company Sergeant Major, to give him his full title, looked me up and down and even walked round me.

He asked, "Can you drive?"

I confessed that I could.

"Sign there, lad," ordered this man of power and authority. In a trance, I signed.

7

"Come with me. We'll swear you in before the O.C.," was his next instruction.

My father was a freemason and took his secrets to the grave, but at this tense moment I felt that his initiation could have had nothing on mine. I certainly had a few misgivings about the swearing part, being brought up strictly Chapel. With a Bible in one hand (Ye Gods, what hypocrisy!) and ("Repeat after me") an incantation spoken so rapidly that it could just have easily have been "Georgy Porgy, pudding and pie", I swore allegiance to King and Country until death do us part.

I was in.

Years afterwards, when my own children had reached the age of understanding, I made quite certain that each knew never ever to sign any document before reading it through fully, no matter how long it took or how inconvenient it might be to the one waiting for it. I insisted on this because, on the evening of 10th March 1939, I signed enrolment papers for the army as a clerk, only to find on 11th March 1939 that I had enlisted as a driver. My gamble of joining up early didn't pay off either because, having done my full quota of drills and a fortnight's camp, I was called up on 1st September 1939, long before many of my contemporaries who were drafted in via National Service.

CHAPTER TWO – A "Terrier"

Could anyone who has been in the forces work up any enthusiasm about drills? There would, no doubt, be some, but to the vast majority drill meant the boredom of standardised movements, in unison, carried out as per instructions in the Army Manual of Training. It was expected that soldiers would, for interminable periods of time, march in threes, form threes, about turn, left turn, wheel to the right and left and, the most useless movement of all, "Salute on the March." This latter gem of drill book idiosyncrasy I never saw used in any practical form. Only since the war have I recognised its significance when the fewer and fewer surviving veterans march past the Cenotaph on Remembrance Sunday and do their best, arthritis permitting, to carry out this movement.

Whenever the Sa`arnt screamed, "Section will salute on the march" I was hard pressed to control the laughter which was welling up inside me because I knew the chaos which would inevitably result. Common sense, one would imagine, might penetrate even the thickest Drill Sergeant`s head, suggesting that to move in one direction whilst looking in another must surely cause problems. One of our first attempts resulted in the leading section marching full tilt into the wall because the order to halt or turn about froze on the sergeant`s lips in horror at the catastrophe he was about to create, and many times after that people lost their shoes or had their trousers ripped by those who inadvertently trod on the heels of the man in front. Nevertheless, we persisted in our efforts to salute Earl Haig to the left and His Majesty to the right.

Eventually, some higher authority gave instructions that our drill could extend to include rifles. There were not enough of these for everyone so we performed rifle drill in small sections. And what a performance! Herr Schickelgruber would have felt pretty confident of victory had he put an agent in our midst.

I was elated the day I was issued with a rifle. I was now in the Modern Army because it was dated 1918.

Being issued with a rifle for drill was an honour, not something to be treated lightly. In a two hour period we drilled for half the time: the rest was taken up with the elaborate business of queuing for, signing for, and collecting The Gun, and then its eventual return in like manner.

Apart from the weight of the rifle and my fumbling attempts to move it to the correct part of my anatomy according to the "one, two, hup" counts, I was also very much put out by the amount of grease and oil which seemed necessary for its preservation. These lubricants left ugly stains on my sports jacket and trousers, sometimes even penetrating through to my shirt and underclothes. Nor did it ever cease to amaze me that no matter which gun the armourer gave me it was always filthy down the barrel – and even more so after I`d cleaned it! Strangely enough, I could never see this dirt, but the Drill Sergeant could. The sight of it turned him puce, much to my consternation, for I feared for the poor man`s health over this completely unexpected discovery!

I`ve mentioned my Methodist upbringing earlier, to illustrate that such a training for life was not really adequate for what I was now facing. I was both innocent and naïve, and an example of this is amongst my many memories of those drill periods so long ago.

Though I did my best, the difficulty I found placing the left foot forward, followed by the right, then moving both regularly to comply with commands which turned us this way and that in what should have been smooth precision, wasn`t an easy process for me to master.

One day, in my exasperation, I replied, "I`m a left-footer" to the question which, with a number of four letter oaths removed, was basically, "Why can`t you keep in step?"

What I probably ought to have said was, "I have two left feet," but in the frustration of the moment I had, quite unknowingly, confessed to being of the Roman Catholic faith – and me, of Methodist stock!

This simple and innocuous remark had an astonishing effect on the assembled company. You could have heard a pin drop. I hadn`t yet become aware that the towns of Jarrow and Hebburn at that time were a "hotbed" (which sounds better than "breeding ground") of Catholics and Orangemen. Their attitude to one another, particularly after a drink, was predictable, and here was I making a proud and public announcement that my allegiance was to Rome. In my innocence, I was ignorant of the expression that a "left footer" was a staunch Roman Catholic. Of course, those Catholics on parade muttered to themselves, "One of us. Reinforcements!" The Orangemen looked at me darkly as though I`d asked them to subscribe to the Pope`s birthday present. Fortunately, I had a friend, an agnostic since birth, who explained later and, at the earliest opportunity, I passed the word around that Charles Wesley was my second cousin twice removed and hoped for the best. I wasn`t 100% successful because there were those who bore me malice until my demob day.

It might be said that, as the weeks went by, we became more experienced and not only in military matters.

Most of the training in those early days was difficult for everyone. The Territorial Army had had expansion thrust upon it rather suddenly and the junior officers and N.C.O.s were neither prepared nor sufficiently organised to cope with the enormous changes. They struggled manfully but they were having to readjust from the peacetime activities of "playing at soldiers" to the rather more serious demands being made upon them to bring the Unit onto a wartime footing, ready for possible action. There was even some talk of the Hun as an enemy, and in the rifle range the roundel targets were replaced with Hitler in a coal scuttle helmet! It became increasingly obvious that someone sooner or later was going to get shot at, and it might be sooner. We`d had the surprise of Austria being incorporated into the Greater Reich, "willingly, for its own protection", we were told by Goebbels. Next, Czechoslovakia was "welcomed" into the fold, despite our sabre rattling and verbal support. The Poles knew they were next on the list to be given "protection for their own good" by Hitler and his henchmen. Should this move come about, our role was certain: we should fly to their assistance. The very thought of the boys from Jarrow in their ill-fitting khaki, flinging their might at the seemingly unstoppable rejuvenated German forces made the mind boggle. The only strength in our armoury was that we could salute Earl Haig on the left and His Majesty on the right, but certainly not with arms sloped. Those rifles had been re-oiled and returned to the armoury lest they get dirty.

CHAPTER THREE – Camp

In July 1939 we went to camp at Halton, Lancashire. To me this was really something, an adventure, the nearest thing to war conditions. We would have to show our mettle and prove that the Territorial Army expansion was on target. The people of Britain would see that they could confidently rest safely in their beds at night.

I don't remember much about the journey from Tyneside to Halton other than that it was made in army vehicles, few of which belonged to our company and none driven by our drivers.

The camp was a few miles outside Lancaster. Rows and rows of bell tents spread across the huge field, down a gentle slope to the river. To one side were marquee tents housing the Company Office and Quartermaster's Stores, Mess, and Guard House. Outside this last mentioned a Union Jack fluttered on the flag pole. Behind were other tents in an area known as the "Officers' Quarters", a sort of Holy of Holies. Officers at this time were

Halton Camp, Lancashire. August 1939.
Vehicle Park in the distance.

still wearing Service Dress with brightly polished Sam Brownes, and those of Field Rank paraded in breeches and riding boots, with sword. They certainly looked smart and dignified but pitifully out-of-date.

On the other side of this great field was the Vehicle Park, half empty on our arrival but by the end of the day filled with vehicles to bring up the strength, temporarily anyway, of two Field Companies and a Field Park Company.

Installed down by the river were those most

Ablutions. Halton Camp. August 1939.

interesting and vital of army amenities, "The Ablutions," in this case, four lines of taps fixed above zinc covered troughs and I was shocked to discover that the "inner sancta" were no more than Hessian screens surrounding holes in the ground. Though I didn't know it at the time, those primitive facilities were vastly better than many I was to enjoy during the next seven years.

At times during the fortnight we camped it rained, and the rain came through that part of the bell tent under which I slept. No sympathy or assistance was shown or offered to me by the other occupants who had very rapidly learned the phrase, "I'm all right, Jack," which cuts across all principles.

The rain turned the entire area into a quagmire which, for part of the time, stopped any movement of transport, this being in the days before four-wheel drive vehicles. Unfortunately, it also meant that we were forever polishing our boots to satisfy the Drill Sergeants, whose own boots seemed impervious to the mud and rain.

As drivers we were not called upon to take part in bridging training which took place daily, all day, on the river, where the sappers erected and dismantled pontoon bridges ad infinitum.

One day, I watched the process which involved a pontoon being manoeuvred out of position by a sapper "walking" it back, away from the bridge. The Lance Corporal in charge was slow to stop the movement and to my horror and, I must confess, my amusement, his poor assistant walked off the end of the pontoon. This floated rapidly away down river, disappearing into quite deep water. Chaos reigned while the sapper was rescued. I did wonder how all this would work under battle conditions, but then I was a driver, so what did it matter.

When the ground had dried out a little, part of our drivers' training was to take each vehicle in turn round a course laid out over a very rough corner of the vehicle park. The 30 cwt lorry was quite easy to handle because it had such a low gear that we could almost get out and walk. The course was so designed that we seldom got this vehicle into third gear so there were no problems. The 15 cwt wasn't too difficult to drive either: again, the gears were low and quite manageable once we had mastered the art of double de-clutching. Fortunately, I have always had a natural ability to drive anything. Double de-clutching didn't worry me as much as it did the others who crashed whole vehicles with the same abandon as they crashed their gears.

One vehicle, however, was diabolical and remained so for as long as it lasted in the Unit. The Ford P.U. which, as far as I know stood for "Pick Up," was for the use of each officer, with a driver provided. I couldn`t begin to try and explain all the faults of this vehicle other than to say that it was too small, too light and really not much more than a flashy, speedy conveyance for two people and their kit. To me it always seemed that the very powerful V8 engine was not mechanically compatible with the gearbox and transmission, not to mention its small body. Had the gears been synchromesh it would have been a useful machine. As it was, the gearbox was "straight" and the only sure way of changing gear without the most appalling clang was to come to a standstill before moving the gear lever – an impossible movement, as any driver will appreciate. Mind you, when the little beggar got going (that is, if we gritted our teeth and crashed through the gearbox into top) a very high speed was possible and the steering was as light as a feather.

Everyone who had one of these pickups eventually took it into the Ordnance Workshops because of a most jarring bump which developed in the front end. The reason was simple: the heavy V8 engine was mounted on a very soft front suspension. The cause of the metallic bump was a bulky round crossbar which, when the vehicle was brand new, ran through the middle of a hole in a flat member at each side of the housing, none of which seemed to serve a useful purpose. After a short time, the round metal bar no long ran though the centre of this hole: it rested near the top edge and every slight unevenness in the road surface caused an irritating metal clang. On my suggestion, the CO had the hole elongated on the P.U. I was given to drive in France. Result: no more bump and no loss of efficiency. Our P.U. trucks were not six months old when we lost them all at Dunkirk, so after that it was something for the Germans to worry about.

A Red Letter Day arrived when a person of high rank paid us a visit at our mid-day meal. We got the feeling in advance that something was different about dinner that day. Perhaps it was the tablecloths which covered the usually greasy, stained, deal trestles. Maybe the flowers on the tables, glasses and water jugs gave a hint. The cooks certainly looked strange in spotless white. Perhaps they had boiled their food-encrusted aprons to put a little body into the soup.

A long delay before the serving dishes arrived, piping hot, heralded "The Brass." The great man, all smiles and surrounded by honoured acolytes and a proud Orderly Officer, made his way from table to table. The dazzling red tabs were awesome to us lowly recruits. Here was power, authority and the holder of our destinies.

"A good dinner, sapper?" or "Aren`t you fortunate to be in this mess?" (I found that just a trifle ambiguous), "We must see you are well fed, mustn`t we?"

There was no answer to that, as the condemned man must have thought as he walked to the scaffold.

It took our gallant leader quite a while to beam on everyone and make his remarks, which were as tasteless as our food. Meanwhile, we sat at attention (a glorious drill movement that!) and looked forward to his passing. Eventually, we were screamed at to "Sit Easy," then "At Ease," then "Carry On." The food had cooled somewhat but it was still undoubtedly different and unusually plentiful. We revelled in this wonderful change of fortune: at least we new ones did. The old sweats smiled knowingly.

The next day we knew, too. Deal tables, bare, soldiers for the use, no tablecloths, no flowers, tin cups, and "Collect your own water if there`s any left." And the food: stone cold, greasy and scarce. The Orderly Officer came in at one end of the marquee and beat all records to get out at the other end.

Later in the war this indifference to the conditions suffered by the ordinary soldier would never happen. In my experience in the Division in which I served, the officers and N.C.O.s moved heaven and earth to ensure the welfare and comfort of their men.

This period, however, and up to the time when we came back from Dunkirk, was certainly not one of those to remember with pleasure or pride. The gulf between the commissioned rank and the "other ranks," a term which itself could have been better chosen, was comparable to the state of the Maharajah and the Indian Untouchables. I know: I was one of the other ranks and I resented very much the method of "breaking them in" or "instilling a bit of discipline into this shower," both expressions I actually heard. Between these two levels were the senior N.C.O.s, most of them of long standing and not a few who were too old to go overseas eventually. Annoyingly, they did nothing to improve our lot when they could easily have done so. Their treatment of the men was sometimes unbelievably unintelligent, even sadistic. Equally, their attitude to commissioned rank was embarrassingly subservient. The result was that all three levels were poles apart and none understood or got close to any other, with rather tragic results when the testing time of battle came along.

There were exceptions, as there always are to any rule, but those exceptions were, in my experience, few and far between. Eventually senior ranks learned the lesson, and attitudes, behaviour, integrity and understanding completely changed when tempered by the furnace heat of war. It`s probable that had this not been so we would not have survived the conflict as victors.

Rather grumpy! Halton Camp. August 1939. Side cap.

In civvies with Larry Sanderson and Alan Thompson. Halton Camp. August 1939.

CHAPTER FOUR – Convoy

The day of "The Convoy" was a day to remember because at long last we, the section of drivers, were to be given our chance to show our mettle. We had not been fully employed in the activities of the camp up to then. Apart from some "driving instruction," which frequently proved the ability of the pupils and the failings of the instructors, most of our time had been taken up with domestic tasks: cleaning, scrubbing and polishing and, believe me, there is no better taskmaster than the army when it comes to cleaning, scrubbing and polishing. When all else fails and if there is still time left, clean it, scrub it and polish it - again. However, now it was our turn. We would drive our vehicles, in convoy, by map reference, as part of a proper exercise. Everyone, officers, sergeants, corporals and W.O.1s, would be practising their role in this great machine and, best of all, we would achieve the satisfaction of a job well done.

The minimum establishment of transport for a unit of Engineers was, at that time, something like one P.U. truck for the officer in charge of each of the three sections and one for the Commanding Officer and his Second in Command at Company Headquarters, one 30 cwt. six wheeled lorry and two 15 cwt. trucks for the movement of essential stores per section, plus two motorcycles for despatch riders, and a bicycle for local shopping!

When we left the drill hall in Jarrow our actual fleet was one 15 cwt. truck and a one ton lorry impressed from the local fish man who had, very obviously, got the best part of the bargain, so it was quite exciting to be marched through the lines of gleaming new vehicles in their camouflage matt paint at the Transport Park and introduced to our issue, more or less just as I've listed. I say "more or less" because the motorcycles had not been delivered, and one P.U. officers' truck had been damaged removing it from the flat-car at the station.

We marched in threes round a huge field past rows of army lorries, stopping at each one (at attention, of course!) while two names were read out. The two named would fall out to stand alongside their new charge. The section moved on, becoming smaller and smaller, until the last six men had faces as long as the distance they'd marched, and I was one of them. I was guessing that, just my luck, one of the non-existent motorcycles would be my allocation, or possibly the P.U., officers for the use of, with the prolapse, but no, the Transport Sergeant stopped, consulted his list and called my name. I`d made it! I`d been allocated a real motor vehicle, ready for war. Well, nearly, because it turned out that I was "second driver," which meant that I was not actually in charge of the truck, but I would drive if the first driver let me or he dropped dead. Nevertheless, it was a start: I had a seat even if it wasn`t the driver`s. I was, however, a little apprehensive about the vehicle – a 15 cwt compressor truck, i.e. a 15 cwt truck chassis with a compressor engine fixed on the back, to be used for drilling holes, cracking concrete or banging in piles, etc. After brief introductions I learned that the first driver was a Presbyterian Minister`s son: what a combination – both the driver and the vehicle full of wind!

We introduced ourselves because my driver wasn`t from the same Unit, and swiftly arrived at the conclusion that we had absolutely nothing in common and would be happy to part company as soon as possible, the sooner the better as far as I was concerned.

A short time later a bevy of officers and N.C.O.s came round with maps and instructions about the proposed convoy movement on our exercise. No troops were being carried in our vehicles: they were for stores only and, of course, convoy drill. I looked forward to all of this. It sounded challenging and stimulating and, best of all, it was doing something constructive: being a soldier, part of a unit formed to protect our country from those who might try to do us harm. I had joined up partly from patriotic motives after all, and I didn`t really like playing at soldiers all the time, not to mention all that cleaning, scrubbing and polishing.

On reflection, I think that the reverend`s son had some influence "higher up" somewhere and I certainly wasn`t sorry about that. Within a short time I had discovered that his attitude to life and the opposite sex were a revelation and his language electric. For the next seven years I was to learn an almost new vocabulary, particularly adjectives, but in those early days army language was, to me, quite horrifying. In this instance it was made worse by its utterance from the most unlikely source, the son of a man of the cloth. Thankfully, a name was called across the park and my undesirable partner left to go elsewhere; I knew not where, nor did I care. I promoted myself to the driving seat determined to be in charge.

Our own M.T. sergeant approached the row of vehicles and gave the "start up" signal. This was repeated all round the field by N.C.O.s from the other companies. What an impressive sound this produced as first one then another and another of the trucks burst into life. A blue smelly haze hung over the whole park as two Field Companies and a Field Park

Company of Engineers prepared to move en masse for the very first time. I was a little bothered about being on my own and would, therefore, have to drive, map read and do anything else required without help, but I could do it, I was sure.

The vehicles had all been loaded the day before by the sappers, a few of whom were detailed to ride postillion, so to speak, but no-one was sent across to me, although I half expected it, my truck having such a vital and complicated piece of machinery in the back.

The next signal was to move out in the order indicated by the officer in charge of the convoy. He stood on the bonnet of his P.U. and issued orders to his sergeant who bawled instructions to his corporals strategically placed near their own lines of vehicles, and slowly the convoy formed up and snaked its way to the exit and out onto the main road.

No instruction came my way, so it appeared that I was going to be somewhere near the end of the line which I found comforting because then I wouldn't have to do much more than follow.

It took a while and the field was almost empty, yet still I hadn't been summoned to move. A last vehicle crawled out onto the road and I stared around the vast expanse of churned up turf. Four lonely trucks remained. One had a puncture and there was no spare wheel. Two had their bonnets off and the drivers were heads down, bottoms up, furiously trying to get the brutes going. And one single compressor truck, not near any other vehicle at all, with me in it, quite stationary.

Everyone had gone and no-one came near me so it seemed only sensible to switch off the engine. What an inglorious anti-climax. I felt so disappointed. I also knew I had a tedious period to fill in, as the convoy and everybody in it wouldn't be back until much later in the day. There was no tool kit on the vehicle, or reading matter, not even a handbook: they didn't exist.

As no-one had given me any orders I supposed that I wasn't absolutely obliged to stay on the field with the compressor truck all day. On the other hand, to walk away across the open space would be very obvious and if anyone in authority was about I would be sure to attract attention.

After half an hour of utter boredom I decided I'd have a walk across to the mess tent and see if I could get a drink. Before I could make this move, however, I saw a party of uniforms approaching. Surely they weren't interested in me? Have you ever seen anyone look over his shoulder when he cannot believe he is the one being addressed? I did that. There was nothing behind me but the whole of Lancashire and the group was definitely coming my way. With a ghastly shock I realised that the group was headed by a Brass Hat, red tabs, polished boots and all. Goodness knows who he was, I never actually found out, but he was important and he stopped in front of me. I threw up my best salute which, through inexperience and shock, was pretty sloppy.

"On your own, driver?" Now wouldn`t you expect him to say that?!

"What a pity. Useful little truck you`ve got there, eh?"

"Yes, sir." I might as well match intelligent questions with intelligent answers.

"Easy to handle, I should think?"

"Yes, sir." The truth surely: I`d had no difficulty handling it so far.

"Well, let`s see the equipment it has, Driver." I liked the fatherly manner, the title "Driver" and the honour of being singled out for attention – not difficult really when there wasn`t anyone else around.

I hopped up onto the back and opened one of the big side toolboxes marked "Drills." It was extremely well fitted out with racks to hold the different drills so they wouldn`t move in transit, but there were no drills! It was quite empty. We all looked at it with varying degrees of surprise – Brigadier, Adjutant, a couple of lieutenants, a sergeant, and me.

"I`ll try the other side, Sir," I said weakly.

The same empty void greeted our gaze. There were other boxes around the back but they, too, were quite empty. I was hoping that I wasn`t going to be charged with their loss but no-one said anything, although the Brigadier`s supporters were obviously discomfited.

"We`d better see if the compressor works for the great day when we do get the tools," smiled the nice old gentleman.

At that moment I started to go off him: he wasn`t saying the right things at all.

Start it up? Goodness, what was I to do? I`d certainly started the vehicle engine but I`d never considered that the compressor engine was my responsibility at all. My idea was that some sapper would do that. By chance, during my half hour`s loneliness, I`d read the instruction plates beside the levers and knobs between the seats which were obviously meant to engage the compressor to the engine of the truck. The group gathered round and glared so I had to make a move. The starting handle soon got the engine running, I let in the clutch, moved a lever, eased out the clutch pedal and – success! The little engine on the back groaned, wobbled and began to chug in unison with the main vehicle mechanism. I'd done it, first time! It was quite touching to see the expressions on the faces of the group. The glares relaxed into something almost resembling smiles. I wasn't being awkward, I wasn't as thick as two short planks – one maybe, but not two – and I did know what I was doing, it seemed.

"Good lad," laughed the Brigadier. "What a little beauty." For a moment I hoped he wasn't being personal.

This spurred me on to better things and I increased the revs.

Suddenly I thought, "If this thing is compressing air, how much and where?"

There was a dial on the back so I dashed round to have a look at it. Zero. Not a flicker of the needle. Afraid that someone else would tumble to this and I'd be exposed, I began twisting knobs and moving levers – all of them. The needle flickered. I'd started the compression of air, although I'd no idea how.

"We must get some tools for your little machine," I was told by the great man.

Very decent of him, I thought: just what I'd wanted all my life. But my immediate concern was what was happening inside this little machine. I was standing, at the salute, with the engine chugging away behind me, waiting for the cluster of commissions to depart, which they were obviously about to do. I could sense the moment. It happened quite suddenly when interest evaporated and, like doctors at the end of a hospital bed, they began chatting amongst themselves as though I didn't exist.

The message was confirmed when the Brigadier turned on the youngest lieutenant with the full benefit of his charm and the words, "Your turn to buy the drinks, Rodney."

Rodney worked up a sickly smile, essential when a Brigadier speaks, and they turned to go. Rodney's smile fell off like a shutter descending as he walked at the rear, no doubt calculating his bank balance.

When the gaggle had gone a safe distance I stood myself at ease then dashed round to look at the pressure gauge. The needle had not only passed maximum, it had passed the red danger patch, and was quivering on the manufacturer's name at 6 o'clock. I flung myself at the driver's seat, declutched the drive mechanism and turned off the motor. For a moment all was gloriously silent, then gurgling and hissing noises issued from the pipes, valves and things in the back. I was quite convinced that I was sitting on a concealed bomb, perhaps a time bomb, but certainly a bomb which, with the slightest wrong move, could blow my "little beauty" and me to smithereens. Somehow I had to release some air pressure from those two long steel canisters underneath the truck. It was muddy beneath the compressor but, throwing caution to the wind, as it were, I wriggled under the vehicle on my back to see what I could find.

At the end of each tank there was a tap with a lever handle. Quite obviously this was a release point and it was high time there was some relief from the danger threatening. I turned the lever and – whoosh! Dear knows how many pounds to the square inch hit me full in the face. I managed to roll away leaving the jet of air to scatter mud all over me and everything else. I found my cap halfway across the vehicle park. Unfortunately, I had to repeat the operation with the other tank, but with that side I was more prepared. It was a blessing in disguise really, because this fiasco might have taken place in front of the Brass and the thought of his riding boots spattered with mud sent cold shivers down my spine.

Tools arrived for the compressor truck later in the week, and a second driver. My self-promotion stood, probably because some higher authority had accepted me as an expert. I had certainly learnt all about Air Compressors and how to work them without a handbook, but the lesson had been a nerve-wracking one.

International news worsened. Czechoslovakia had been overwhelmed without a finger being raised to help, and it was plain to see that Poland was about to follow. In the background, Molotov and Ribbentrop played fast and loose with pieces of paper called Treaties. None of this did anything for my peace of mind because, despite the fact that I had volunteered to serve King and Country and was now part of the fighting machine, unpatriotic as it seemed at that time, I really didn`t want to die in a war which we were assured would be far worse than the last one. Bombing during the Spanish Civil War had demonstrated what horrors could descend upon the civilian population, and I didn`t go along with that happening to the people of Britain one little bit. Each day`s news seemed to make the possibility more certain, however, and I felt very despondent as the camp ended and we returned to Tyneside, home, and the Coal Board office.

CHAPTER FIVE – Called to the Colours

Britain and France decided that should Poland be attacked by Germany, war would be declared. After some blatant and obvious provocation on the border, Germany invaded Poland and, towards the end of August, the British government took the drastic step of making its declaration public.

I shared the national gloom and prayed that a conflict would not come. Like all British people throughout that warm and pleasant summer of 1939, I desperately hoped that something would happen at the last moment and all would be well. Sadly, nothing did. To make me more fearful and my immediate future more certain, papers arrived from the War Office telling me I was to report to my Unit for active service on 1st September 1939. Being "Called to the Colours" was the expression, a phrase from another war but just as meaningful.

Since 1936 when my father died after a long illness, I'd lived with my mother, just the two of us. The loss of my father had all but destroyed her. In fact, had it not been for my youthful presence Mother, who was not young, would quickly have followed her husband, her heart being quite broken and her life empty. At the moment war was declared she was on holiday with my sister and her family, staying with relatives in the south of England. I knew very well how she would be feeling about the outbreak of war, miles away, and me at home alone. Frankly, I didn't feel any better about it, having visions of my rapid departure overseas to repel the

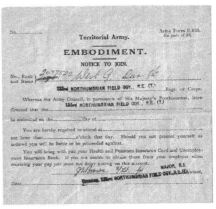

Call up papers.

Call up papers' envelope.

wicked Hun without even the opportunity of waving goodbye to the only person in my life who mattered.

I had to inform the secretary of the coal company for which I worked that I was to report to my Unit for active service at once. He couldn't make any objections, of course, but he had his priorities in order because as he shook my hand formally, he said to make sure I'd balanced the petty cash, all 12/6 of it, and got a receipt from the cashier when the key was handed in.

Saying farewells made me feel like a hero before the war had properly started, but it was some years before I appreciated the sincerity in the faces of the old soldiers in the office as they shook hands and said, "Good luck."

I felt a great sadness as I locked the door of my home on the evening of the 31st August 1939, and stood outside on the pavement. I was, I think, really and truly alone for the first time in my life and felt it. I looked at the house in which I'd grown up for nineteen years and wondered whether I'd ever see it again. I glanced up and down the street at houses where my friends lived. We'd played together and enjoyed our childhood there. Many of those friends were doing the same as me, off to the army, navy or air force. Despite my pessimism at that poignant moment I WAS to see my home again, but other houses in the street were completely demolished by German bombs, and the people within them killed.

I stayed that night with a friend in Shields who had joined the same Unit of Royal Engineers in Jarrow, and his company helped a great deal towards overcoming my deep despondency.

On 1st September 1939 at 9 am precisely I went to war, by taking a threepenny bus ride to Jarrow. By 11 am, equally precisely, I was back home in South Shields, having been thoroughly registered, having sworn more oaths (official ones promising to do this, that and the other until death do us part), and having been issued with instructions about returning the next day with the necessary requirements to stay the night, the next night, and every other night after that. It was certainly something of an anti-climax, but I was thankful for another sleep in my own bed, even if it was to be the last one for a while.

The next two days were taken up with issuing uniforms and no-one could pretend that mine was a good fit, anywhere.

The uniform was, of course, the new style battledress, a shock to the old sweats who felt that this was an undermining of the true soldier of the King, and a weakening of moral fibre. Furthermore, not one button in the whole outfit would polish! The greatcoats, however, were their salvation, being 1914-18 issue and liberally scattered with brass buttons and the letters RE on each epaulette. Having lain in store for many years the brass was dull and green. The drill sergeants positively gloated over this windfall knowing the amount of polishing that would be needed to get a mirror finish on each button.

In the past, soldiers had always worn flat-topped caps with a peak. Now we were given the "fore and aft" side hat. Their newness and stiffness made them the devil`s own to keep on. Our infantry, the Durham Light Infantry, solved this problem by wearing the side hat absolutely centrally over the crown, a fashion which was inclined to make the onlooker gasp with incredulity at first sight. We in the Engineers took the name more literally and wore the side hat in the traditional position, on the side of the head, held in position merely by the size and position of the right ear. A strong wind or an over-vigorous salute played havoc with the effect and they were off more than they were on until some of the stiffening was knocked out of the material.

For the first time ever, some of us (and I was one) were being made to wear boots. They were, like the greatcoats, of early manufacture, unfortunately; ugly, heavy and terribly uncomfortable. Advice was freely offered on how to soften the leather and make them bearable. To the innocent and naive (me, for instance) some of the advice was designed to make a fool of those who took it. It might have been effective but it was also crude, insanitary in the extreme, and only tried by the feeble-minded whose sense of humour had become warped. Most of us attempted, as far as possible, to soften the leather with liberal applications of polish, leather soap or dubbin, while toughening up our feet in any way we could. It was a couple of years before I finally got used to wearing boots and by then I had to admit that they were the right footwear for the job.

We had been medically examined when we first joined the Territorial Army earlier in the year, by a local doctor who was probably middle aged in the First World War. No doubt he had served with distinction in the Medical Corps and been retained over the years as Unit M.O., receiving acceptable perks as such. Six of us reported to his surgery and were medically examined in as many minutes. The procedure was:

"Feel fit, do you?" (no time for an answer)

"Drop your pants. Cough. Excellent. A1. Next."

At the time I couldn`t understand how a request to cough could reveal a chest complaint so low in the anatomy.

During the first two days of our "call up" we were again medically examined. This second examination was much more thorough and one or two men were actually rejected, although no-one knew why. No doubt they reappeared later in the war as spies or Quartermasters somewhere. I was declared horribly fit in all departments and wasn`t sure whether to be pleased or sorry.

Originally, we had been told that from 1st September 1939 we would be placed on a War Footing and billeted in the school opposite the drill hall which had been taken over for the purpose. It seemed that the organisation and administration of this had been overstretched because it was announced that anyone who wanted to could sleep at home after the divisional parade each evening, so long as they were "on parade" in the morning at 9 am. Furthermore, the catering facilities were inadequate for the whole company and a number of us had to buy pies or fish and chips nearly every lunchtime.

September 3rd 1939, "The Day War Broke Out" as Rob Wilton used to say, was a very solemn and sombre day for everyone who had any imagination at all. We knew that the Prime Minister was due to speak to the nation at round about midday and loudspeakers had been connected up to a radio in the drill hall. The whole company was assembled in ranks to listen to the important announcement. Everyone, officers, NCOs, cooks, orderlies and office staff, was on parade. The CO stood on a small box and made a little speech about the lights going out in Europe for a second time in thirty years, about duty, loyalty, discipline, sacrifice, patriotism, etc., until the wireless announced the Prime Minister, the Right Honourable Neville Chamberlain MP, was about to speak.

His words had a profound effect upon the listeners. Not that Chamberlain was a particularly impressive speaker, but it doesn`t fall to many people to say, "Today Britain declared war on Germany."

We had known what was coming, of course, the whole country did, but hearing it directly from the Prime Minister`s mouth was very final and put paid to any thought of turning back or compromise. This, at last, was it and every one of us standing there was well and truly committed.

I wasn`t to know then but, out of the two hundred and forty men who stood there at that awful moment, listening to the words which sealed their fate, only fourteen would eventually return to Tyneside unscathed, and I was one.

Barely had the Prime Minister finished speaking than, of all things, the air raid sirens wailed out their warning. Ye Gods! They hadn`t waited long to obliterate us. Surely, we weren`t to be wiped out before we had even fired a shot? Two or three men actually fell down in a faint and, I must admit, my heart missed a beat. There might be bombers overhead but as we had no air raid shelters there was nowhere for us to run so we just stood still like good disciplined troops and waited for the next order. What rubbish! We were all rooted to the spot in terror and had someone rushed for the door there would have been a stampede. Those who had fainted were unceremoniously dragged away and the CO very coolly, I thought, announced that we would march out in orderly fashion, in threes, and lie flat round the field at the back – also in threes, I suppose. In the event, it wasn`t necessary because almost immediately the All Clear went and we were told to stand easy and listen to a lecture on the dangers of venereal disease – at which even more men fainted!

So ended The Day War Broke Out.

CHAPTER SIX – In Limbo

That air raid siren had a predictable effect on the higher echelons. Although the "raid" had been a false alarm, with not an aircraft in sight, friend or foe, it was vital that some form of shelter was constructed urgently to protect the Company. Plans were very quickly drawn up and displayed for all to see: the grassy area to the rear of the drill hall was to be excavated and turned into a labyrinth of tunnels and chambers which could hold every man Jack of us in comparative safety. The design laid out for our safety and retreat in an emergency was the brain child of the CO. He was a civil engineer by profession so it was to be expected that he could think of everything and produce quick results. All the officers in the Unit had some sort of engineering qualification but it wouldn`t be often, I felt sure, that their civilian knowledge of sewage disposal and incineration would be called upon while they were in the army.

Drawing plans is one thing: achieving the end result is another. In those early days we had no machinery: everything had to be done by hand. So, next morning, after parade, all were marched to the rear of the drill hall and graciously given a choice – a pick or a shovel. I had never handled either in my life, having picked nothing more than my teeth on occasion, or shovelled more than sand into a toy bucket to make castles on the beach. Not that it mattered anyway because we interchanged between the two tools at regular intervals thereafter.

One man, a driver, murmured disapproval on the grounds that he had joined to drive not dig. They accepted his complaint and for the rest of the week he "drove" a heavy, loaded wheelbarrow up and down a plank and wished he`d kept his mouth shut.

From 4th September for about a week we worked every day from 9 am until 6 pm with a short break for sandwiches and tea at midday, and tea at 4 pm, loosening the soil with a pick and throwing up the spoil with a shovel until we had completed a nine feet deep trench right around the grassy area behind the drill hall which was of field size. From this trench, which was designed never to be straight for more than a few yards, "rooms" were dug out in the centre to house offices, signals equipment, stores, food and water, medical equipment and armaments. The rooms were completely covered with strengthened roofs and they all interconnected with each other. All trenches and rooms were beautifully revetted at the sides so that no soil showered down, ensuring they would not cave in easily. The main trench was only partly open at the top, and the floor was duck-boarded throughout against wet weather. It was really an expert job which gave everyone considerable reassurance that we would be safe should any bombs fall.

At the same time, it was the hardest of work, particularly for those of us who had never before done any physical labour. Needless to say, we neither expected nor received any sympathy from the miners, shipyard workers, labourers or men who were tough and hardened to this kind of work, but many a time I had to grit my teeth and exercise the absolute maximum of determination to keep going. There were blisters on my blisters and muscles ached where I didn`t know I had muscles. The journey home by bus each evening (because I was, thank goodness, still living at home) was torture and convinced me that the bus had been manufactured with square wheels and no springs.

My mother had returned from the south by then and had the boiler stoked up so that I could take an immediate hot bath. Afterwards I was fit for little else than to lie on the bed or the settee. Even that was agony. I suffered, of that there is no doubt, but I think my mother suffered more, seeing my extreme discomfort without being able to do much for me. She probably felt that "this is what the war is doing" but it was a mere nothing really compared to the discomforts I suffered before it was all over. Thank goodness my appetite had not been affected. Quite the reverse, in fact, and luckily in those early days nothing was in short supply.

By the end of the week I became aware of a change in my physical health. My hands were healing and hardening so that it was no longer excruciating to hold a pick or shovel. Not only that, but I`d mastered the swinging action required for these tools and could shift my quota of soil without difficulty. I was able to walk upright once again and take an interest in the world around me. I felt physically fitter than I`d ever felt in my life and was beginning to enjoy, with some humour, this different environment.

Not long after it was completed came the baptism of our air raid shelter system.

It happened just as we had formed up for "voluntary" church parade. That must be the most anomalous of all army ceremonies. All denominations, including at that time the Roman Catholics, were marched to the local Church of England where they were dismissed to attend their own places of worship.

As we were called to attention prior to moving off, the air raid warning howled. If there's any one thing we probably all remember vividly about the war, it is the sound of an air raid warning. That ghastly warbling sound sent cold shivers of apprehension through me. It was a hateful sound. Instead of marching to the church to be rescued from sin, we marched to the air raid shelter for salvation, and I don't remember anyone complaining.

Everyone took cover except the two men on the Lewis gun, together with one officer who was the lookout, and his runner. Guess who was the runner? The four of us were the only ones above ground: the rest cowered in their burrows while we scoured the skies with our binoculars, searching for the raiders. We found them, almost overhead, silver wings glinting in the sunlight. The call of "Take Cover" echoed round the whole area and I was instructed to grind out our own personal warning, only to be activated when there were aircraft immediately overhead and an attack was imminent.

No bombs dropped and the aircraft sailed on unhindered. The All Clear sounded and we followed it up with ours. It was too late to parade for church so we were dismissed to our own devices.

It was disclosed later that this, too, had been a false alarm and no enemy aircraft had crossed the coast. No-one would admit to seeing "at least twenty five planes with great black crosses on the wings," but I knew who it was because he knew everything better than anyone else and never failed to say so.

During the next few weeks nothing of great importance occurred. Each day we drilled and marched and were inspected in one of the school yards. I reached a state of efficiency which ensured that I would not turn left when I should be turning right and Earl Haig and the King were saluted more efficiently than before war broke out, but no matter how many times I pulled an oily four-by-two through my rifle the barrel always seemed to be chock full of filth when the officer looked down it.

Repetition of the daily routine was boring but eventually it became evident that we were not, after all, going to stagnate in Jarrow for the rest of the war. Stores began to arrive, boxes of ammunition, more Lewis guns and, best of all, army vehicles, two 30 cwt trucks and three 15 cwts.

The 30 cwt GS lorries were most interesting. GS was an abbreviation of "General Service"; in other words, they could be used for anything. Although brand new, there was something left over from the First World

War about them; perhaps the high load carrying area at the back, wooden slats on angle iron uprights, or maybe the square, flat radiator. Likely it was the driver's only protection against wind and weather: a canvas hood held in its stretched out position on a metal frame by two long leather straps fastened to the front mudguards. These lorries had power and their bogie of four driving wheels at the back suggested that they wouldn't stick in soft ground easily which proved to be very true. An increase in our vehicle strength must surely mean we were becoming at least partially mobile.

More stores had to be collected from the station one day. The "impressed" fish lorry was detailed to collect them and a driver chosen at random to do the job. The random choice was both ironic and, in the event, unfortunate. The man in question was a local fishmonger who had a distinct aura. We very soon became aware of his civilian occupation and, as most of us were living at home after duty, we were equally aware that he must still be carrying on his fish business.

The grinding of gears attracted my attention and I looked up to see the one ton fish lorry heading towards the open gate at a speed which could only be described as foolhardy. It would have passed between the gateposts safely had the gates been six feet to the left. As it was, the nearside front wing crumpled, then the door, glass flew, and finally the left side of the lorry destroyed itself and the gatepost before coming to rest in a cloud of splinters and dust. Our fishmonger friend stepped out unharmed. Only then did it come to light that his ability as a driver was limited to one horse power – literally. He had never been behind a wheel in his life and no-one had bothered to ask for his driving licence. Shortly afterwards he left the Unit for I know not where, perhaps the cavalry but more probably the Catering Corps.

The incident did have the effect of a pebble in a pool, however, and the ripples touched us all in the form of a stiff driving test, the issue of a War Office driving permit for those who passed, and a course of training in the handling of army vehicles large and small. I enjoyed all this and learned a great deal.

The period between the outbreak of the war and the "next move" was a very strange time, a sort of limbo. We were, so we were told, part of the army yet it didn't seem so. We had very little equipment, our armaments were First World War vintage, matching our drill, Manual of Training, attitude of higher ranks to lower ranks, and even the new transport had hardly been brought up to date. These doldrums were quite frustrating:

we certainly didn`t feel like efficient soldiers, part of an army preparing to fight the mighty war machine of Hitler`s Germany.

An example of these irritating frustrations was the implementation of an Army Regulation which must have gone back even further than the war period of 1914-18. Pay Parade.

Pay Parade took place each week. In preparation, a trestle table was set up at one end of the largest school yard. An army blanket was then spread, almost ceremoniously, over the table top, smoothed into place and weighted with something suitably tasteful like a couple of bricks, a pair of boots or a Bible. On another table, not so covered, large loaves of white bread were piled high. The Pay Officer then arrived with a large bag of half crowns and shillings which were stacked on the blanketed table in neat piles. After a great deal of saluting, shouting of orders and stamping of boots on the yard, we were lined up in single file corresponding with the payroll list. As each man`s name was called, he marched smartly up to the table, saluted, and in a loud clear voice, identified himself, and stepped right up to the table. At this point, the Pay Officer put the man`s pay directly into his outstretched hand, plus a half crown, the officially designated amount of money for a week`s "subsistence," and proffered a large white loaf, uncut and unwrapped. One took the money in one`s right hand, transferred it in a swift move to the left hand, pocketed the money, then received the loaf in the right hand, transferred it to a position under the left arm, saluted, about turned, and marched away, all this done to the well known army formula, "One, two, hup!" and with absolute seriousness. It took a good deal of self control to prevent myself from bursting into the loudest laughter. Carrying that loaf home on the bus was not only awkward but also embarrassing and it wasn`t long before I found a number of Jarrovians who were only too delighted to relive me of my burden. I got the impression that not a few of them must have lived solely on a diet of dry white bread.

CHAPTER SEVEN – The First Move, to Yarm

We seemed to be in Jarrow a long time before we finally made a move. Autumn came, the weather began to get cold, foggy and damp, so it must have been towards the end of October that the rumours became fact. We were, at last, on the move. More stores and more vehicles arrived, so many for each section and so many to Headquarters, one of which was a compressor truck and guess who got that?! I don't think it was any coincidence either.

The move was to Yarm, in North Yorkshire but only just. At the end of the town a bridge crossed the River Tees and on the north side it was Durham, to the south side Yorkshire. I had never been there nor, to be honest, had I heard of it. It was still, in those days, a small country market town noted chiefly for its annual horse fair. Even during the war it still managed to keep up this tradition and horses were brought in for sale from miles around, many of them owned by gypsies. The town itself comprised the cobbled main street with a small amount of more recent building spreading out behind. I was struck by the number of pubs there were in the place, some of which rejoiced in the more elegant title of "hotel", "inn" and "coach house".

The distance from Jarrow to Yarm is certainly not great but it seemed to take an age to get there by the time everything was loaded and checked, the convoy formed, and we had crawled down to Yorkshire. We'd had very little practice moving in convoy and our efforts were much frustrated by civilian vehicles splitting up the column, together with those bright sparks who couldn't read a map.

Our arrival in Yarm was so late that darkness had fallen by the time I'd carried my kit and bed roll along to the drill hall. This was down a picturesque alleyway which ran at right angles off the main street. We were all billeted in the drill hall for the night. It was the local HQ of the Green Howards but they must have been moved to be near the other infantry Units of 69th Brigade. The floor was hard and it wasn't warm. An awful lot of people seemed to talk late into the night and others moved around all the time so I don't suppose any of us got much sleep that first night.

Next day, I was moved to the local village hall on the other side of the main street. It had a stage at one end and my bed space was on the stage. The place had a very musty smell. The facilities most lacking in those early days were those for bathing, washing, and toilets. Two hand basins and two toilets weren't nearly enough for thirty or forty men, particularly when we were expected to be neatly turned out and clean shaven for parade at 9 am each day.

There was very little to do in Yarm. I think this must have been the first time in my life that I went into a pub. Three or four of us found our way into one of the many pubs in the town shortly after arrival. It was bright and warm and the people were friendly which was really admirable of them since they had been "invaded." I tried beer and disliked it intensely but I found cider much more to my taste and was to drink nothing else for a very long time.

Yarm seemed well endowed with village halls or similar which might be why we had been moved there. The Mess hall was at the top end of the town, quite a long walk from our billet. At this stage of the war, if there was any rationing, it certainly wasn't noticeable. I remember going into the cookhouse store which was quite extensive, and seeing sides of beef hanging, rolls of good bacon, stacks of fresh white bread, and many large tins of preserves, tinned meat, butter, and so on. It came as something of a surprise to all of us, therefore, when we sat down to breakfast.

A large aluminium tray appeared, containing a lake of rather greasy liquid in which floated, flabbily, five or six pounds of overdone sliced onions and a few rashers of fatty bacon which, because they had been cooked in the liquid with the onions, had neither taste nor colour. A ladle was provided for sharing this horrible mess out on to our tin plates which were stone cold, or course. Supplementing this unappetising slush was a white loaf and a plate of margarine lumps and marmalade, served as one. Tea came to the table to be dished out by the "cook's assistant" direct from a large dixie. It was pre-sweetened, very much so, but there was no alternative for anyone who didn't want sugar. I did my best because I felt that, having joined the forces, so obviously different from my normal life, I'd better accept the bad with the good.

The mid-day meal was the main meal of the day so we felt it had to be better than breakfast and, anyway, I'd seen those sides of beef hanging up. Stew arrived in the same metal trays with serving ladles, but as this was dinner, there was an extra tray containing a veritable mountain of mashed potato and boiled cabbage. I'm fond of both mashed potato and cooked cabbage, but when cabbage is boiled and boiled until it loses its colour, shape and taste, one cannot work up much enthusiasm for it. Whereas the cabbage was overcooked, the meat certainly was not and much had to be left uneaten. Dessert was dried fruit and watery custard made without salt or sugar.

I discovered in November 1939 that our cook had been a blacksmith in civilian life and his culinary efforts reflected it! So there will be no day-to-day menu details hereafter because there was only one variation of the two meals mentioned previously. At breakfast, tomatoes might be substituted for bacon, and for lunch, swede or carrots might replace the cabbage. These meals remained unchanged for weeks on end. Probably the only big difference ever made was for Christmas Day. I wasn`t there: I`d made my own arrangements, and it wasn`t very long before most of us were giving the Mess (how well named) a miss. A number of local cafes cashed in on this failure by the army to provide appetising meals, and we were able to buy very good and varied food for quite reasonable prices there. Our attendance at these cafes was so frequent that the proprietors could make a really good job of providing filling, tasty food and some comfort to go with it.

One might ask, what was higher authority doing about this waste and failure? Very seldom did one see an officer to whom one could complain, but it could be that, as their Mess was in a very palatial private home four miles in the opposite direction to our dining hall, they hadn`t the time or the inclination to show interest. More probably, they left the matter in the hands of the CSM and his senior NCOs. They had a private room at the end of our dining hall, the door was always closed, and I cannot remember any one of them interrupting their meal to see to our welfare. I had occasion to enter that room once and saw a white tablecloth, good cutlery and glasses of beer. The meal was over so I cannot make comparisons, but I do remember a framed text on the wall. The text read, "By prayer and perseverance and a bottle of sweet oil, the snail at length reached Jerusalem." The CSM was very fond of quoting this gem but I never could read any significance into it, nor have I any idea why it hung in the sergeants` mess at all because it didn`t fit in with the attitudes of anyone in there, other than that most of them had brains which moved at the speed of that small slimy creature.

The weather was becoming much colder now and the nights were often frosty. I liked the countryside in winter and Yarm was very rural. The morning parades were a trial and the whole procedure could be quite drawn out. Of course, it was all conducted according to Army Regulations and I suppose the CO was following the form of what a Regular Army unit would do when it gathered to pay him his due respects each morning. Standing still, in line, holding a rifle, unable to speak or relax for anything up to an hour was very hard going and could be physically quite painful when it was foggy and frosty. Occasionally, men slumped to the ground with a clatter.

One of the good things that came out of forces life for me was the friendships I was lucky enough to form. Perhaps we were thrown together in adversity and clung together for support but, whatever it was, I found myself part of a small group. Four of us seemed to find the company of one another enjoyable enough to want to see and do things together. A friend from Darlington, Bert, was one of the first National Servicemen to be drafted to us. Another, Robbo, from Jarrow, had worked as an accounts clerk like myself. He'd been in the main Co-Op offices. The third was a South Shields fellow, Larry, a little older than the rest of us, who had more experience as a driver having been a lorry driver in civvy street. We all had similar tastes in our way of life, came from similar homes, liked the same food and disliked with the same intensity the army "cuisine." Only Larry, the ex-lorry driver, was married and perhaps his maturity was a steadying influence on the rest of us. I was the only one to return home unscathed. Bert suffered so much from "near misses" he was returned to England later in the war as unfit for active service, a polite way of declaring someone shell-shocked. Robbo was invalided out when some idiot accidentally pumped half a dozen shots into his leg when messing around with a Sten gun in North Africa. He lost his leg. Shortly after we'd celebrated the birth of his twins, Larry Sanderson, was blown up in his Jeep running over a mine in the desert. He spent months in hospital having suffered serious leg and arm injuries, was left deaf and his hair turned pure white.

However, the war was just beginning and we knew nothing of the future. Our concern was to go out together in Yarm, have a drink and find a cafe with a roaring fire, there to eat a good meal before returning to the rather bleak conditions of the stage in the village hall to sleep until another day dawned.

I had never met people from an environment other than my own and it came as a bit of a shock to come up against characters like our Motor Transport Sergeant and his Lance Sergeant.

The SgtMT (as he is officially known in RE army jargon) struck me as a very smart and able soldier. He was always immaculately turned out and "polished." Whatever was polishable he had had polished by some lacky. He was a big man in every respect. Shortly after war was declared and we were in frequent contact at Yarm, I realised his front was all show. He obviously had very little knowledge of the workings of the internal combustion engine or the mechanics of even the most ordinary vehicle. He had two interests: the consumption of beer and the consummation of his lust for women, and in both subjects he was an expert. We were soon made aware that his prowess lay elsewhere in his anatomy other than between his ears. At the same time, I really felt very sorry for him when I got to know his unfortunate secret – he was illiterate. This, of course, presented considerable problems for the man responsible not only for the practical side of running the Transport Section, but also for its administrative organisation. The section was still very small but the prospect of its imminent growth must have given him nightmares.

The SgtMT knew my record: someone in the Company Office would have given him my details. I suddenly found his "on parade" attitude softening as he began a campaign to cultivate my assistance. Needless to say, I was only too pleased to be cultivated, knowing that an improvement in my way of life would result. It didn't pay to give way too easily, but I did allow some gradual co-operation. Eventually I was made a firm offer: would I become the MT Clerk, establish an office, and run the paperwork because "I am so busy," as the big boy put it?

And thus I became almost my own boss, answerable only to the SgtMT, and he was so dependent upon me after a week I knew I could keep at bay anyone below the rank of full Sergeant. I moved into my own office, well away from the billet, in a disused building contractor's premises known as Danby's Yard. It had a table, chairs, a bed and, best of all, a fireplace on which I could cook. Absolute luxury.

My success wasn't everyone's joy. Almost from my first day, before the war even began, I had clashed with the MT Lance Sergeant, the second-in-command of the section. Not openly, because I was only a driver, but I soon came to realise that I was never going to have a peaceful life with this NCO around. I could not think of a particular reason why, but he took an immediate dislike to me, and was soon using every opportunity to "get at" me. Intellectually, he was as thick as two short planks, just like his senior but, unlike his boss, this one was sly, cunning, vindictive, and, I knew, dangerous. He was out to trick me into overstepping the mark or into giving him some excuse to put me on a charge. Anything would do, just so long as he could parade me before the CO, make me look small and guilty, and exact a punishment. Naturally, I wasn`t going to be tempted into falling for his blatant attempts to entrap me, but it wasn`t at all pleasant to be walking on a continual knife edge. I`ve often wondered why he took this attitude towards me. Maybe it had to do with an exaggerated idea of some class difference between us, and in this view he may have had a point because I would never have considered myself to be of his gutter level. Enough is to say that he hated my guts and the feeling quickly became mutual. He was, without a doubt, a little man in all senses of the word but, oh boy, he had a big mouth with stinking language and breath to match. My move to Danby`s Yard, the disused haulage contractor`s place, was a move in the right direction because it removed me from this lance sergeant`s clutches.

I really wasn`t looking forward to Christmas, my first away from home, and not in the most comfortable or happiest of surroundings, but there certainly wasn`t any talk of leave. Our little group had decided that our best chance of "getting our feet under a table" was through the church. There was only one other way and that was to "click" with some lass in the pub who would want to take us home for whatever reason, and none of us fancied that sort of entanglement, not even for home comforts!

The nearest non-conformist church was in Stockton, so each Sunday we made the trip and, sure enough, the ploy worked. Two ladies, one middle aged and the other in her late twenties, invited all four of us home for a meal after the service. They had a very comfortable place, or rather their elderly mother did: warm, well lit and obviously middle class. We went each Sunday a few weeks running and enjoyed it. The meals were tasty and generous, and the three ladies were pulling out all the stops. We were all most grateful for their hospitality but it was sometimes hard work. Before the days of television, Sunday night`s radio wasn`t all that exciting and one couldn`t very well eat a good meal and dash away so it was whist, rummy and chat. It did become a bit of a trial to be jolly through a couple of hours of songs round the piano, but they were kind and, knowing what was at stake, we stuck it out.

We didn`t have a great deal in the way of off-duty entertainment in Yarm but the local ladies got together and decided to throw a dance, concert and "bun fight" for anyone from the Unit who might like to attend. We were sceptical, I`m afraid, but the food was an attraction and we went. Those who preferred to enjoy the magnetism of their local pub were sorry later because it was a much better social occasion than anyone had anticipated. Admittedly, as with all affairs of this sort, it was slow to start but as the night progressed and all had enjoyed a very tasty and filling meal, everyone relaxed and tried hard to show gratitude.

I don`t remember how it was done but Bert, one of the four of our group, myself and another fellow in the Unit were invited to spend the next Sunday with a farmer whose two daughters were part of the army of lady volunteers looking after us that evening. We were collected by one of the daughters in her father`s car to be taken to the farm. From then until we left Yarm I knew that that would be the one day in the week when I could relax and be looked after in conditions that were "homely" to say the least. Sadly, I cannot remember the name of the farmer or his daughters.

After the war I took my wife back to the farm to express my thanks and show her the lovely surroundings of that short, happy period. I found the farm but both the farmer and his wife had died. The daughters had married, one to a fellow from our Unit, but they`d all moved to other parts of the country and the farm was being run by the son who was a young lad in my day and of whom I knew little. It was sobering and somewhat sad that so much had changed but those older people and their daughters did make our Sundays days to remember. Christmas Day was a real Yuletide with turkey, wine, Christmas crackers, funny hats, charades and lots of laughter. Larry, the married one of our group, stuck with the ladies in Stockton for Christmas. The fellow from Darlington, Robbo, and I were more cavalier and we chose the hospitality which suited us best.

After Christmas the severe weather started, first some very heavy frosts, then snow, then both. I was glad to be in my little office despite the many rats, creaking rafters and pitch darkness all around. I had organised the admin to run very smoothly and knew the running of the MT section from A to Z. The SgtMt was delighted and left me to get on with it unhindered. When the day`s work was done, the lorries were parked around the yard and the drivers had gone back to their billets, I was able to shut my door, build the fire up, lie on the bed and read. The rest of the world, the war, the sergeants and WO1s could safely be forgotten.

Meanwhile, it got colder and the snow got deeper. Work and parades virtually came to a standstill because we were in the grip of one of the worst winters. I got `flu. The fire went out. I was too unwell and it was too cold to go out for food and, because I`d made my own life for myself away from the others, no-one came near me for a few days. Then two of my friends, Robbo and Jack, arrived. They got the fire going, brought soup from one of the cafes and heated it on my fire. I had reached a low level of despondency but my friends had come to the rescue.

Eventually the snow turned to rain and floods. When the weather faired nature awoke to Spring 1940.

CHAPTER EIGHT – The Battle of Danby's Yard

Danby's Yard was all my own place; no other fool would have lived there. Because it was so well away from the rest of the Unit, it was only necessary for me to leave my sanctuary on a few occasions like weekly parades, pay day, collection of mail, etc.

The single room office had a fitted wash basin and WC, electric light and my own comfortable bed with unlimited blankets. Because of my isolation and distance from the Mess, at least a mile, the Cookhouse supplied me with tinned food, bread, tea, sugar and butter. I bought milk, eggs and fresh food out of my own pocket in the town shops, to ensure good meals daily. The windows of my room looked onto a patch of ground where early spring flowers bloomed. There was no dampness but if I was careless and let the fire go out the place rapidly became an ice box.

Danby, the builder who owned the yard, probably made a tidy income from letting the enclosed and secure area to the army. He had his own lorries parked there but there was still plenty of room, despite the fact that we had quite a few vehicles to tuck away in all the corners. There were also large areas for the storage of timber, cement, gravel, bricks, window frames, steel joists and general rubbish. A large part of Danby's Yard was under cover with a workshop and sawmill above, supported on steel pillars. Pigeons, small birds, a cat or two, mice and even rats tolerated each other and me quite happily.

Each morning the Unit's drivers would collect their lorries and drive away to work with the sappers on some job or other. I was more or less left to my own devices, keeping the paperwork of the Transport Section up to date and making cups of tea for anyone who dropped in. The fire had to be stoked and I enjoyed listening to my portable radio which kept me in touch with world news. In the late afternoon the lorries returned and by then it was almost dark.

All was contented and peaceful until we had the "Battle of Danby's Yard," an event which may seem unbelievable now but in the circumstances of the time, was not altogether surprising.

The HQ building in the Drill Hall and our vehicles in Danby's Yard had to be guarded. Each evening a detachment of four sappers and a junior NCO marched into the yard. Two men wandered off on individual patrol, ensuring the safety of the Company's valuable equipment in every nook and cranny. The other two men and the guard commander relaxed in the wooden hut provided until it was their turn to take over on patrol.

It was a black dark night. The wind moaned round the building and the lorries. An owl hooted somewhere. Rats and mice scrabbled over some corrugated iron before an owl swooped. A solid body fell from the rafters, thudding onto a wood pile. All normal night time sounds to me, but to the young lads on guard these unexplained noises left them transfixed, eyes popping and mouths open. Darkness and things-that-go-bump-in-the-night set their imagination running riot.

Cartoon posters had delivered a lot of propaganda saying things like,

"Careless talk costs lives"
"Be like Dad: keep Mum"
"Don't talk to strangers"
"Are you sure it wasn't Hitler sitting next to you?"

These stirred up a liberal helping of Spy Fever so it wasn't surprising our guards were distinctly jumpy.

One of the patrol saw a figure just visible against a stack of light-coloured timber. He pulled back his rifle bolt to "put one up the spout." The other guard heard the metallic click and assumed, understandably, that he was about to be sniped at.

I should say at this point that very few men in the whole of the Unit had ever had the opportunity or doubtful privilege of firing a rifle. Maybe 20% had visited the shooting range at Whitburn, and another 10% had been in the company long enough to have fired on the range at summer camp. In Yarm, only the men actually on guard duty were issued with five rounds, and these had to be handed back and counted when they came off duty. All this explains that if we did have any crack shots they were unknown and hardly likely to have developed that skill in pitch darkness. So 70% of our establishment were, as far as rifle shooting was concerned "virgin soldiers."

The soldier with "one up the spout" saw the cloaked figure of the sniper run across the gap, took the chance and fired, then tried to utter,

"Who goes there?"

He realised that the sequence was in reverse order but consoled himself with the knowledge that with his throat constricted in fear the sniper wouldn't have heard him anyway.

The other guard heard the unintelligible shout, thought, "God, a German spy!" and fired towards the sound of the enemy. His bullet went well wide, ricocheted off a steel pillar and drilled two holes n the guard house as it went in and out. The NCO and his two companions inside completely lost interest in relaxing and very smartly flung themselves out of the door and onto the ground.

A junior NCO had to show initiative and take command.

"Germans! Parachutists! There they are! Open fire!"

I`d hit the ground after the first shot and as the telephone fell with me, my call for reinforcements was almost instantaneous. It took far longer to convince the senior NCO on duty at HQ that war had broken out for a second time in six months than it did to start the battle outside.

All being rotten shots, no-one was hurt and the fight ended very quickly because five rounds don`t last long. Both sides came out with their hands up, and an argument ensued over who had fired first. By mutual agreement it was decided to stick to the story that intruders had got in but had escaped after a united show of strength.

The NCO I`d frantically called at HQ, not having one of the sharpest minds, got it all wrong.

My hasty call had been something like, "We`re in a right mess here. There`s firing broken out. We need help!"

He had called out the Fire Brigade which was a rather slow and complicated process, led them to the cookhouse at the Mess where they put out the fires the cooks had stoked up for breakfast. By the time he arrived at Danby`s Yard all was quiet and under control and I was in bed.

The outcome was that the guards were charged with "Firing rounds of ammunition without permission" and having dirty rifle barrels. I hoped that they mightn`t be inhibited by these consequences when we later reached a battle that wasn`t in a builder`s yard.

CHAPTER NINE – The Second Move and We're On Our Way to War

Time passed. The sappers continued to train, blowing up trees for example, to learn how to handle explosives. The MT section practised convoy work and they certainly needed it. We all had to take part in route marches and I can't say that anyone derived much benefit from these. We probably became better soldiers for our efforts but since no more equipment appeared we didn't feel that "active" service was anywhere in the offing.

Meanwhile, we listened to radio reports of the "phoney" war across the Channel. Although war had been declared between Britain and Germany, it almost seemed from the actions of the two protagonists, that neither wanted to offend the other in case one became upset and went berserk with a gun. Personally, I was in no hurry to be nasty to the Nazis: if they kept quiet so would I and I would be quite happy to see out my war in Danby's Yard, Yarm.

There had been no leave so I hadn't seen the folks at home since the previous November when we left Jarrow. I was delighted, therefore, when the CO sent for me and told me that he was going back to his home on Tyneside, would be staying overnight, and that I would drive him and have the privilege of going to my home, also for an overnight stay. I felt this was very thoughtful of him, to choose me from the whole section for the task. It was also quite an honour, not to mention a pleasure, to drive him in his staff car. We hadn't yet been supplied with a car for the Commanding Officer, but the army had the power to impress whatever transport was necessary for the efficient working of the Unit. The CO had impressed for himself ("impressed" could be interpreted as "taken") a 16 hp Austin saloon. It was a pretty new vehicle, maroon in colour, very roomy and incredibly powerful. The CO let me take it out for a run to get the feel of it and I was thrilled to drive such a beautiful motor car.

I spent a very pleasant 48 hours taking the CO to his home first, then proudly going off to Shields on my own in this lovely private saloon.

I had another similar short leave but this next time I was taking the second in command and he had merely a Morris 10. Beggars can't be choosers, however, and it was another 24 hours at home, which was more than the rest of the Unit enjoyed.

Everyone, at long last, paid a visit to the rifle range to fire five rounds only. As each round was fired, the spent cartridge had to be handed to the controlling sergeant who entered it in a log. The procedure was so wrapped up in red tape that it occurred to me that my five Germans would have little to worry about if the sergeant wasn't around with his little book. The worst features of target practice were, a) the kick of a .303 Lee Enfield was enough to discourage anyone from firing it except in case of a dire emergency, and b) it wasn't worth the fun of firing at Hitler as it took too long to clean the darned gun afterwards. Once again, my rifle was declared to be full of cobwebs by the officer in charge, both before and after my shoot.

New transport was added to the strength so that each section now had its full complement of three 15 cwt GS trucks, two 30 cwt lorries and a 15 cwt compressor. We still had not been issued with a special vehicle for each of the officers and they continued to use private cars.

The time to go eventually caught up with us all and there were, as there always are at times like this, lots of farewells, last meals and drinks. The convoy of our Unit formed up along the main street in Yarm and very impressive it looked, too, now that we were nearly complete. The vehicles were heavily laden because there was no coming back this time and everything had to be jammed aboard somewhere.

The sappers and all the officers, except the Captain and one other, were to march to Eaglescliffe Station and travel to our destination, Southampton, by train. The two officers left behind were to be in charge of the convoy, one at the head of it, the other at the rear to deal with accidents and breakdowns. There were, of course, more drivers than vehicles and we were allocated two to each truck so that we could share the driving. I managed to get onto a 15 cwt truck with Robbo from Jarrow and it was much more agreeable to be with a good friend on a journey like this.

It seemed that the whole of Yarm turned out to wave us off: after all, it wasn't a very big place. Many friendships with the locals had developed and several fellows were to marry girls from the town. People can be very sentimental on such occasions and, with the memory of the First World War still in the minds of the older people, tears weren't far away as young men went off to war. It was a very strange feeling to turn the corner at the top of the High Street in Yarm for the last time but I wasn't sad to put behind me the shadow of the village hall and its onions, hoping that I'd never have to taste their greasy, sloppy flavour again in my life!

It was a long way to Southampton and I`d certainly never driven there before. We knew that the journey was going to be in stages but at that period of the war communication between officers and troops was practically non-existent. Apart from knowing that our ultimate destination was to be Southampton, any movement instructions for the journey were in the minds of only a few. I don`t think it bothered us particularly. All Robbo and I had to do was follow the lorry in front and not lose it. Someone else would do all the map reading and organising. It was something of a surprise when we reached our first day`s destination, Catterick – 18 miles from Yarm!

There were no motorways in those days but I remember travelling a fair distance on the A1 and then on good secondary roads which would be in as direct a route as we could take to the south coast. Each day the journey was long and slow and very, very cold. It snowed heavily a number of times. The vehicles in those days did not have enclosed cabs: the only protection for those in the front were two small individual windscreens, so small that one looked over the top, and neither of which had wipers. A sort of canvas apron could be clipped onto the dashboard which offered a little protection for the hands and legs but, even so, in a blizzard or driving rain, one became either a snowman or a sponge in no time. Unfortunately, the faster one travelled the more uncomfortable it became. The passenger could crouch down behind his small windscreen but the driver had to peer over the top and suffer.

When we finally pulled in the next night everyone felt pretty miserable and thought very unkind things about the designer of the lorries.

I cannot remember exactly where it was we stopped, perhaps half way between Catterick and Southampton. We were billeted in a large house standing in its own grounds. The owners, if there were any, certainly didn`t reside there which was perhaps just as well: an awful lot of mud and slush was tramped into the rooms on heavy boots.

Someone in the army had things well organised for once. The rooms in which we were to sleep already had blankets and straw-filled palliasses laid out in neat rows. A hot, tasty stew was dished out as soon as we got into the house after parking our vehicles in a side road. We didn`t have to do anything except eat and prepare for sleep and most of us were ready for that.

At this point I want to digress from the story, to go back to the period before the war when Neville Chamberlain stood by his aircraft waving his useless piece of paper and muttering those futile words, "Peace in our time." We young people in 1938/9 weren't nearly as optimistic as he was. Admittedly, British character thinks, "It might never happen," and we tried to pretend that whatever did happen it wouldn't be to us but, deep down, we knew that Britain was on a collision course. Perhaps this feeling of impending doom prompted me to remember vividly two dreams I had had some time before September 1939. I could not normally recall the details of dreams but these two dreams I did remember and I recount them for good reason.

In the first dream I was dressed in khaki uniform of First World War vintage, carrying the equipment of the time. I was marching in file with many other similarly clad troops down a street at the end of which were docks and ships. As we moved down the street, I looked to my left at a shop selling sheet music and musical instruments. My eye was caught by a particularly attractive guitar hanging from a display hook. Had I been able to, I would love to have left the ranks and bought the instrument even though I couldn't play it. This was quite impossible, of course, and we marched on to the docks and filed aboard a ship. That ended my dream. It was short, not really very interesting, but extremely clear in all its details.

The other dream was set by a canal. It was a canal rather than a river because the sides were vertical, supported by wooden piles, and a towpath ran along the top of each bank. Across the water was a row of objects which looked like large stepping stones. I was on one bank side with other people when a girl came to the opposite bank and waved vigorously. Probably in the dream we would have liked to cross to her if the waving was an invitation but as there was no way of doing so other than via the stepping stones, none of us did. This also seemed a rather uninteresting dream and, at the time, I could think of no reason why I should remember the details.

We stayed in a school in Southampton. Parades took place on the large playgrounds and there were long waits while we were checked, rechecked, numbered, and our details entered on sheets which, I suppose, were sailing lists. Eventually, after a boring few days of inactivity, we set off in convoy to motor down to the docks for the cross channel ferry to Le Havre. As we neared the terminal, our slow moving line of vehicles passed down a narrow street and there, on the left hand side, giving me quite a shock, was a music shop. The window was full of sheet music and musical instruments and, right in the middle, hung a guitar. Even the metal cellar grating in front of the shop window was exactly as I had seen it in my dream. I was in khaki, in full equipment, with other troops. The only details which didn`t fit were that we weren`t marching, nor were we dressed in the uniform of the other war. It was an eerie feeling because everything struck me so forcibly, as though I`d actually been there before and it made me wonder what other thoughts and fears I`d experienced might come true.

As we turned the corner at the end of the street a vast shape loomed before us, a black hull lined with portholes, white upperworks and three huge red and black funnels. For the first time in my life I was looking at one of the great Cunard "Queens," an awe-inspiring sight. She was still in her peacetime colours not yet having begun those famous and adventurous trans-Atlantic troop-carrying voyages. This wonderful example of British ship building was not for us, however. Much further along the quay, two rather grubby ships belching smoke and steam from all their seams were obviously our means of transport.

First we had to drive up to a petrol pump, not to be refilled but rather to be unfilled. The nozzle sucked out all the petrol from each tank, leaving only enough fuel in the system to drive our vehicle a few yards onto a net. The four corners of the net were then drawn tight as a crane sailed the truck mast-high then lowered it deep into the hold of the transport ship. There was no crash or sound of breaking glass so I assumed my little 15 cwt compressor truck hadn`t been smashed to pulp.

Next, to the Customs Shed. Our country was at war but one didn`t leave these shores to face the enemy until one had been instructed to read the list of declarable goods and had made one`s true and honest statement to the official dressed in a flashy uniform, looking rather like an admiral of the Salvation Army, I thought. I was sorely tempted to confess that I was carrying a Lewis gun and four Mills bombs, not to mention a rifle, ammunition and a Brownie camera. Instead I looked him steadily in the eye and declared,

"Nothing to declare."

I`m sure he disbelieved me: officials are like that with me even though I always tell the truth. We all had to pass through the customs barrier and I don`t recall anyone being caught smuggling.

We didn`t cross the Channel on the same boat as our transport. Our journey was made aboard a peacetime ferry. I have crossed the Channel many times since on my way to continental holidays, often in quite crowded conditions, but none compared with the squash aboard on that occasion.

It might be an exaggeration to say we had to be seasick by odd and then even numbers, but it was a fact that the facilities for this awful affliction left a lot to be desired. Unfortunately, the crossing from Southampton to Le Havre is a long one even when the ships are travelling flat out to avoid being torpedoed. By the time I'd reached the Isle of Wight a torpedo would have been a blessed relief from the misery of seasickness. It was a fine April but the waters were hardly as calm as a mill pond so, as no German submarine caused any diversion, we suffered the boredom and the discomfort of seasickness all the way to disembarkation.

CHAPTER TEN – Vive La France

I had been to France once before, as a schoolboy, and I looked forward to visiting again. It wasn't really very long since I had left school and I could still remember some French so I felt well equipped to enjoy all France had to offer me for a second time. Despite the fact that somewhere in France there was war and danger, the nearer I got the more excited I was.

It was a relief to set foot on solid ground again. Although the vehicles were unloaded and returned to us remarkably quickly, refuelling took some time before we could begin our journey into France.

For all of us in April 1940 driving on the "wrong" side felt anything but "right" as we rolled onto French roads.

"Rolling onto" the roads wasn't the way to put it: "limping" would have been better. The loading at Southampton, or perhaps the channel crossing, had bent two of the larger vehicles rather badly. One had a burst radiator and the other had twisted steering. Two of the 15 cwts couldn't be started at any price, and another had a puncture. We didn't exactly look like conquering heroes as our convoy left Le Havre towing or lifting one another, so it was perhaps just as well that we didn't go far on the first hop, to Bolbec.

This first French town was exactly as we'd imagined. We parked our vehicles in a large square, at one end of which was a rise, atop which stood a most ornate and grand church, marble steps climbing to its entrance. Around the square, houses, inns and shops of all shapes and sizes nestled cheek by jowl. Some buildings jutted out, some were set back, and most were painted with a wash varying in colour and texture. It was most picturesque.

The people of Bolbec were swift to take a closer look at the "new" Tommy and we were quite happy to be the centre of so much attention. Before long their hospitality extended to wine, coffee, cheese and, of course, French bread, which has no equal.

We were told that we were to spend the night in the square in Bolbec. We weren't really prepared for camping out which meant unpacking the blanket each of us carried in a sausage wrapped around our large pack, and it was at Bolbec that most of us put to use the gas cape in a way for which it was never designed, the first of many, many times in the near future when it would keep us warm and dry. Each driver, NCO and officer found a corner in a vehicle to snatch some sleep. Not that we retired early to bed: the local hospitality was too enthusiastic for that, and it got better by the minute.

The British are pretty good at making friends and none better than Geordies. Not a few actually slept in beds between sheets that night. I wasn`t so lucky or perhaps I should say that I wasn`t given the chance, but I learned the beauty of French wine and its strength, not to mention some of the variety of cheeses matured in Normandy. There is no doubt we had been made most welcome and it seemed sad that the reputation of the British Expeditionary Force was badly tarnished not many weeks later. For the present, however, we were enjoying ourselves.

The weather was now much improved, perhaps because we were further south than where we had started our journey. The sun was warm and Spring was

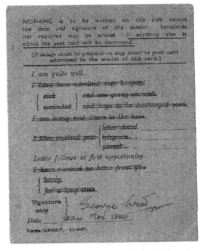

Postcard sent from France at the beginning of the Phoney War.

Reverse of the postcard.

certainly visible in the trees and countryside. Sleeping almost in the open was a new experience but, well fed and glowing with liquid refreshment, we hardly noticed the lack of cover.

Somewhere between Bolbec and Yvetot there was a linen factory. It stood in a valley, nestling between the hills in very much the same way as did the mills of Lancashire and the Scottish Borders. We pulled in to this factory which was to be our home for three nights, probably to give the rest of the Unit time to catch us up.

The linen factory was empty. The machinery was there but there was no workforce and no cloth, processed or otherwise. All we required were water, light, and covered accommodation.

The water was probably 100% pure, but British suspicion of foreign plumbing meant that every drop we used from a tap had to be boiled then sterilised with chemicals which made tea taste and look like iodine.

Had we known, it might have paid us to carry a few light bulbs because those left in the sockets at the factory were little more than 60 watts. That sort of candle power in a warehouse-sized dormitory only served to prevent anyone walking into a door, and I liked to read a book at bedtime.

The "dormitory" was made up of row upon row of racks which had once held linen bales. Those drivers five levels up on the racks got all the light from the bulbs: those lower down had less distance to climb and equally less to fall, but very little illumination. At least we were under cover and all together.

It was quite a pleasant interlude and we had free time in the evenings. Not that we did much during the day, but the army says that troops must be kept gainfully occupied so we cleaned, polished or refurbished whatever came to hand.

By crossing two fields then walking up a hill it was possible to reach a small estaminet where drinks were extremely cheap. I still hadn`t acquired a taste for beer but I did like Normandy cider. The little estaminet was very hospitable and had a good atmosphere when the locals were in. For a meal we walked to a village nearby where we found cafés to supply the ubiquitous egg and chips.

In the village was a dance hall decorated with bunting and artificial flowers. A floor of wooden blocks, about as level as pavé, created space to "trip the light fantastic" and fantastic it turned out to be. I am no dancer but I had the rudiments and a few of us felt this was an activity we could enjoy rather than drink all night.

The dance hall was slow to fill and we had to occupy some time with a tipple after all, this seemingly being the done thing.

For a dance to be a dance, of course, men need girls for partners. We were there, some of the local blades were there, but no girls. We sipped our cider and listened to the "band," a kettle and a bass drum with piano accordion accompaniment, in that order of volume. The tunes played by this ensemble were those jerky Latin-type ditties much favoured by tourists and which one associates with Montmartre. "J`attendrai" and "Parlez-moi d`amour" were thrown in somewhere, too, at least I think they were. They must have been. They were bound to be, I`m sure.

For the first hour it seemed that it was going to be an all male affair. Then slowly, almost fearfully, a few of the local girls put in an appearance.

Of course, our lot weren`t slow to snatch the opportunity of dancing with a real French girl, but the real French girls obviously hadn`t got the same idea. Maybe it was the approach. Maybe they weren`t used to being asked to dance with encouraging phrases like,

"Howay, hinny, put yer kitten doon" or

"Is yer rabbit deed, lass?" delivered in broad Geordie.

Whenever one of us tried to take a partner, the result was either a look of horror followed by a rapid retreat behind the nearest potted palm, or the lady in question literally doubled up with mirth, along with any other girls standing nearby. The British are nothing if not persistent, however, and we all continued to try until eventually it worked. The ladies discovered, either to their relief or disappointment, that the purpose of our request was dancing not rape.

Dancing, French style, may have changed since the war but in 1940 it was not quite what was expected by any of us who had learned the English way. To begin with one held one`s partner at least two feet away – nothing personal one might say. There was none of this "left arm around the waist, right hand clasped with arms bent." The expression "cheek to cheek" would have been looked upon as being positively erotic. No. The dancing stance was roughly two feet apart, nearly three if you are tall, both arms outstretched, and hands firmly grasped. When the music began the body was jerked as a puppet on a string and the arms pumped up and down alternately as though one was trying to pump water on the village green. No regard was paid whatsoever to dancing steps, other occupants on the floor, wear and tear on clothing or footwear, physical peculiarities, or the music of the band. The music only heralded the start of the dance and might have some small bearing on the end of it should one not have fallen exhausted by then.

We had to concede defeat in the end. It may have been that all the French young people at the dance were from the local village and were naturally shy. Perhaps our uniforms, different looks and attitudes were inhibiting, or maybe we weren`t as welcome as we thought. It was disappointing, chiefly because we hadn`t enjoyed our first real night out as much as we had hoped.

The second of our two nights in this place was so much better. I went for a haircut and found that, like French dancing, it was a completely new experience. At least, I was able to sit still while the hairdresser danced attendance. My hair wasn`t long – it wasn`t allowed to be – but I thought that, as the opportunity had presented itself, I`d take it. The most surprising part of the haircutting procedure was that the whole time the scissors snipped, my head was being doused with powder. I feared at first this powder might be Keatings, used as a preventative measure, but its heady strong perfume (and French perfumes are pungent!) soon indicated it was more to do with the cutting since all the other customers, all male, were sitting in clouds of powder no less perfumed than mine. In those days my hair was quite fair but when I left the hairdressers one might have suspected that I`d suffered a severe shock – but I smelled glorious!

CHAPTER ELEVEN – War Zone: The Somme 1914-18

Next day we moved off. No-one said where to, just follow the vehicle in front. Not a very sensible arrangement, but we were still suffering from this rather old-fashioned attitude that the troops didn`t need to be told anything just as long as the officers had their orders. They were commissioned to lead and the rest of us would follow. We did, as far as possible, like glue, but it was all too easy to get lost and then there was a long delay while everyone waited for the stray to catch up or, as more often happened, someone had to go and find the "lost sheep." Equally stupidly, it was always the one who got lost who was blamed.

I was beginning to notice around this time that our SgtMT was acting in a rather morose fashion. He was usually brash, noisy and full of his own importance, though he didn`t bother me whatever his attitude was to others. Now he was quiet and retiring, not his usual self at all. At the same time, his cunning, loud-mouthed Lance Sergeant became more obvious around the place, chucking his weight about unnecessarily and, worst of all, his superior didn`t make any attempt to curb him, unusual indeed. There seemed to be a lack of interest on the SgtMT`s part in all that was going on. Orders weren`t issued, checks weren`t made, he didn`t want to see the daily routine administrative work for which I was responsible. Neither did the Lance Sergeant, but that wasn`t surprising; he wouldn`t have known what it was all about anyway. He hated the idea that I could do something and know about something with which he couldn`t begin to cope. I tried to find out from the SgtMT what was bothering him but it wasn`t easy to get through to him at the best of times. Just now he wasn`t able to, or wouldn`t, communicate.

It was quite a long journey from Le Havre to Albert on the Somme and we drove through some attractive countryside and pretty villages. There were a lot of very sobering First World War cemeteries in this area and the nearer we got to Albert the more cemeteries we passed, some of them holding many hundreds of graves. This brought home to us very clearly the results of war, the purpose of our being here.

We were led to understand that after its almost complete destruction in the First World War, Albert had been rebuilt in its original form. Towering over the town centre is the beautiful church with the golden Virgin Mary topping the dome. The story went that, in 1914-18, if the statue were to fall, the war would be lost. Apparently, the Germans did their best to make the story come true but although she slipped, tilted and rocked, Our Lady never fell, partly due to some expert shoring up by British Royal Engineers.

Our destination was beyond Albert, one and a half miles up a very narrow country road to Bécourt. Bécourt was barely a hamlet, consisting only of two or three very old rustic cottages, an estaminet, a farm and a chateau.

The chateau was the focal point. We weren`t officially designated as a bodyguard but, being the only troops near the place, it must surely have been expected of us because the occupants of the chateau were our Brigadier and his staff.

It wasn`t a huge building by chateau standards but it was very elegant and well kept. A large white gate opened onto a wide drive up to the front door. Weeping willows, poplars and Cypress trees graced the front, and behind the chateau stretched a vast lawn around which ran a gravel road flanked by huge old trees, oaks, elms, sycamores and chestnuts. It was a beautiful setting, well away from any major habitation. To the left of the main gate was the "factor`s house", or whatever a chateau-keeper`s place is called. Next to it was a smaller cottage in which lived the local postman and his very attractive daughter. Beyond was a tile floored conservatory complete with palms and semi-tropical plants, outside which stretched a considerable kitchen garden with a soft fruit plot and orchards.

I really took the place to heart from the first moment and enjoyed almost every minute of our stay in this sleepy little place. I looked forward to a long stay.

The vehicles were parked round the great lawn at the back under the trees and our first firm instruction, issued by the Brigadier himself no less, was that no-one, repeat no-one, would walk anywhere across the expanse of grass. Our reaction to this, as one might expect, was "What`s special about that grass?" but it wasn`t quite like that. The reason for this order was that if we constantly walked from our vehicles around the perimeter to the cookhouse, the office and the latrines, all of which were situated under the trees, the grass would eventually be flattened into tracks, and tracks would betray our exact position to any enemy reconnaissance aircraft. Quite sensible really, and I`m sure the Brigadier had our safety in mind.

The weather was improving. The days were warm and even at night the temperature was quite comfortable.

On the side of the lawn where our al fresco kitchen was located, we discovered a network of trench works. Most were overgrown with tangled weeds and brambles after twenty odd years but they were clearly recognisable for what they'd been in 1914-18. Along the tops of these trenches most of the angle iron and corkscrew posts still stood, albeit somewhat awry. The rusting barbed wire was still there and strong enough to serve its original purpose.

Living right on top of this piece of land, which must have seen so much close combat in that earlier war, was quite fascinating. There was an atmosphere about the place one could almost feel, particularly in the stillness of the evening, and many of us were absorbed with imagining what it might have been like at that time. Poking about in the undergrowth, we found "souvenirs" lying where they'd fallen. Their owners probably hadn't time to retrieve them or, in the case of helmets of both friend and foe, with a tell-tale bullet hole, had no further use for them.

The entrance to a dug-out came to light one day. Steps, carefully constructed, led down deep into a tunnel. It looked safe enough but none of us wanted to risk further investigation.

Years later I read war books about this earlier period and it seemed that our temporary home had been the front line of both sides, or very near it, as battle had raged back and forth. Judging by the direction the entrance faced, the deep dug-out was almost certainly of German construction.

One day I went for a walk with Robbo. We crossed some fields to reach a slight rise, only pausing to hide in some bushes as an aircraft droned slowly overhead. It was almost certainly German because we never saw British planes. I doubt if we spoiled his photographs with our rapid movements, but we weren't taking any chances. Anyway, we reached the rise and looked over the top. A surprising sight staggered us. The rise was part of the lip of an enormous crater yards and yards across and so deep it was quite scary to look to the bottom down its steep sides. It was the result of a First World War mining explosion, one of the biggest ever blown. What went up with it when the bang occurred, goodness knows. Thirty years after the Second War, I stood on the same spot again with my wife and family just to prove to them that my stories were not made up!

We didn't go into Albert every night but when we did, usually at the weekends, our number one priority was food, maybe because we were hungry or perhaps because a café gave us the chance to relax in a different atmosphere. Two or three shops had caught on to the fact that English

Tommies were partial to chips but there was not much choice about what to have with them. It amounted to chips and egg if finances were low, or chips and steak if one wanted to be rash.

It was during one of my chips and egg meals that I got talking to Madame, the owner of the café, about music. I cannot play a note or read music but I am fond of it and I suppose I must have shown the right sort of interest. It resulted in an invitation to come "back shop" and listen to the music of an ensemble in which she played. There were a couple of violins, a cello and a woodwind instrument, and they were quite good. Their repertoire ranged from someone`s violin concerto to selections from musicals. I particularly enjoyed it, as much because it was something personal and different. I also had visions of having my "feet under the table," so to speak, but it wasn`t to be because for us time was running out. That was my first and last musical evening and the last supper out, which may have been fortuitous because soireés were really too stuffy for a twenty year old at war!

So, we tried something else. A few of us happened to be down in Albert during the day, a weekday. There was a very large High School at the end of the town, a sort of cross between a secondary school and a college. It stood at the end of a long wide drive with seats on both sides. The drive and the seats were open to the public so we sat down to wait. The idea was that when the students came out we might be able to prevail upon some of the girls to show interest. In the course of time, the young people from the school made their way down the drive in twos and threes. Strangely enough, they didn`t walk down in mixed company but it mattered not, we only wanted to talk to the girls. Their response was slow but eventually a little group stopped and as soon as they did, a passing group of boys made some remark which immediately caused the girls to giggle and walk on. I`m afraid our success at chatting up girls was on this occasion no better than our efforts at Yvetot.

It is quite possible that individual members of the Unit found companionship with the opposite sex if their rather lurid stories were to be believed, but we were inclined to favour safety in numbers and never had the inclination or courage to go it alone. It wasn`t particularly important that we made friends with the civilian population but it would have been interesting and I suppose we felt a sense of frustration that it never worked out for us. We were young and inexperienced and the French were understandably reticent.

On our way home that night there was the father and mother of a thunderstorm just before we reached Bécourt. Its approach had been very obvious. The sky grew black across the whole horizon and the wind dropped to a calmness and stillness that could be felt: like this period of the war, the calm before the storm. We hurried past the little war cemetery on the right and the wood of small tress that hid the stack of howitzer shells from the '14/'18, and just as the chateau came into sight, lightning flashed and thunder rolled around us like an artillery bombardment. The rain was torrential.

Signs were just beginning to show that our time at Bécourt was getting much shorter, although we didn`t know it.

Next day we had to go to a vehicle park some distance away to collect five 5 cwt pickup trucks for the officers. These PUs were the small powerful personal vehicles I`ve already described. It meant things were moving.

A gun pit was dug at each end of the great lawn and sandbagged. Each emplacement contained a Lewis gun on a tripod, cocked and ready to fire, another sign of expectancy.

There was much coming and going at the chateau. The Brigadier, who was not usually seen, made a number of excursions with a comet`s tail of vehicles tearing after his staff car at top speed. He was even seen walking in the grounds deep in thought. It may have been a touch of indigestion but I had a feeling that his discomfort was not physical. There was something more in the wind.

Life had to go on and many of our Unit continued with their daily challenge of trying to be the one who made the grade with the postman`s daughter who lived in the chateau lodge. This had been an occupation eagerly pursued since we first arrived at Bécourt. Despite great dedication on the part of all who tried, none had made the slightest progress. She was an extremely pretty girl and no-one could be blamed for trying. Every time she appeared, and that was quite frequently because not only did she keep house for her father, she was also a waitress at the Brigadier`s table, everyone stopped, turned and whistled or found some suitable French remark to make if they knew one. Mademoiselle never looked to right or left, never smiled, and never faltered from her mission, whatever that happened to be. The rejected, rebuffed and frustrated in our ranks reached the point of accusing this pretty lass of being a spy or in the 5th column. She may well have been, in retrospect, but I doubt if she`d have been much use with such a complete absence of contact or communication with the men. Of course, the spadework might all have taken place in the chateau: we soldiers didn`t have many secrets to give away but who knows what the Brigadier and his staff had to offer.

On the night of 9th May the Captain for whom I was driver had a dinner date. This wasn`t particularly unusual: he often had a night out, but there was a bit of a problem. Shortly after taking over his PU truck, the Captain had decided to have a bunk bed built by the Unit joiner into his vehicle across the back behind the cab, installed ready for the time when we would take on our mobile rôle. The Captain had never slept in this bed because he had a much more comfortable one in the chateau, but I had. My allotted place overnight was in a tent with others or sometimes in the back of one of the larger vehicles. Neither of these places was very comfortable so I`d become used to using the 2i/c`s bunk. Now that he was going out for the night in his PU my bed was going with him. He went, with all I possessed except a blanket! Fortunately, when the weather was warm, the tiled floor of the conservatory at the end of the cottages wasn`t too uncomfortable and that night it was warm.

CHAPTER TWELVE – Bombed!

Normally we got up at about 7.30 am but on May 10th we were awakened at dawn. It was just light and the sky was filled with that de-synchronised drone easily recognised later in the war as German aircraft. The sky seemed full of them but perhaps there weren`t more than fifty. They were slow moving, on a bombing mission, and the first hostile aircraft we`d seen. It struck me as rather sad that only twenty years had passed since the nations who had fought each other to a standstill over this very ground should be about to start all over again. And here was I, one of the next generation, about to receive similar treatment from the same enemy in exactly the same spot in yet another world war.

We threw ourselves out of the glass-walled conservatory into the slit trenches as the black war planes wheeled slowly round and began their dive towards us, their engines making a steady crescendo. The bombs started their curving fall and, because this was our first experience of an air raid, we felt that sure that each missile was meant for us. Perhaps some shut their eyes but I didn`t: I was curious to see what hit me. I watched the bombs passing over and onward to fall beyond the hill about two miles away. It might have been comforting to think that the Hun had missed, but it was soon obvious that they hadn`t; their objective was the aircraft factory at Méaulte, two miles down the road just over the hill. To prove their success a large pall of smoke rose from that direction as the planes climbed away to the north east.

There was almost euphoria as we climbed out of our slit trenches. The war had started: we`d looked the Germans in the eye, been attacked, and survived.

Shortly after breakfast the 2i/c sent for me.

"How`s your French these days, Driver?" He, too, knew something of my background and that I`d taken French at school.

"Rusty, Sir," was my reply.

"Someone has unexploded bombs in their back garden and I need your assistance," he went on. "Get the PU."

We made our way to Méaulte, past the factory which was still smoking. French Air Force personnel were busy among some ruins but the damage was very little considering the number of aircraft and the noise of the bombs. We weren`t concerned with that, however: our task was amongst the houses.

Méaulte was quite small really, hardly more than a village, but some of the bombs had strayed into the streets surrounding the aircraft factory.

The garden to which we were directed had, sure enough, had three bombs drop in it, creating apertures about the size of rabbit holes. Captain Osborne and I were told by the very upset householder that they had had a narrow squeak, surviving only because the bombs hadn't gone off.

I did what was expected of me, offered words of comfort, assurance, courage and thanks for showing us the holes – in French – none of which carried much conviction as my English probably lost a bit in translation. The house owners beat a hasty retreat, slammed the door and we saw their faces peering round the curtains! That showed the general ignorance about explosions at that time in the war.

Meanwhile, my chief stood over one bomb hole, feet astride, and looked intently down the cavity. He was the man in charge and the Engineer, so I stood astride the other bomb hole and tried to look down equally intently.

Our Captain was quite ruthless about certain soldierly traditions in service life, but I was happy that I had someone to serve who had a sense of humour. His came out in many ways, often just when it was most needed. I was very glad when, later in the war, he was made Colonel RE.

After a minute's consideration of the hole, he took three or four paces back, bent his knees and lined up the cavity as would a professional golfer down on the green before making a putt.

"What do you think, Driver, a niblick or a spoon to get mine out of the rough?"

I knew he'd accept any reply I made as long as I didn't overstep the mark.

"Don't know about yours, Sir," I said, "but I think I'll use a Driver, screw, bomb for the use of, on mine."

His next instruction was so unexpected I obeyed it without a second thought.

"See if you can touch it. It may not be deep."

I put my hand down the hole and at arm's length my fingers could close around the fins.

"Pull it out, man! Pull it out!" he shouted excitedly.

Out of the corner of my eye I saw the householders disappear from the windows.

I did as I was told and pulled out the bomb. It wasn't much bigger than a mortar bomb and we were pretty sure that the housing area had had a sprinkling of anti-personnel bombs.

Before the faces reappeared at the window, we rapidly filled in the other holes with soil and left, carrying our trophy cradled on a greatcoat in the back of the PU. Later, sappers blew open the bomb and discovered it was full of sand! Strangely enough, this happened quite a few times during the war when we had to blow up unexploded bombs. Some were filled with sand or other non-explosive materials, some had not been fused, and a few were quite empty. We liked to think that there were Germans who weren`t fervent Hitler supporters, or maybe the slave labour workers, gathered from all over Europe, had been at work. These bomb failures saved many lives including the Captain`s and mine, without a doubt, because a certain civil engineer with pips on his shoulder and a certain driver with nothing on his shoulder except cares, were not particularly brave that day, just plain idiots who hadn`t yet learned the dangers of war.

The following night our little group made a trip into Albert for a meal. For some reason we decided to splash out on steak and chips with eggs and a bottle of wine. It turned out that this meal would be our last in this pleasant café, but we didn`t know it. There had been another air raid. We`d seen the planes swooping down on the town last evening. No-one had been killed but the station building had lost a lot of tiles and glass, and the rails in the goods yard looked a mess. People living and working near the station were out clearing up the debris and all had serious and worried looks. Anyone living near a station as the war progressed knew that it was only a matter of time before it was their turn to be hit.

The owner of the café, which was quite near the station, was really agitated when we went in for our meal. We tried to offer some comfort and consolation that the damage was, at least, confined to the railway.

We learned that the attacks on Albert and Méaulte were only part of a much larger plan that was to have far-reaching results. The radio had broadcast news that on 9th/10th May the Germans had begun a thrust through the Ardennes at Sedan, though the French army was containing it, with heavy casualties on both sides. Military commentators suggested that the German High Command in general, and Hitler in particular, had played a predictably dirty trick by trying to break through at the place where there was the least defence. They knew perfectly well that the Maginot Line had been built specifically keep them out and they`d ignored it. Not only that, but the Germans were fully aware that the gallant BEF was deployed across the Low Countries to combat a repetition of the 1914 Schlieffen Plan and they`d ignored that, too. Instead, the dirty rotters had made their attack through the forests of the Ardennes which Marshall Pétain had clearly and distinctly stated were impassable.

We enjoyed our meal, one of the best ever, and our expressions of enjoyment and general "devil-may-care" attitude probably became slightly exaggerated. The atmosphere, the news, and the gloomy faces of the locals in the café told us that things were about to happen, and our answer to it all was to act the part of protectors, brave heroes, and tough, hardened campaigners. It was the wine, of course, the good food and that comfortable feeling of well-being when one is replete. I like to think that we spread a little bit of entente cordiale around the place that night and, hopefully, the Albertians in the café felt they had less to worry about than they'd thought, even though disillusionment was to come with an awful thump soon afterwards.

We'd had so little personal contact with local people since we came to France, it was something of a surprise when, on our walk home that evening, an elderly gentleman hailed us from his garden gate.

Just outside the town, along the country road we took back to the chateau, there were a number of small cottage-type homes with pretty gardens. No matter how small the house, each had a substantial protective fence or railing with the gate kept locked, something we found unusual because it certainly discouraged visitors.

Anyway, this old boy opened his gate and beckoned us in. It was really quite an honour to be invited in, even if it did seem like stepping into a cage. He was pathetically charming, however, and the purpose of his invitation was to ask my advice. He'd seen us pass a few times, going to and from Albert, and must have decided that we looked reliable and sober enough to approach, together with the fact that we carried the badge of the Royal Engineers on our caps and arms.

Would I please look at his self-constructed air raid shelter here in the garden and pass judgement on its design and safety? Well, I ask you! Me, ex-accounts clerk, sometime Sunday School teacher, now a driver even less than sometimes, and I was being asked to pronounce on a piece of engineering for safety, but it's amazing what a piece of flattery can do and I'm just as susceptible to it as the next man. Before I could think of all the ramifications of my actions, I'd crawled into the shelter, poked the roof, felt the joists, kicked the sandbags and murmured snippets of technical jargon I'd heard the sappers use like "revetment" and "stress" and "stepped support," etc., all very grand phrases that meant very little really and I couldn't translate into French anyway. The old boy obviously viewed me as the expert and that's what made it pathetic, but my conscience was eased by the fact that he knew far more about engineering than I did. He'd made a really good job of his shelter and only wanted assurance, I felt sure. I gave him that willingly and in all honesty because the place would have been safe from everything except a direct hit and that wasn't altogether likely. The only thing I wasn't happy about, which didn't seem to be part of Air Raid Precautions Equipment, was a sporting rifle propped up in the corner and two hand grenades, one a Mills bomb and the other a stick grenade of 1914-18 vintage. I mentioned this in as jocular a fashion as I could muster, my French vocabulary being somewhat sketchy for such a situation. His answer wasn't in the least light-hearted: in fact, it was a veritable tirade of invective most liberally sprinkled with words I did understand like, "dernière guerre" and "salle Bosch" or "vache", "mort" "sacre bleu", etc., etc. By which I took him to mean that if and when the Germans passed that way he intended to use his souvenirs left over from World War 1 on the same enemy in World War 2. I was glad I came under the heading of an ally.

The sincere but fiery old Frenchman's thanks took the form of a glass of good wine - private stocks always seemed better than the bought stuff – all round. My two friends, who had been interested spectators in this charade, had at least benefited from their support even if it was silent, and we then went on our way, pleasantly refreshed, up the hill.

Two nights previously we'd walked along this country road to the crash and rumble of a thunderstorm. As we reached the crest of the slope this time we were again to hear a crash and a rumble, but it wasn't thunder.

Away over the distant horizon, too far for the naked eye to see, was the Ardennes. It was a long way to the source of the noise, but the sound of an artillery barrage, particularly one of this magnitude, carried many miles. It was also just possible to distinguish heavy black clouds in the same direction. We were seeing and hearing land war for the first time and, as with the thunderstorm, we knew then, with absolute certainty, that it would eventually roll our way and we would be caught up in it.

We stood on the top of the rise just above the quiet little war cemetery by the wood with the stacked artillery shells that would never be fired, and wondered what the future held for us. I know a cold shiver ran down my spine as I watched and I'm sure it was the same for my friends.

As the rumbling rose and fell we hurried away down to Bécourt and temporary security.

The news of events was now grave and it seemed that things could happen quickly. I wanted to keep up to date but as no-one in authority put us in the picture in those days, the answer was to listen to regular news bulletins. I had a radio, the only one in the Unit, bought originally with my Territorial Bounty money. It was a good one, covered in blue leather, with two wave bands, a lot of power and a wide range. I`d used it a great deal in Yarm.

Portable radios were in their infancy in those days and the power was supplied by a rather cumbersome battery and accumulator, both of which fitted into the back of the set. It was made more efficient by stringing an aerial across a room or between two trees. The Unit joiner, for a consideration, made me a good strong box which took the radio, two spare batteries and a spare accumulator in such a way that all were held firmly, and the set could be used without removing it from the box. There was only one snag, however, which I discovered when I got to Bécourt in France. It turned out that I wasn`t allowed to have a radio. The CSM informed me of this regulation shortly after our arrival. He said that it was his duty to confiscate it but, as he wasn`t a hard man, he was prepared to let me "store" it in his room for the time being, on condition that I didn`t object to him using it! As a special concession, which he would only do for me as I was so co-operative, he`d let me listen to any particular programme I wanted to hear, or the news. He assured me it would be perfectly safe in his hands and he wouldn`t say a word to anyone about my breach of regulations in bringing a forbidden radio set into France. There was another small point that would help him with his "understanding", and that was that I would see to having the accumulator charged each week and the battery renewed when necessary. I bowed to the inevitable. A few times I went to his room in one of the chateau`s cottages to listen to my radio, but he was "out." I knew this because the door was locked and the sound of music drifted through the keyhole. Now that the war was hotting up in the Ardennes, however, the CSM became a little more receptive about me going to listen to the news and commentaries on the hostilities overall.

The news was not good. The Germans were throwing a great weight of hardware onto the French at Sedan. Their air force was keeping up continuous daytime bombing, and tanks were massing for a breakthrough. Stronger French forces opposed them, in troop numbers and artillery, but the French army was very immobile and their equipment was neither modern nor designed for the kind of fighting the much better trained and rapidly moving Germans had perfected, blitzkrieg. Valiant defence was put up by the French divisions but German tactics and the skilful use of aircraft was telling. Everyone, even we in our sleepy little French village with little or no fighting experience, were aware that sooner or later the line would crack and what then?

I decided to pack. It seemed to me that when the balloon went up there would be a mad scramble and I didn`t want to be caught unprepared. First of all, I wanted my personal belongings all together in my small pack so that I could grab it in a hurry. I`d bought a number of small souvenirs and presents for the folks at home. These I packed into the box made for my radio where there was a little space. I did not intend leaving my radio so I left empty the section built to take it ready for its collection at the last minute. I knew there would be a good deal of driving to do so I packed away my heavy army boots and wore civilian shoes. Army boots were so cumbersome and made it difficult to drive the temperamental little PU. In odd corners of the PU I tucked away things like chocolate, bottles of cider, wine, water, a couple of packs of toilet paper, a few books to read, two tins of corned beef and some packets of hard tack biscuits, and a couple of extra blankets, with the full approval of the Captain with whom I might have to rough it. I felt I`d more or less done all I could for the moment.

The next morning I had to take the CSM into Peronne about something or other. It didn`t take long. On our return, as we turned into our country road from Albert, we heard a considerable amount of small arms fire both in the region of the chateau and around the area where other Units were stationed. It was alarming. I speeded up. Suddenly, over our heads, tree top height, flashed three aircraft, one behind the other. They were jinking from side to side. Three biplanes but, to our horror, we saw the black crosses on their wings! For the first time ever it seemed we were really under attack by German war planes.

I pulled the 15 cwt we were using under some trees and we beat a rapid retreat into the woods. After a moment or two we felt brave enough to have a peep. The CSM went one way and I went the other to the edge of the wood where we could see the chateau and a fair stretch of countryside beyond. Quite a sight met our eyes. There was an aerial attack in progress right enough, by about a dozen of those little biplanes, type unknown. At the time my aircraft recognition was limited to black crosses or roundels.

The planes were diving and swooping, machine-gunning not only the chateau and its grounds but also the numerous villages round about where the British army units attached to Headquarters were located. It seemed strange that the pilots of those aircraft knew exactly what they were doing. Someone had done some homework, and every British army position was accurately pinpointed. Time and again the planes swooped down like angry wasps and let fly with their guns, although I didn't see any bombs dropped.

We got back into the truck and set off again up the road, arriving at the chateau just at the tail end of the last straff, aimed at the Brigadier.

There was, naturally, great excitement in the camp when I drove in. A lot of broken glass and bullet holes but, miraculously, no-one had been hit, although a few suffered from flying glass splinters, bumps and bruises.

No-one had fired the Lewis gun at the far end of the big lawn, but the other, in front of the chateau, had been manned very bravely by the Company Quartermaster Sergeant. He'd shot off about half a drum, pretty accurately by all accounts, then the thing had jammed. The Lewis gun manual gives page after page of possible stoppages and how to clear them. The CQMS had struggled to clear the fault but the raid was over before he'd got to Page 4, much to his annoyance. How many Lewis gunners suffered the same frustration? Only later did we appreciate the advantages of the Bren gun over the Lewis but at that time we had no Brens.

To the best of my knowledge no aircraft were brought down. The damage to the buildings was not serious but there is no doubt that everyone had had a fright and had been made aware of our vulnerability.

I should here mention again the problem of the SgtMT and his strangely morose behaviour which had intensified as the days went by. It turned out that he must have been told some time previously that he did not have the capacity to run and be responsible for a complete Field Company MT section on active service. It was no more than the truth. He had never been capable since I first came into contact with him before the war, and it was always a wonder how he had remained in that position, particularly when we moved into the war zone. His inefficiency would be a danger, not only to the section itself, but to the whole Unit. It wasn't really surprising that he had been told that his career with us was over but it must have come as a shock to one who had held the top job for so long.

He didn't discuss the matter with anyone. I don't suppose he could have done anyway. One day he was gone, bag and baggage, quite unsung, without any farewells, and not many noticed his absence. The post of SgtMT was filled by one of the section's Lance Sergeants who had been in this rank since territorial days, and long before I joined. I knew little about him other than he came from my home town, was a Local Government Officer with at least a sound administrative knowledge, quite the opposite of the "dear departed."

It didn't affect me much because administration had fallen to a low ebb. It was still unofficially on my shoulders but I had little time to attend to paperwork that nobody wanted. I still had a few drivers who would come to me with a question, "What shall I do about ...?" and I helped them as far as possible. Now that we had a new man, however, I absolved myself of responsibility and passed the buck with, "See Sgt. Johnson. He's taken over."

There was more and more activity at the chateau. All this, the air raids, the news and the many rumours flying around meant that the balloon was about to go up.

Days and dates from this point on until Dunkirk are very confused in my mind. It all began about 13th May 1940 and ended when I landed back on British soil on 2nd June 1940. Only the events remain clear and it is those events I now recall, more or less in the order they occurred.

CHAPTER THIRTEEN – The Rot Sets In

An officer, his sergeant, a corporal and two sappers arrived at the chateau one morning in a 15 cwt. They had been brought in from one of our other sections because they were experts, the most experienced explosives experts we had. The other ranks had been in the TA for some years and one had been a regular RE and was quite elderly. The officer's notoriety was for quite a different reason.

The officer, who rejoiced in the nickname of "Little Tinkle," was well known to me, though not socially, I hasten to add. In civilian life he worked for the same coal company as I did but whereas I worked in the Accounts Department above ground, Tinkle worked in the mine below ground, and never the twain shall meet! I wouldn't say I hated his guts and he couldn't stand me: rather it was that I couldn't stand him and he hated my guts. Things had never been easy since I'd brought him his pay packet.

At the beginning of the war, for some reason both he and I continued to be paid by the coal company for several weeks and as I was the very one who made up Tinkle's pay in civilian life, the Accounts Office gave me his pay packet to give to him when I collected my own money.

Miners' pay was a most complex business. The underground workers pre-1939 had a pay structure second to none. Our ledgers were huge, with hundreds of lines and columns, each for a different worker and a different job. I'm quite sure the purpose of the whole business was to ensure no-one knew what anyone else was earning. In point of fact, the only person who had any accurate idea was the pay clerk who made up the wages – and that was me. Friend Tinkle knew this, and when I delivered his pay packet he got quite a shock because I had to go to the Officers' Mess, knock on the door, salute smartly, hand over his pay and get a signature. He hated every moment of it and showed it, but oh boy, did I enjoy it! He probably thought he got some of his own back when I had to go up to him at the pay table, salute smartly and receive my pay, army rate, the princely sum of 14/- a week, but I know who found the pay business most distasteful.

Tinkle was an explosives expert. He was the official in the pit responsible for bringing down a section of coal seam with explosive for the miners to remove to the coal tubs or conveyor, and it was a tricky and dangerous job where men's lives were at risk. Our friend must have known his job well enough and I admired him for his expertise. His working conditions were far more hazardous and uncomfortable than mine at the coal company. He had a mining engineer's qualification for which, no doubt, he'd worked hard both practically and theoretically, and this gave him the right to a commission. Nevertheless, he had assumed a role of the greatest importance and self-inflation. Perhaps the cause of this was his very small stature: I could easily look down upon his 5 feet nothing.

The small party debussed, to use the army expression for extracting oneself from a cramped truck, and lined up. The Brigadier, his staff, our CO, his 2i/c, the CSM and Uncle-Tom-Cobley-and-All stood to one side while the party was given its orders and wished success.

Tinkle was the last to appear. His entrance had a similar effect on the audience as Madame Melba's entrance would have had upon the stage at La Scala in Milan in her heyday. Considering the mission which was being mounted, his rig-out was, to say the least, pretentious. We were all in our everyday battledress looking rather crumpled. He was wearing his best gabardine service dress with highly polished Sam Browne and leather pistol holster. His buttons and brass were quite dazzling. The side hat, which was named for its position, he wore directly across the top of his head like a coxcomb and it looked exactly like one, being the dress version of a RE officer's side hat, bright red. Eyes popped as they travelled down from the scarlet crown. They didn't have to go far to see that this peculiar little man was wearing riding breeches and, of all things, shining brown leather laced riding boots, the like of which the Chief of the General Staff would have been proud to wear at Buckingham Palace.

I managed, with difficulty, to bottle my laugh but a few onlookers behind the bushes gave vent to very audible chortles of derision which Tinkle thoroughly deserved. The poor Brigadier was certainly sartorially outshone and I felt embarrassed for him having to accept the "All Present and Correct, Sir," from his underling in fancy dress.

Some arrangements must have been made because I was told to collect the 2i/c's PU truck from its place under the trees. We were to use this instead of the 15 cwt. It was a good thing in one respect: the PU could move when it had to, in top gear, but it would be a very uncomfortable squash for the men who had to ride in the back. It was not for me to reason why and, no doubt, the switch had been made without much regard for anyone's comfort except Tinkle's.

We were told we had a long way to go, beyond St Quentin, to an RAF aerodrome which was in danger of being overrun by the rapidly advancing

Germans. The task for Tinkle and his sappers was to blow up the bomb and ammunition dumps and any planes that could not be flown out. A codicil to this order was that, should the Germans be in possession of the aerodrome, the dumps still had to be blown!

My job was to get the party there and back as quickly as possible and, hopefully, in one piece. There was one small snag, we were informed: it might be difficult, a British understatement if ever there was one, because no-one knew where the Germans had got to. We might bump into them or even have to make a dash through their lines of communication ... and back.

My preparations were almost complete. The only thing I had to do was take my radio box out of the 2i/c`s vehicle. I kept my radio, spare batteries and accumulator with me, however, because I felt it would be handy to keep up with the BBC news bulletins, our only source of information. The radio and its equipment fitted nicely into a recess between the seats.

The previous evening when I knew no-one was watching I`d dug a hole under some trees down the little lane by the stables. I hurried down there, put my box of precious belongings into the hole and covered it up with earth and leaves. It still looked rather obvious but I felt sure it couldn`t be seen and I would rescue it later. It was twenty five years before I was able to go back for it.[1]

I said a few farewells, trying to appear jocular which was far from the way I felt. My friends seemed genuinely concerned for my welfare, going on this sort of job with so many imponderables, and in the charge of an individual as unpopular as our Tinkle. I wasn`t his greatest supporter by any manner of means but if he didn`t come back neither did I, so I was on his side that far, at least.

The NCOs and sappers arranged themselves in the back of my vehicle with their boxes of explosives and detonators for footstools. I was lucky in that I had a padded seat and a view all round. Those in the back had a choice between a view to the rear only if the canvas canopy was fastened to the sides, in which case they had to suffer the dust from the roads which in those days was the norm in France. The alternative was to close the canopy, see nothing, and cook as the hot sun beat down on the canvas. For the sake of the explosive as much as anything, they chose to strap the canopy back. Tinkle stretched out comfortably in the passenger seat and we were off.

---

1 Appendix – Dad`s Box

My battle began immediately, with the little beggar I was driving, not with the officer – that was a separate skirmish. No, it was the PU truck with which I had to fight. Changing gear quietly was almost impossible and even with double-declutching it could only be done by allowing the revs to fall very slowly to almost nothing in between each gear movement, a very slow business, and we hadn't time for such nicety.

It was early when we left Bécourt. I was told we had about two hours of fast driving over unknown roads, so it was a question of stepping on it and to hell with finesse. I really did hate this method of crashing through the gearbox. When there was a lot of gear changing to do, and there was with such a load on, it became quite painful on the left hand. Each change sent a jarring shudder up my arm and it was a wonderful relief to get into top gear. Then the little so and so would really move.

We went through Albert, which had had another air raid and debris was well scattered around the square near our café. The main road to Péronne was crowded and I had to push my way through the stream coming in the opposite direction. Most of it was refugee traffic: farm carts, barrows, people pushing prams, private cars (their owners having found petrol from somewhere) most of which had a mattress tied to the top. Whole families trailed along on foot.

After about three miles the traffic suddenly stopped and we noticed, well ahead, that there was something on fire, giving off volumes of thick black smoke. It turned out to be a petrol bowser, nationality unknown, well alight and completely blocking the road. Some of the refugees and farm carts were making their way around it through the fields but this was no use to us. There was a side road very near to the burning vehicle which seemed a possibility. I wasn't given any time to ponder. Tinkle simply ordered,

"Take that side road, Driver!"

Thinking more about the possible effect of the heat from the burning bowser on the explosive than anyone's comfort, I yelled to those in the back, "Hang on!" and put my foot down.

Thank goodness for the power of that Ford V8 engine. It responded well and I was to be thankful for this more than once. No doubt you've seen television programmes of car chases where someone turns a right angled corner on two wheels: I'd never ever tried it before but it worked that day. Mind you, those in the back had a lot of rude things to say, and went on shouting them for some distance after the turn until Tinkle screamed at them to shut up. I didn`t stop to enquire how everyone was keeping in the back but at least I knew that we hadn`t blown up.

Progress was quiet and slower for a while but eventually we had to rejoin the main road again which, by now, was becoming really packed. In some respects we had an advantage because all the traffic was coming towards us and our difficulties were being caused by those trying to overtake, double banking or just spreading across the road onto our side.

The next bit of excitement happened so quickly it was over and done with before we realised what might have been its consequences.

I was pressing on against the tide at about 25 mph which was quite fast in the circumstances, when I noticed the traffic dead ahead stopping and people running in all directions on both sides of the road. Never having experienced straffing by aircraft before, my action was just to wonder and keep going. It didn`t take long to learn that one should bail out and dive for the nearest ditch or tree, even if the truck was still moving. On this occasion, however, I kept going and within seconds I was looking at an aeroplane head on. I felt as a mouse must upon coming face to face with a cat unexpectedly. Everything was crystal clear: the spinning propeller glinting in the sunlight, the pilot`s face behind his windscreen, the sparkling red points of light in the wings of the plane, remarkably small when seen close to, then the plane flashed overhead. Spurts of dirt jumped up from the road and grass verge before my eyes but I didn`t feel any sense of danger or fear. I never got the feeling that the airman was trying to kill me, nor that he would and, thank goodness, he didn`t. The lot in the back didn`t even know we were under attack until they saw the Messerschmitt disappearing down the road.

Very often, we found out afterwards, such a plane would come back for another run, but this one didn`t. Anyway, I just kept going and it was only later that I found a couple of jagged holes, one through the wing on my side which, fortunately, had missed the tyre, and the other through the top of the canvas canopy between the two front seats. Miraculously, that one had gone out of the back somewhere without anyone being aware of the peril. I was very proud of those bullet holes and, as time passed, came to realise that I was leading a sort of charmed life.

All the people who had abandoned their carts, cars and belongings to flee from the straffing plane slowly returned to the road. It was pitiful to see the distress and fear which showed in their faces. No homes, no future and no hope. We, at least, had a little more than that.

All over Northern France at that time this frightening experience was being enacted, and people – old men, women and children – were being wounded and killed. Some may have been cut down in this raid but we didn't stop to find out: we had to press on.

I made quicker progress during the lull when the traffic stopped and the refugees were still slowly sorting themselves out, but it didn't last long. Once again our speed was drastically reduced to a crawl by the heedless mass. The delay was obviously raising Tinkle's blood pressure and he kept shouting,

"Go on, go on! Push them to one side!" rather like a jockey in the Grand National.

This was all very well but one cannot nudge a huge farm cart with a flimsy 5 cwt PU without damage, and damage would have brought us to a much more permanent halt. Nor did I feel inclined to bump human beings out of the way. They had had enough to suffer from the enemy without injury by an ally. So I ignored Tinkle's mounting fury and did the best I could, getting slower and slower. He was an officer with orders to carry out a mission so I suppose he had every right to make the next move which, to say the least, shook me rigid.

"Get out of the driving seat," he barked and slung open his door.

I stopped, which didn't take much doing, but I really didn't think he was serious. He was. He came round to my door and snarled,

"Get out!"

I got out. He didn't ask me to get in again but I wasn't going to be left so I hurried round and got into the passenger side. Our charming friend then got behind the wheel and, revving the engine full blast and with hand on horn, he charged the oncoming mass of people and traffic. Human beings leapt in all directions at speeds governed by their age and ability, as he ploughed forward.

To begin with I thought, "You beggar. You're ruthless but it's worked!"

I felt a number of bumps and dull thuds and prayed they were inanimate objects causing them but then, looming ahead, was a huge farm cart. Our speed didn't slacken. For the first time on this trip I felt fear. After all this, am I going to die squashed against a hay wain with not a Constable in sight? I could only stare helplessly and hang on as the gap between us narrowed. There wasn't really room to get through but these PUs were quite small. That, together with some very rapid heaving on the horse's reins by its French farmer owner, left the absolute minimum space for us to scrape through, literally: I heard the paint being scraped off the side.

"Stupid bloody French," was all the poor farmer got from Tinkle for saving our lives.

Just past where this happened there was a gate into a ploughed field.

"Open that gate, Driver!" was the next urgent command.

I restrained myself from questioning the absurdity of attempting to drive our heavily loaded vehicle, which was certainly not designed for cross-country work, across a ploughed field. But an order was an order and it would have been foolhardy of me to make any objection. I had been taken over by higher command and, providing he didn`t kill us he could, as far as I was concerned, drop himself up to the neck in the mire if that`s the way he wanted it.

I opened the gate for us to make this clever by-pass of the traffic on the road. The ground was completely flat for miles and miles and the traffic stretched as far as the eye could see. It was, therefore, going to be a long detour to clear the build up and the route before us was rough ploughed ground with the spring green of early crops showing here and there. Trees weren`t a problem, the only trees being those lining the road planted by Napoleon to shelter his troops from the sun as they marched. Those same trees, grown very tall since Napoleon`s day, did offer a small measure of cover and protection, but from a different attacker. Neither were there any hedges to bar our progress: French farmers don`t feel the need for such boundaries. I was fairly certain, however, that if we did manage to make progress across this ground we were almost bound to come to ditches as field ditches in this countryside were quite common. They were deep, had few crossing places, were not marked in any way and, as a rule, lay hidden until one was right up to the steep sides.

As soon as the gate stood wide my PU`s engine rose to a scream. Then, as the clutch engaged, the vehicle charged through into the field. It occurred to me, quite without reason, to wonder what on earth was the purpose of the gate anyway? There was neither fence nor hedge on either side of it, nor was it likely to keep cattle in or stupid officers out. I left the gate open and moved to join the rest.

I never knew whether or not Tinkle intended to stop and pick me up. The vehicle certainly showed no signs of slowing down. With a most appalling whining, it charged across the rough ground, slipping and sliding, the men in the back bouncing around like peas on a drum. Their faces when they saw me standing by the gate were a study. I like to think they would have been happier with me at the wheel.

The end, of course, was inevitable. A rear wheel drive vehicle, built as low as the Ford, and with its strange gear ratio, was absolutely bound to dig in at the first piece of soft ground, and it did. Racing the engine only made matters worse and before I caught up, the back wheels had dug in deep and that was that. As I arrived to join them, everyone was out looking at the poor old truck knee deep in mud. His Lordship was giving it a kick. I'd no particular love for the vehicle but for once it was completely innocent.

With job in hand still to complete and aircraft around it was no good just standing there so the Sergeant took charge. First of all, he dug out the wheels, then got us all round to more or less carry the PU to the gate and back onto the road. Tinkle seemed too abashed to object and his boots were absolutely filthy by now, so his deflation was complete, temporarily at least.

I took the wheel again and we actually made some progress.

About an hour later we were climbing a rise to meet a crossroads and something made me pull in. My officer was dozing but the braking woke him up and, not unreasonably, he asked why we had stopped. I hesitated to answer and that didn't go down too well but I just wasn't sure.

Ahead, on the skyline, passing along a road at right angles to us, more or less in silhouette, was a string of nose-to-tail traffic. The road was the usual tree-lined stretch and the traffic was horse-drawn with a few motor vehicles interspersed, and there were people, lots of people. That all seemed normal: we'd been bothered with this sort of traffic movement all day, but the goods on the carts looked different, the vehicles were not Citroens and the people were all male, in uniforms, with coal scuttle helmets.

Tinkle had his binoculars on the road by now and he whispered, "My God. Germans. Sit still. Don't move!"

He didn't need to tell me: I was rooted to my seat. It would have been most difficult to turn round in so narrow a road and it was straight so I'd have had to reverse a long way to find an opening. In addition, any movement might well have attracted attention. We sat still. Fortunately, the German column wasn't expecting any opposition and they certainly weren't likely to get any from us. They didn't look very war-like and my morale was raised just a little by their apparent lack of aggression.

When the tail end of the column disappeared into the distance I started up the engine and dashed across the crossroads without even knowing how I got through the gears. We sped on like a bat out of hell and hoped we weren't followed.

In due course we reached our destination, the RAF airfield.

All was furious activity and warlike preparations. My first impressions were that everyone was either Flying Officer Kite or related to him, and that the airfield was Much Binding In The Marsh not an obscure makeshift aerodrome no more than a big field somewhere in France.

Dodging taxiing aircraft, we drove from group to group of airmen busy with ammunition or bombs, and finally ran their Commanding Officer to earth.

The contrast between our leader and theirs was as amusing as it was enormous. Tinkle marched smartly up to the regulation distance from the RAF CO and threw up his most vibrating salute. This was acknowledged with a casual wave of his pipe by the tall fair-haired flier.

"Reporting to blow up your dumps, Sir!"

"You don't have to worry about them, Old Fruit. Before we fly out our last plane will take up what's left and shovel the stuff out onto the Bosch."

I'm sure he meant business. He exuded confidence absolutely and his personality didn't need a red hat and cavalry breeches to show it. We left with our tails between our legs, or at least Tinkle did.

Now that this episode was all over I was in a hurry to get back to Bécourt and wherever possible I put my foot down.

We were returning through a small farming village when I saw, to my horror, a huge cart coming slowly out of a walled farm. From the gate to the road there was a slight slope. In a flash I realised that there was no horse in the shafts, it was being pushed. This meant that when it reached the slope it would quicken and reach the road at the same moment as we would pass. My choice was to brake and hope we would stop before hitting the cart broadside, or speed up if possible and hopefully get clear. I chose the latter and nearly made it, but not quite. The cart did as I expected and just caught the back nearside corner of the canopy. There was an almighty clang which threw the truck to one side. We wobbled some yards and skidded to a halt.

Tinkle was cursing something but I was already out to see how they had fared in the back. By the most amazing stroke of luck, the sapper sitting on that corner had just moved into the middle to sit on the floor. I shudder to think what injuries he might have sustained otherwise. The canopy was well and truly mangled and the corner of the bodywork bent. The farm cart wasn`t even scratched, needless to say. My luck had held again.

We all got aboard and, very shaken, set off again. I knew Tinkle was going to be either critical or sarcastic, but before he could say a word I grumbled,

"Stupid bloody French," which was exactly his remark after his brush with the French farm cart earlier. That shut him up completely and we motored back to Bécourt in silence.

CHAPTER FOURTEEN – Leaving Bécourt

Back at the chateau all was chaos and despondency. The calm and control we had left that morning had gone. People were dashing hither and thither; no-one had time to stop, everything was urgent, desperate, immediate. I managed to pin someone down long enough to find out that the order had come to pack up. We were moving – in a hurry. It seemed that the Germans were likely to, were actually now, or were about to march through Holland and Belgium and probably into France, not to mention the fact that they might have, or had, or were about to break through the Ardennes at Sedan. We could never be sure of the facts, although there were many who swore on their grandmother's grave that what they knew was the truth.

Our orders were to leave all kit and possessions in the barn at the big farm in Bécourt and carry only arms, ammunition and small pack with soap, towel, toothbrush and emergency rations. The latter, incidentally, were in a sealed tin box, rather like a tin of sardines. On the lid it said, "Never to be opened under any circumstances except with the express permission of an officer. Penalty for improper use, imprisonment in The Tower," or something equally threatening. I mused upon the slow and painful death by starvation of a section of unfortunate troops because there was no officer present to say, "Open your emergency rations."

I joined the rest and dashed hither and thither collecting my toothbrush, soap and towel, but I had no intention of leaving anything except the box I'd buried. I was in for a shock.

I went to collect my radio set from the 2i/c's PU we'd been using on our jaunt to the RAF airfield, only to find that Tinkle had gone off back to his section in it and my most valuable possession had gone with him. It was some days before I managed to contact Tinkle and I made haste to ask him if I could collect my belongings from the PU. Casually, too casually I thought, he told me he'd had to lighten the vehicle for more speed and had thrown out my radio, boots and other things I'd left in it.

"Oh, and by the way, I gave your bottles of wine to the NCOs and men who went with me to the airfield."

I was absolutely speechless! What could I do? One doesn't tell an officer what a dirty rotten sod he is and I knew he'd love me to make that sort of mistake. I saluted and, in silence, turned and left him. Fortunately,

I never saw him again though I do know he didn't get back to England from Dunkirk. I did.

Some lucky people were detailed to act as a rear guard in Bécourt. The idea was that they would look after all the heavy equipment which was being left behind to await some troop carrying RASC vehicles, but right then we had to travel quickly and fill in a gap in the defence line before the enemy swept through. This meant no room for greatcoats.

Had I been asked, I'm certain I'd have been only too happy to be one of the rear guard, but I wasn't asked. Since the 2i/c's PU had gone off with Tinkle I was now out of a job because the other PU was off the road. I was given a 15 cwt to drive instead.

Once more Lady Luck smiled upon me. We moved off on our dash into Belgium at about 9 am and one hour later the Germans swept into Bécourt and put the whole rear guard in the bag. It must have been a shattering experience for them, and utterly unexpected. They were prisoners of war until 1945, a very long time indeed.

Meanwhile we headed north, I knew not where at the time. I have since found out that we were to take up positions on the Escaut Canal.

The only thing I can remember about the journey is passing the Canadian War Memorial at Vimy Ridge and being moved at its striking design and position overlooking the plain in the direction of Lens.

We passed through this coal mining area, so reminiscent of my own home landscape with its slag heaps and pit head winding gear. It was here for the first time I saw the full use of artillery.

Our convoy was snaking up a hill (and there weren't many natural rises hereabouts), moving slowly enough for me to see and hear the flash and bang of a battery of British 25 pounders. Five or six miles away at a guess, the bursting shells showed as white puffs of smoke against the dark background. We were all fascinated and horrified to think the enemy was just over there.

Our destination was in the middle of a wood. Remarkably, someone always knew where we were going and more wonderful still, someone knew when we had got there. Equally impressive was the regularity with which the Quartermaster and his staff produced meals and the trick of having the rations to do so.

The rumour was that from our wood we were going forward to do some bridging across the canal. How things changed as the war went on! It was only a rumour that this was our task: no-one actually told us. It was only after Dunkirk that more and more detailed information was to be made known to us so that we were aware of exactly what the future held. The confidence this gave us and the resulting ability to cope with unforeseen difficulties made the risks of the information falling into enemy hands quite justifiable.

The rumours seemed correct for once. The senior NCOs went into a huddle. Boxes of explosives, detonators, etc. were moved to a 15 cwt and we stood around full of curiosity, ears flapping, waiting for the all important piece of information next due – who was going on this job?

While all this was going on something else happened. Ever since the guns first began to rumble in the Ardennes when we were still comfortably settled in Bécourt, no-one had seen a British aircraft. We now know that the RAF was not only there in the skies above France but also shooting down German planes right, left and centre. I could vouch for the fact that the pilots on the airfield we visited were doing their stuff to the point of exhaustion. Nevertheless, our planes were not to be seen here.

Above our wood, quite suddenly, came the sound of low flying aircraft and bullets clipping the branches. We hadn`t dug any slit trenches so there was no alternative but to throw ourselves flat and hope for the best. I don`t think the aircraft were intent upon bothering us, we just happened to be in the line of fire of a private fight. After the noise had moved over we got to our feet and one or two of us tip-toed – goodness knows why – to the edge of the trees. There we had a grandstand view of one lone RAF plane, a Hurricane, wading into a flight of German twin engine bombers. The British pilot didn`t need our shouts of encouragement even if he could have heard them. That little plane fastened onto the Dorniers like a terrier worrying three Alsatians. Of course, the Germans fired back and the row of rattling machine guns was terrific. How our pilot wasn`t blown out of the sky I don`t know, but he wasn`t. On the contrary, he eventually got his man: a Dornier started to pour smoke. It went into a shallow dive, the pilot doing his best to reach base somewhere over the horizon. It looked as though he might make it but the constant pounding from the Hurricane put paid to that. The German suddenly tipped over and drove smack into the ground with a great gout of flame. We cheered.

That wasn`t the last time we saw the RAF before we got home. A few days later a Blenheim bomber accidentally unloaded a stick of bombs on us!

A little demolition party was detailed to go forward to the canal, and guess who got picked? Why me? I don`t know because these jobs were usually given to another of the three sections, all of which had any number of drivers.

I was called to drive the 15 cwt carrying the senior NCO and sappers who were going up to the canal to blow the bridge, but "not before you see the whites of their eyes" as the 2i/c said jokingly. He was like that: fair and just, with a keen sense of humour.

So we motored along isolated country roads with not a soul to be seen until we came to the canal and the bridge. The sappers got out their explosives and got to work placing the charges under the girders in positions which they knew would bring the whole structure crashing down when the plunger was pushed.

I had no part in this, of course. My job was to get them there and, hopefully, to get them back. Half of my task had been completed so I turned the truck round ready to depart in a hurry, after which there was time to look around.

The bridge was a miniature version of the Tyne Bridge, a homely thought. The canal was wide but the water in it rather low. It did occur to me that it wouldn`t be difficult to cross even without the bridge.

A few civilians and one or two army vehicles crossed the bridge as we were busy. No-one was interested in our affairs and they disappeared rapidly to the rear.

After an hour or so the sergeant in charge said that the bridge was ready to blow but he didn`t seem to be clear about when he had to bring it down. The only answer seemed to be to sit down and wait. All traffic across the bridge had now ceased and an ominous quietness descended upon the place. We waited and the sergeant checked his charges.

To me, as a layman, it seemed rather pointless to blow a bridge to deny passage to enemy troops but do nothing to prevent them immediately crossing the canal by pontoon bridging or something of that sort. There was absolutely no defence of the canal bank on our side, not a soul in sight except us. Our bridge was only one of quite a few to our right and left. Maybe the enemy wouldn`t be interested in ours, we hoped.

We heard the sound of a vehicle engine. The sergeant put his hand on the plunger. I fired up my truck and got ready for a racing start. The approaching vehicle made its appearance, sure enough, but on our side of the canal! There it was, a staff car containing the Brigadier. It was a relief to see someone and, in a way, we felt honoured to have a visit from a person of such high rank. He had come to see us!

I was always amused at the skill of people like Brigadiers. Not only have they the know-how to fight battles using people like ourselves who are neither belligerent nor militarily intelligent, but they also exude confidence in situations which they know are completely hopeless.

Our Brigadier positively glowed with bonhomie. A smile creased his face and he shook each of us by the hand, an action designed to put us at our ease. To me, it felt more like seeing the black cap put on by a judge before sentence was passed.

He looked at the charges on the bridge, checked the wires, asked a few trivial questions, then came out with an instruction which rocked our sappers back and left me with the feeling that I might very well turn out to be the sole survivor of this escapade.

"Wait until the first enemy vehicle is on the bridge then hit the plunger! If, however, the electric charge doesn`t work, Sergeant, you will have to fire your rifle into the biggest charge point blank! This order applies to all your party down to the last man because this bridge has to be destroyed."

It then occurred to me that I could be the Last Man. Perish the thought!

With a cheery wave the big man left.

There wasn`t long to wait before we heard something else, that all too familiar drone in the sky heralding the approaching aircraft. Not the most comforting of thoughts when one has half a ton of explosive under one`s feet.

Sure enough, enemy planes arrived and wheeled in line overhead. This was it: we were definitely the target.

The canal bank was pretty bare at this point, just lots of fields, a few knee high brambles and one spreading chestnut tree. No village blacksmith could have got under that tree more quickly than our party of one sergeant, three sappers and a driver. As the planes circled overhead lining up their approach, we five circled the tree trunk, all pushing and shoving, hoping that the entire party was completely hidden by the spring green above and the two feet diameter trunk. Very soon we`d beaten a well flattened track in the grass round the tree and at one point in our perambulations I saw the funny side of our efforts at camouflage and burst out laughing, getting some very dirty looks!

Perhaps it was the five crazy Englishmen playing "ring-`a-ring-`o-roses" in the middle of a serious war or perhaps the German airmen were offended because they thought we were laughing at them, but they suddenly climbed away and flew down the canal to knock hell out of the next bridge.

Things were quiet now, too quiet, ominously quiet.

From the houses on the other side of the bridge a figure emerged. We weren't feeling at all hostile so we allowed the figure to approach as he had his hands up, quite unnecessarily as it turned out. He was a British officer and there was a Bren carrier behind him with troops in it. Our sergeant went across to talk to him. Apparently, he was from another RE unit and had been detailed to relieve us so we could return to our Unit. My engine had been warmed up since before the Brigadier's visit so it didn't take long to pile aboard the truck and beat a hasty retreat from what, undoubtedly, would soon be a very hot spot.

In retrospect, I wondered if the officer was genuine and did our sergeant check his bona fides? There were certainly many Fifth Columnists around. We saw an infantry unit arrest a civilian the very next day and he had a non-British uniform under his overcoat. I watched as he was made to strip off the outer garments to reveal his true identity. Whether or not he had parachuted in I don't know, nor do I know his fate except to say that he was being told at the time that his actions put him into the category of being a spy, the punishment for which was immediate execution. On the other hand, I have since read accounts of quite a large number of very brave acts of defence by the French and Belgians on the canals as we fell back to Dunkirk.

Many engineers and infantrymen who were called upon to wait until they saw "the whites of their eyes," fought hard, died or were captured. A few succeeded in making an escape. Was that officer and his men of the latter, after all? I like to hope so. What I do know is that we didn't need a second bidding to get the hell out of it.

In the wood they were surprised and, I think, pleased to see us back safely. The QM dished out an extra ladle of stew on the strength of our courage! Unhappily, in our absence the CO, who wasn't a young man, had had a serious heart attack and been evacuated. I never knew whether or not he recovered but his position was rather remote from my social circle so his passing left no gap. In his place the 2i/c was promoted to Acting Major and being a substantive lieutenant, temporary Captain. Unfortunately, it meant that I was to have very little contact with him from then on which was a pity as I did respect him. He had been particularly fair and approachable whilst 2i/c.

CHAPTER FIFTEEN – Retreat

Over the next few days we moved a few times, mostly during the day, from wood to wood. French woods are very thick and offer marvellous protection if their camouflage is used correctly.

Occasionally we moved at night, travelling a long distance in convoy but, unbelievably, seeming to arrive back almost at the same spot by morning. Each move had some purpose, no doubt, but I never knew what it was.

How exhausting it was, driving all night without any lights at all. I would have said it was impossible had I not actually done it many times. It was amazing how much vision the human eye can manage in the dark. To begin with the night seemed totally black and all-enveloping. We are afraid to move. Slowly, however, we begin to see the shapes of trees and houses, the sky above the shapes becomes lighter, and the road reflects light depending upon its surface. To drive on a moonless night was possible but very tiring on both mind and body. Fortunately, by May the nights were shorter which was a blessing. Later, when on foot, we would have been happier with longer hours of darkness.

Sometimes the column stopped. Flashes, gunfire or the noise of vehicles or metal tracks usually meant that the front vehicles had "bumped" the enemy, but that had been prepared for. Frequently, however, we had no idea of what was going on at the head or the rear of the column but we were getting past caring.

One night, after a particularly long slow move weaving in and out of little villages and down side roads, the convoy ground to a halt. We stopped on a straight stretch of road and, as it was particularly dark, I couldn`t see beyond the vehicle ahead and had no inkling of the reason for the stoppage. It didn`t matter: there was no fighting, bangs or flashes, so we sat and waited. I suppose after a while we dozed a little, but, on waking, the truck in front was still there and there was no sign of movement. As lightness changed the sky from night to early dawn I got out of my seat to stretch my legs. Behind me the convoy was motionless. In front was one 15 cwt truck, and nothing else! Sometime during the night the front end of the convoy had moved off but the driver ahead of me was asleep and never heard them go. He was, even then, still asleep and, naturally, horror stricken when I shook him awake. There was nothing we could do. To move off would have been foolhardy and in any case, where to? We were never told our destination, or the route, and no-one wanted to motor "into the bag." Fortunately, the convoy leader had discovered us missing at some point and sent back a guide. No word of recrimination resulted. There was probably nothing in army regulations to cover it.

Nowadays when I look at a map of the area of our advance and retreat, the names of places bring back memories of here or there. I recognise that we must have travelled many miles in all directions on our way to Dunkirk but I can`t attempt to arrange our movements into any chronological order, nor retrace the routes. One or two places still remind me very clearly of something, however. For instance, before we set off for Ypres and the Belgian frontier to plug some gap in the line, we got mixed up in the fight for Arras, watching the tank battle from a safe distance.

Anyway, to recall ...

Our Unit alone, some two hundred Engineers, found itself in a little village called Farbus near Vimy.

HQ, including me, settled into a farm and my bed was in a most comfortable hay loft. The food was good, there being quite a few hens around for eggs and for cooking, and cows for fresh milk. We had a farm hand in the Unit, Walter Selly, who performed this tricky task, as much to relieve the animals as to give us sustenance.

All seemed quiet and restful until suddenly a Despatch Rider arrived from somewhere to say German tanks were coming our way. The Durham Light Infantry had taken up positions across the road in the woods and the East Yorks were just up the road, but if the tanks broke through we had to stop them. That set everyone quaking.

On arrival in France, each section had been issued with a gun called a Boys Anti-Tank Rifle. It was like a giant-sized rifle and it fired very large bullets, said to be armour piercing, but no-one had ever fired the thing. And why, you may ask? Rumour had it that the Boys had a kick like a mule and, reputedly, could do more damage to the firer than to a tank.

There was one corner in the village where the roads met. A party of likely lads was detailed to set up the Boys rifle and knock out any tank which made its approach. Guess who was one of the party? Why I always got picked for these jobs I don`t know, but picked I was and tried on the rifle for size. It fitted like a glove and I thought there goes my shoulder. What a funny way to be wounded: self-inflicted, perhaps.

We settled ourselves on the corner and waited. We didn`t have to wait long, but it wasn`t a tank that struck: almost without warning aircraft came in low, bombing and straffing.

I really thought, "This is it." It wasn`t us they were after, however, but the infantry up the road and in the wood. They were very badly hit.

As suddenly as the planes had struck they left, leaving vehicles, trees and some cottages burning, and a lot of dead British troops to mark their visit.

Hard on the heels of the departing enemy, another DR roared into Farbus warning us to bail out. I needed no second bidding and that was the nearest I ever got to stopping a tank and breaking my shoulder.

We stopped in another farm, always welcome for the extra food. As at Farbus, we were being called upon for a last ditch stand at another canal. There was no bridge to blow, nor cover, but we were instructed to spread out to defend the near side.

All was quiet. I looked around. The canal, which appeared to be almost river-like at this point, looked vaguely familiar. The bank on the far side was vertical and supported by wooden piles, but on our side the bank sloped down to the water. Debris from damaged cottages had fallen into the water and it was obvious a crossing could be made over these bits and pieces, hence our presence.

At that moment a girl came out of one of the houses on the far bank. She hurried to the edge and waved furiously as though she wanted us to either go away or come over. We had no intention of crossing over there, nor could we depart, much as we would have wished. It then struck me: I had seen this scene before – in a dream. The second of my two pre-war dreams had come true! The same canal, the same houses, the same girl waving; the only difference was that there were no stepping stones to cross, but there was that debris which could serve the same purpose. The girl ran away when we didn`t respond.

Half an hour later we heard the noise of vehicles from the far side of the houses and, horror of horrors, German soldiers appeared in full view. What to do? Here is the enemy, as large as life, almost within spitting distance. As soldiers we were trained to kill, and people in coal scuttle helmets were the legitimate target. We looked at each other. Should we open fire? If we did they`d shoot back and they were real soldiers not amateurs like us, but we were supposed to kill Germans because they`d kill us if we didn`t kill them.

No-one dared move in case they saw us.

Then one very clever Royal Engineer whispered, "We are detailed to defend the canal so if those Germans don't attack we can hold our fire."

I admired the man's reasoning. He was right, of course. Anyway, the British are good sports after all: they never shoot sitting ducks.

We waited, pointing our Lee Enfields very belligerently at the German army until a message arrived from somewhere to say withdraw, bail out! Everyone was packed and waiting when we got back to the farm.

The RAF appeared again, this time in the form of a Lysander Army Co-operation plane which flew very low round and round the farm. We assumed he was connected with the battery of 25 pounders which was firing from a position just beyond the cow byres.

We hadn't moved 200 yards down the road when a terrific shelling by German artillery descended on the farm and the 25 pounders, swamping everything. We debated whether that Lysander was British or had been captured and was in enemy hands.

Many towns suffered damage during this period, some from battle in the streets, most from aerial bombardment. When a town stood astride the junction of main roads it was an acceptable act of war to bomb it and block the roads, the transport of the retreating enemy thereby slowed or even stopped and, of course, that meant us. I had the experience of seeing two French towns suffer this fate. One, Poperinge, was attacked just as we approached it.

It always seemed personal. As the planes approached, I felt that they had set out solely to find and destroy none other than me. I took cover accordingly and waited for the bomb or bullet which was inscribed "George West." Of course, it came as a relief when the falling whistle passed over and on, leaving me shaken but unharmed.

When the planes dived out of a beautiful blue sky, I was out of my cab quicker than greased lightning, having had considerable practice by now, but discovered that there was no ditch alongside the road. Far quicker than it takes to write this I was through a hawthorn hedge only to find, to my chagrin, that I'd chosen a field of three inch high green wheat as my refuge. There was no time to look for safety elsewhere: I could only dive to the floor and lie still, hoping for the best. In this rather exposed position I found myself a spectator of the bombing of Poperinge, about half a mile ahead. Again and again German bi-planes, quite slow by later standards, plummeted out of the sky to drop their bombs. There was a little small arms fire in retaliation but eventually the enemy had no opposition. The planes only departed because they had nothing left to drop or shoot, but they left behind a burning town.

We tried to pass through the town but the work had been well done: we couldn't get through. Homes were wrecked, fallen, burning and blasted, and rubble blocked the roads. Most of the French people had already left to swell the multitude of refugees on the roads so I doubt if there were many deaths. We did see some Red Cross workers carrying out errands of mercy in the main square. It must have taken many years and cost a great deal of money to rebuild French towns and villages, and the people must have lost most of their possessions.

We had our own affairs to think about and the convoy had to remain together. With some difficulty we turned our vehicles round and made a detour by side roads. We hadn't been completely stopped but certainly delayed.

The other town, Armentières, suffered a very similar fate to Poperinge, and the pattern of destruction was the same. We were a little further away when it happened but still saw the place disappear in a vast cloud of smoke. When the smoke cleared Armentières was still there, however. We passed through during the night and the town continued to burn furiously in many parts. So hot were the fires that our faces were scorched as we drove through and later I found the paintwork on my truck had blistered. No attempt was made this time to bypass and the bomb holes in the streets were difficult to negotiate. People had been killed and there were quite a few bodies lying around, mostly covered and lying in rows, the darkness shrouding them.

The war was hotting up and getting much closer.

News finally filtered through that we were making for the coast or rather "falling back to the coast in a series of defence lines."

We'd arrived in France as part of the 23rd Territorial Division but over this period of backwards and forwards, up and down, advance and retreat, we seemed to be attached to various private armies like Petreforce or Frankforce. As far as I could make out, we'd now become part of 50th Division. No-one really knew, below commissioned rank anyway, but speculation was the spice of life at that time. One thing we did know was that the Belgian army had packed up and left us in a rare pickle with an impossible gap to hold. I remember seeing Belgian troops throwing their rifles in a heap by the roadside and a Belgian officer openly weeping. We didn't weep: we were horrified.

The French seemed little better than the Belgians but they should have been as it was their country which was in danger of being over-run next. I was amused by the way they went into battle – in buses. There were busloads of French troops going this way, other busloads going the other way and some busloads not going anywhere. Unfortunately, those busloads caused an awful lot of problems on the roads. They were so big and wide that when two met on a narrow road everything stopped while first the drivers and then the troops indulged in furious arguments over who should give way. Meanwhile, we fumed at the delay. Had I known then what I know now about how many divisions in the line the French army apparently had, I'd have been even more shocked at their collapse.

When it had been decided that the BEF would fall back to the coast, the High Command passed orders to all units that no transport would be brought within the Dunkirk perimeter. This was understandable, the perimeter being small, too small to hold an army's vehicles as well as all its men. At the same time, it was a tragedy that so much valuable equipment had to be sacrificed.

The SgtMT, our new one, announced that today was our last day for riding on four wheels. We were going to ditch our vehicles in a special collecting park where Ordnance Fitters would systematically and thoroughly destroy them beyond any possible use by the enemy. It wasn't far to go: an hour's slow drive and there was the place, with dozens of lorries neatly parked.

Our vehicles had been new just a few months before and they still looked good. It was unbelievable to think that we were actually throwing them away. We drove into the park and I followed directions to the place indicated.

The wheels stopped rolling and I had just put my hand on the handbrake when Bang! Bang! Bang! Three explosions rocked the truck and splinters whizzed past me.

This was shattering. My first thought was, "They might have waited till I was clear before they started to smash the trucks. Typical Ordnance." Then I realised those bangs were meant for me and the person who had caused them wasn't Ordnance. They were mortar bombs: I could smell the cordite. Needless to say, I didn't wait to let them have a second go. Grabbing my small pack, rifle and tin hat, I tore off in the direction of the nearest ditch. I never saw my 15 cwt again and, no doubt, when the Germans arrived they would be pleased with its pristine condition, even with the engine still running.

We set off to walk. Now I was no longer a driver, just a Royal Engineer and one of a section of thirty British soldiers in the charge of a Sapper Sergeant, making our way home via Dunkirk.

Walking was really slow after riding for so long. My first miserable discovery was that my feet hurt. I'd never worn boots: I'd never had to and, anyway, I found driving in them too difficult. Brown shoes were my usual footwear. Twenty mile route marches were hell in civilian brown shoes but I was stuck with the situation. My boots, unworn, were still in the 15 cwt.

For nearly a week we walked, following the rest, everyone going the same way. The section was split into squads of half a dozen and we walked in alternate groups on opposite sides of the road in single file. Not being used to marching I found it exhausting and painful, mile after mile. The weather was hot and the roads were dusty. We could only scrounge food: a few biscuits here, or the odd tin of meat from an abandoned truck there. Occasionally we found eggs or some stale bread in a farm. Now and then French people who hadn't fled gave us scraps to eat but, generally speaking, we were starving. Somehow it didn't matter as long as we could get water. I'd packed quite a few packets of hard tack biscuits into my small pack and two tins of bully beef specially for such an emergency as this. I nibbled the biscuits but hadn't yet reached the desperate stage, at least not so desperate that I couldn't keep going.

I never felt that I wouldn't survive. I knew I would suffer danger, hardship and privation, but I knew I would survive. I even considered the possibility that I might be taken prisoner. I thought deeply upon that. I'd escape, too, somehow from somewhere, and get home.

I had worn a wrist watch for long enough but it was time to consider the future which could very well be difficult. I took the works out of my watch and threw them away. Behind the face I packed some French currency notes of high denomination that I'd saved from my last pay day. These I would use to buy food and exist until I could escape from France to England. Fanciful? Yes, very fanciful indeed. Whether I'd have had any success with this venture is extremely doubtful but, although things were drastic, I never felt defeated and tried to appear confident because some of my friends were feeling very low indeed. I learned much later that it was common practice, both on our side and the enemy's, to remove watches, pens, cameras and money from captured prisoners. My watch and money wouldn't have lasted five minutes!

As we got nearer Dunkirk, marching in the daytime became suicidal, so we would set off at about 11 pm when it was dark enough for cover and march until dawn. As soon as lightness touched the sky we looked for a farm or a barn to hide in and sleep until it was safe to move again.

Most nights our luck held but one night, to find shelter from the rain, I had no choice but to kick some pigs out of their sty to find a bed. It was shelter from above but somewhat damp beneath. After a while I even got used to the smell. I took some of that back to Britain with me!

I blessed the War Office official who issued the order that every soldier would at all times carry his gas cape. It was the most perfect waterproof invented and large enough to cover one completely, tent-like. It kept out the heaviest rain and even preserved body heat on cold nights. I slept inside my gas cape on numerous occasions both at this time and later during other campaigns.

I was beginning to agree with the unwritten Army Regulation which said, "When in doubt have a fag and wait and see." Fags were in short supply but waiting at that time was plentiful.

CHAPTER SIXTEEN – Dunkirk

31st May 1940 was the worst day I had experienced up until now. In the naivety of youth, I wasn`t to know just how bad things would get later.

We`d almost reached the "last ditch" canal line which encircled the port of Dunkirk. Time was running out and we knew that failure to reach the beaches meant being left behind. Everyone had abandoned all idea of camouflage and we marched most of the day in the open with barely a halt.

Sometime about midday I found, to my consternation, that the brown shoes in which I`d been forced to march were about to fall apart. A piece of string held one upper to what was left of the surviving sole, whilst the other gaped uncomfortably with every step. Without a miracle, it would be stockinged feet for me before long.

My salvation was literally "Dead Men`s Shoes," the gift of an ally, a dead Frenchman who had no further use for his most magnificent pair of brown leather boots. In a trice I`d removed my tattered pieces and laced on "les bottes Françaises." Beggars can`t be choosers so I wasn`t in any position to complain that he took a size smaller than me. At least I had footwear of soft leather and in good condition.

The unfortunate man also had a long rapier-like quatre-foil bladed bayonet which not only looked like a good souvenir, but would also be a lethal defensive weapon. British issue bayonets were toothpicks compared with this one. I pondered for a moment upon the wisdom of the extra burden and decided it was worth it, though I shuddered to think what it would have been like to use it in earnest.

As dusk fell the Luftwaffe was very much in evidence but they weren`t interested in anything other than their target of Dunkirk. Wave after wave of bombers droned over, their noise frightening. They flew slowly, heavy with bombs, to join the constant rumble and great clouds of smoke away to our left.

By now the roads were completely crammed with tired, shuffling troops and the ubiquitous French buses. Here and there a civilian moved in the crush. I spoke with a man who was a War Graves Commission gardener, accompanied by his family. He was, naturally, hoping to be evacuated with the rest of us. I often wondered if he was, though he could have been mistaken for a Fifth Columnist.

There was still a long way to go to reach the town of Dunkirk and, although we were very tired indeed, we agreed by the roadside to carry on through the night.

It grew dark and the sharp details of men and vehicles merged into the night. Moving shapes, black against the navy blue sky, reminded us we were still a large mass.

Only noises meant anything now: slow, grinding engines, some belching diesel fumes, some petrol, clanking metal tracks betraying a Bren carrier or armoured vehicle, the noisy beat of a motorcycle, aero engines overhead, voices all around, English voices in many dialects, Yorkshire, Cockney, Geordie and Scots, French voices, quick and excited, and other tongues, perhaps Belgian, Flemish or even Moroccan.

The firing started. First some bursts of small arms, then a star shell lit the sky. Surely it must be British, but was it? If the firing wasn't from our side then the Boche must be pretty close. A pop in the opposite direction. Another whine overhead and another star shell. Everything and everyone on our road was very clearly illuminated by these two incandescent lights hanging in the sky.

I readied myself for what must follow. There was, thank goodness, a ditch on either side of the road but this would become pretty congested when everyone took cover. I was determined to be one of the first into it if a shell didn't land on me personally. There wasn't long to wait.

Almost simultaneously the skylines to the right and left burst into flame and shells began whining towards us, many of them tracer and clearly visible as they sailed in perfect parabolas. I was all ready to make my leap for cover when I realised that the shells from both sides were passing over us. We were marching down the centre line of an artillery duel. Whether they were tanks or field guns, I couldn't tell, nor did I care, as long as the shells kept going. The odd one did fall short and there were shouts and moans, but we didn't stop.

As suddenly as the battle started, it ceased. We plodded on, in a sleepy daze and very footsore. I was feeling the effects of wearing boots one size too small.

Midnight came and went. When dawn broke we were still marching, albeit much more slowly, and had reached the last canal bridge to cross into the Dunkirk perimeter.

Our rear guard troops seemed well dug in on both sides of the bridge and the canal, and their high vigilance suggested that the enemy couldn't be far away.

The number of German bombers had increased from an intermittent gaggle to a constant shuttle service of massed planes. Some of these straffed the troops marching into the perimeter and all too often we found ourselves diving for cover. It was more puzzling than ever to see that so many vehicles had found their way into the confined space of Dunkirk, despite orders that all trucks would be parked and destroyed in regulation collecting points well clear of the defence area. We were miffed to recognise that having carried out these orders properly and having walked so far, others ahead had made the journey in much more comfort, and were probably back in Britain by now.

Roaming the fields nearby was a number of horses, well cared for and groomed. To the best of my knowledge, the British Army didn`t use horses in this campaign so the animals must have been French. They were a nuisance during air raids, charging down the road, tails and manes flying, wild terror in their eyes, foaming at the mouth, scattering all before them in their fear, poor things. At times, the explosive rain from the sky made us feel rather like those horses.

It had been emphasised that to lose one`s arms was a court martial offence. For this reason, I was still carrying my rifle, heavy though it was, and so were all the others in our section. We carried them back to Britain. There were many who didn`t, however, and stacks of perfectly serviceable Lee Enfields littered the roadsides. I can`t say it bothered me particularly then, but later, in Britain, I was to learn that there was a desperate shortage of rifles and we had to be issued with a very old-fashioned American weapon which was only one step advanced from the muzzle loaders used in their Civil War. The few perfectly good rifles we`d brought home were taken away from us to give to "fresh fighting troops."

I was taking my turn to lead our party when, about mid morning, we topped the rise at Bray Dunes and there, at long last, was the sea. Bray Dunes was somewhere between twelve and sixteen miles from the town of Dunkirk, along a wide (at low tide), straight stretch of sand. The rest of that day and the next were spent covering that distance. We trudged on with frequent dashes for shelter in the grassy sand dunes when the Stukas came over to straff and bomb. Bombs fell quite close yet did remarkably little damage because sand has a very safe cushioning effect. Once we became reconciled to the appalling noise of a diving plane, the actual fall of the bomb and its explosion was something we almost got used to. No-one in our section was hit but there were other troops around us who were killed and wounded. So many men filled the area some were bound to be under or near enough to the missile to suffer its effects, sand or no sand.

The constant screaming of planes and bombs, the rattle of machine guns and the patter of bullets kicking up the sand were undoubtedly unnerving if one didn't attempt to "hold on." I was absolutely scared stiff but I was even more scared of anyone seeing or knowing that I was scared stiff. I hadn't often been under fire: this was more or less my baptism of concentrated attack. I suppose youth and the strong belief that I'd get home gave me confidence. I tried my best to put on an outward appearance which looked much more casual than how I felt on the inside.

At first, we marched, or more accurately, shuffled, near to the dunes ready for a hasty retreat if need be, but the sand was soft and dry here and progress was far too slow, so our section sergeant, having long since decided that he was taking us off the pier at Dunkirk harbour where we'd be sure of safe transport, directed that we walk on the hard sand near the water's edge.

A fine man was the sergeant in charge of our section. He was much older than the rest of us, maybe even thirty years of age, and took charge like a mother hen protecting her chicks. Nothing ruffled his feathers and there was never a mention of defeat or despondency. His catch phrase, which stuck with me for the rest of the war, was, "Don't worry. It may never happen!" When he gave an order, everyone obeyed without question. No-one would have considered he was wrong or that we'd suffer by following his instruction. He never was wrong. Not one of us was disadvantaged by any decision he made and I aver that his responsibility and devotion to duty got us home. More than likely he saved our lives many times. He wasn't a brilliant academic nor a man of the professions. Before call-up he had worked in a Jarrow shipyard. Just as he was unknown to anyone other than some men in our Unit before the war and a few more during it, that good man would return to the shipyard in 1946 unsung and unrewarded.

Some distance along the beach a strange pier stuck out into the water. Lorries which had reached the perimeter and would have been abandoned anyway had been run out from the beach as far as they would go until they were waterlogged. Along the canopies of these nose-to-tail trucks, planks or duckboards were laid creating an instant jetty. The tide was too far out now for this makeshift pier to operate but it was certainly a brilliant idea and would serve its purpose each time the tide rose.

The sea as far as one could see in both directions was dotted with ships of all sorts, shapes and sizes. The warships kept moving rapidly all the time, being the most vulnerable and valuable craft. Cargo ships, ferry boats and vessels of similar size were stationary. Between the large ships and the shore small boats, whalers, cruisers and motor boats, many from the Norfolk Broads and Thames, plied back and forth, overloaded with their human cargo.

The beach sloped very gradually seawards and only those boats of very shallow draft could reach the shore line. Every soldier had to be ferried into deep water and heaved aboard a merchant ship or a destroyer for passage to Britain. Men stood in quiet queues up to their necks in the sea waiting for rescue, just to give some boat the advantage of a few feet of water and save it from grounding.

All the while the enemy bombed and straffed the waiting thousands. There were quite a few bodies slopping back and forth in the wavelets splashing near our feet as we plodded on to Dunkirk.

Surprisingly, some units sacrificed safety for parade discipline. The latter might have been acceptable in its place, but on the Dunkirk beaches it was nothing more than thoughtless suicide.

A short distance past the lorry pier, shells and mortars began to fall and we took what cover there was in the dunes. Not so a company of infantry who were being marched in step, in threes, parade ground fashion, along the sand. It didn`t take long for the German gunners to drop their shells or bombs right into the marching phalanx. Officers called for ranks to be held and they marched on, leaving stretcher bearers to deal with the dead and dying. We could only watch, horrified, as again and again great gaps were blown in the column when the explosions took their toll. In the end, discipline was overcome by the common sense of the survivors. They broke and ran. The firing ceased and we moved on, straggling and spread out but safe.

Not many actually see the end of a warship but it was my sad experience.

A destroyer, despite its high speed and skilful manoeuvring, was caught by a flight of dive bombers. Several bombs screamed down, clearly visible to us on the shore, and one plummeted neatly down the ship`s funnel. We could feel the dull vibration of the explosion through the sea and sand. Almost immediately, the stricken ship slowed and showed the first signs of sinking. When a warship sinks, depth charges and torpedoes have to be set at "safe" if anyone in the water is to be saved. There would have been very little time aboard that warship to do anything, I imagine, but some quick thinking individual must have given the order to fire all torpedoes.

The first indication we had of this action was when someone nearby shouted and shakily pointed seawards. Eight fast moving frothy tracks were heading straight for the beach in a wide spread, directly at us. It was instinct to run away from these approaching torpedoes, but what a short distance one can cover in sand from a standing start even when being chased by something moving at such a high speed. We didn't reach a safe distance or anything like it! Fortunately, the big steel fish were either set to "safe" or the fact that they simply shot up the beach twenty five yards meant that the firing mechanism didn't activate. Had they gone up there would have been nobody to recount this tale but I remember thinking at the time, would my next of kin not be puzzled to learn that I had been torpedoed ... on dry land?!

There were times during our long walk to Dunkirk on that never-ending stretch of sand when I wondered whether or not I could stay the distance. My feet were seriously raw, partly due to the considerable distance we had covered in the last six days, and partly due to the size-too-small boots I'd been bequeathed. There was no option, however. I either gave up and sat down to await capture or worse, or I kept going. I kept going.

None of us had had any food. Even my last reserves had been shared out. Of all things, during an enforced stop due to some of the bombing, I came upon a RASC driver who was fascinated by my souvenir French bayonet. I had almost reached the point of throwing it away to lighten my pack, but the driver made me a cash offer. I asked him what was the use of cash at a time like this, suggesting perhaps we could do a deal for something to eat. Being RASC he had made sure he had adequate food supplies. After some haggling, the bayonet changed hands for two tins of corned beef and a large packet of biscuits. It was not a lot between twenty odd men, all starving, not having eaten for 48 hours, but such rations were a banquet and we disposed of them there and then before he changed his mind. We each got only a biscuit and a mouthful of meat but it relieved the pangs of hunger and we struggled on.

Our sergeant had decided on evacuation from the port but from the amount of smoke, the flashes and the noise it didn't look to be the healthiest of places. Just before we reached the wooden pier-like structure known as The Mole we were warned by an MP crouched by a gap in the concrete promenade barrier, that we would have to make a dash across this shell hole. Apparently, some sniper had ranged on it from the top of a church tower in the town and he was "popping off" every so often. Proof of this lay covered in blankets at our feet. Four or five pairs of protruding army boots bore sad witness to those who hadn`t made it across the gap. They wouldn`t be making the journey home now. All our section survived that lethal obstacle although the marksman had a go more than once. Again, we had the common sense of our sergeant to thank for our safety. He wisely staggered the timing of our dash across so that the sniper couldn`t rely upon any regularity to shoot at us.

At the landward end of The Mole, which we reached once past the sniper`s gap, all was feverish activity. Within moments of our arrival a salvo of shells crashed down around our ears. Some landed in the water sending up tall fountains, some on the rocks beside the pier, and rock and metal splinters flew everywhere, adding to the casualties. Some of the shells burst in the midst of the troops climbing up from the beach and promenade, with horrible result.

After the smoke of these salvoes cleared and we took stock, we found our section had, by a miracle, survived unscathed again.

A number of RN and army officers had the responsibility of directing arriving troops. Our little lot were told to board a destroyer lying further along The Mole. The Mole was never intended to be used as a quay for the berthing of ships, and vessels had the greatest difficulty manoeuvring alongside. Even after they`d done this, the deck was twenty feet or more below the level of The Mole`s planking at low tide. The only method of boarding then was by means of ladders tied together.

The journey along the pier was distinctly hazardous. Shell holes had been blown in it leaving gaps to negotiate with a considerable drop to the water if anyone took a false step on the ladder laid across the hole.

On arrival at the destroyer, which happened to coincide with another shower of bombs from the ever-present Luftwaffe, we were just in time to hear, "Full up. Catch the next one, mate!" and the warship rapidly backed out, twisting and turning delicately around sunken craft.

A hospital ship ablaze with lights and covered in red crosses pulled out, too. One of these ships, maybe this one, was sunk during the operation. They were all attacked, despite their markings.

Had we missed the bus, was the question? Resigned, we made our way landwards again, scrambling back along the ladders over the open gaps. The area at the shore end of The Mole was even more crowded and salvoes of shells continued to arrive at frequent intervals, so regularly, in fact, that a naval officer warned through a megaphone, "Take cover," almost as though he was about to fire the German guns. Everyone scattered for whatever shelter was available and, sure enough, with a whine and a swish, the shells came in with precision timing. Frequently, during the war, we found that this German characteristic of regularity and precision could be used to our advantage.

Our return to the shore coincided with the arrival of a fleet of British ambulances carrying some very seriously wounded men. The drivers hastily unloaded the stretchers and departed in a cloud of dust, anxious either to collect more wounded or to get away from the shelling, or both.

The cases on the stretchers looked utterly pathetic, covered in blood-soaked bandages, most of them barely conscious. What hope must they have had? In retrospect, not many did have much chance, knowing the fate of the hospital ships that were to carry them.

One of the movement officers shouted an order that all able-bodied men, people like ourselves, would carry the stretchers along The Mole to be loaded onto another hospital ship which had appeared outside the harbour.

Carrying a stretcher with an inert man on it was heavy and awkward, made worse by having to teeter along the rungs of horizontally placed ladders over a drop of twenty feet or more into the sea below as, once again, we negotiated the shell holes in the wooden planking of The Mole. I have no head for heights at the best of times and that slow, terribly difficult journey back along the pier carrying a badly wounded man on a stretcher was absolutely hair-raising. We made it eventually and put our burden down in what shelter there was beside the fencing of The Mole on the sea wall side. I don't mean shelter from the weather which on June 1st was pleasantly warm and calm with barely a ripple on the sea. No; the shelter I was fondly seeking was from the bombing and straffing by every aircraft the Luftwaffe could muster, not to mention shells from their artillery, all of which rained down on us without respite.

CHAPTER SEVENTEEN – Home Again

Crouching in mortal danger as we were once we'd got to the Mole, we didn't want to be hanging around any longer than we had to.

The hospital ship hadn't managed to get into the harbour and, by the way things were shaping, it seemed unlikely it would. We squatted down beside our patient and waited.

I discovered that the 2nd lieutenant I'd helped to carry came from a village in the coal mining area of Durham. He hadn't been in France long, and had a nasty shrapnel hole in his back and side. Frankly, I didn't think he had much chance of survival judging by the amount of blood he'd lost. He gave me his name and address and I said I'd contact his home if I reached England, though I couldn't think at the time what I'd say when and if I did write. This was hardly the place for passing the time with chit-chat, though it turned out we didn't have much time to pass.

A small collier had edged alongside The Mole. I recognised it straight away as one of the Tyne Tees Line which usually ran coal from Newcastle to the Thames. All the vessels were called the "Something Castle" and this one was the "Craster Castle," named after one of the many castles in Northumberland. Craster is noted chiefly for its wonderful kippers. Such a familiar ship struck me as being the omen which was bound to bring salvation, a boat from my own doorstep, one that I'd probably seen from my home on the Tyne many times.

The skipper leant out of his wheelhouse and yelled, "Get yourself aboard, lads. I'm already fully loaded and can't take many!"

We didn't need a second bidding although there was a snag. The ship was only small, it was low tide and it lay too far below the level of The Mole to jump aboard. Someone grabbed a ladder from one of the shell holes and lowered it to the deck. Unfortunately, it was about 6 feet too short of reaching the planking of the pier. Thinking of it now I couldn't imagine myself performing the feat, but "needs must when the devil drives" and he was certainly driving a hard bargain at that moment. Hanging onto the pier planking by my fingertips, I managed to lower myself, complete with rifle and small pack, until my toes touched the top rung, then somehow scrabbled down that ladder onto the collier. A slip would have ended, rather pathetically, all the traumatic experiences of the last few weeks and made the lucky escapes quite pointless. Had I stopped to consider the stupidity of what I was trying to do and how impossible it would be to do it, it's more than likely I would have slipped and fallen backwards or become paralysed with fear on the top rung. As it was, I set foot on that little collier and immediately felt safe.

The "Craster Castle" had set out from England to take NAAFI stores to Calais, at the time a safe port behind the lines. When the ship had arrived, however, Calais was a beleaguered garrison on the point of collapse. It surrendered before the stores could be unloaded and the skipper left hurriedly under a barrage of shell fire. He was then directed to Dunkirk in the hope of rescuing at least a few troops.

The skipper, a jolly kindly Tynesider who exuded confidence with his calm bravery, took the covers off the ship's hatches and announced that the more we could eat of his stores, the more troops he could get aboard and the more cover we'd give ourselves as we progressed downwards among the crates and packages. To men who had not eaten for days this was a land of milk and honey. We gorged ourselves on meat and veg accompanied by beans, tomato sauce, pickled onions, new potatoes, steak and kidney pudding, garden peas, baby carrots and Hamburger sausages followed by pears, peaches, cherries, grapefruit and tinned milk, cream, rice pudding, ginger pudding ... and to follow there was every make of chocolate and a huge variety of boiled sweets and toffees. For those who wanted it, bread and fresh butter, cheese and chocolate biscuits. To top it all off, we could help ourselves to cigarettes of all makes, beer and spirits. Not a penny to pay and eat your fill. We did.

While I was helping to empty the hold, I happened to mention my blistered feet. A crew man promptly brought me a bucket of beautiful hot water, soap, a towel and some ointment. There were boxes of socks amongst the NAAFI stores and I was able to make myself comfortable for the first time in days. I remember sitting on a box outside the galley with my feet in a bucket of water, a corned beef sandwich in my hand, a large tin of fruit salad swimming in Carnation milk by my side awaiting attention, and a big box of Cadbury's milk flakes open ready for "afters," all the while half a dozen Stukas screamed down to bomb the harbour. All hell was let loose as shipping fired back and those who could be bothered to fire Brens or rifles joined in. I took a bite out of my sandwich, sipped some milky juice from the fruit salad, allowed a milk flake to melt slowly in my mouth and shouted, "Can't touch me!" or something equally puerile, as much as my mouth would allow.

We were chased on a very erratic course all the way home, bombed and straffed by planes above our wake, but the Craster's skipper threw his little ship around like a paddle boat on a children's pool. Not a hit or a casualty did we suffer. The noise woke me up once or twice but, by and large, I slept all the way back to Britain. I'd never once doubted I'd get there. We've had faith in those who go down to the sea in ships ever since the days of the Armada's defeat and I hope we'll never lose it.

June 1st 1940 had been a long day. I had other harrowing experiences before the war was over but none left quite the same impression. It seemed to me a victory. Although everything around indicated defeat, it didn't strike me as such one little bit.

The British have a great capacity for organisation; whether it be a state occasion or a catastrophe we are, undoubtedly, experts. Somehow or other, no matter how unexpected, someone somewhere has it all buttoned up and there is machinery ready to swing into action. Dunkirk and its aftermath was another example of teamwork, co-operation, and forethought. The well-oiled cogs of a smooth running operation provided incredible relief and comfort for those like myself who arrived back in Britain exhausted and shattered by our experiences.

I stepped ashore at Folkestone. It should have been Dover but we were chased away by a fast moving destroyer with a bellow from its bridge in very forthright terms, "Get the hell out of it! Dover's being bombed!" Of course, we could see that so we did as we were told.

It was evening, light enough for British Movietone News to record my arrival. The sun was setting on a very pleasant warm June day. We had a short walk along the quay before climbing onto a long corridor train.

As soon as the train was full we moved off on a short journey to some isolated sidings where grass grew between the rails and birds sang their evening chorus. It was quiet and so very, very peaceful.

Trestle tables stood alongside the rails and we were invited by ladies of all ages in WVS uniforms to eat our fill. Sandwiches, sausage rolls and cakes with lashings of lovely English tea to take away the taste of what we had left behind in France.

RT officers addressed us in the gentlest manner, informing us that our train would remain in this quiet haven for the rest of the night. We could get back into the carriages and sleep. Such luxury, such kindness; it was quite moving.

Of course, there was a lot of chatter about what this one had done and what the other had seen. Our trainload was a complete mixture of units. None of our company engineers was on it at all. An officer came along and took particulars of who we were, how many of us there were in any party, and to what regiment we belonged. After that, we weren`t long in falling into the relaxed sleep of safety.

To be back in Britain was the finest of feelings. Imagine how it felt to wake to another beautiful day with the smell of bacon and eggs wafting through the train windows. It was no trick of the imagination. The ladies of the WVS had been up very early and worked hard. All we had to do was to step outside the door to be handed a plate of bacon, two eggs, bread, butter, marmalade and tea. Even latrines had sprung up overnight!

After breakfast the train moved slowly out of the sidings, accompanied by much cheering and waved farewells. Choruses of thanks echoed from every window.

All that day we rattled along. Most place names on the stations had been removed and it seemed as though the driver was merely taking us on a tour of beautiful England hoping he could find some place to stop for the night. There was, of course, a plan. We knew this because we stopped for coffee at a station mid morning, then lunch at midday when tables laden with pies, sandwiches, cakes and trifles lined the platform again. Once more the food was delivered to us by female volunteers.

Postcard issued to survivors from Dunkirk.

Some very thoughtful Lady Bountiful stopped at every carriage and handed each of us a ready-stamped postcard. All we had to do was address it and put a brief message on the other side for the recipient. That card was the first communication my mother had received since weeks before the Dunkirk evacuation. Although she was sure she had seen me on the Newsreel, only the postcard made my safety a certainty. She had, sure enough, seen me on the newsreel! I`ve seen it since myself!

Reverse.

For two days we toured Britain on the train. It finally came to rest in Pembroke at the most south westerly tip of Wales. Buses were waiting to take us from the station to an AA training camp outside the town.

There was a strange occurrence on the way to the camp. People lined the streets but as our buses passed by, they banged on the sides and on the windows with the flats of their hands. I never learned why they did this. The rest of Britain cheered, clapped, sang and rejoiced at our return: the Welsh banged on the sides of our buses. A strange expression of welcome, if that's what it was.

The camp provided baths, a change of clothing, new boots and a chance to sleep and eat. All these were necessary and we were slowly revitalised.

It seemed ages, but it was probably only a few days, before leave passes began to be issued. Needless to say, mine wasn't among the first batches. I have suffered from my initial "W" all my life. Eventually, the eagerly anticipated piece of paper arrived and with such few belongings as I possessed, new kit chiefly, I was allowed to set off for home.

The journey from Pembroke in South Wales to South Shields in North East England would be a long one in peacetime with normal timetables and regular routes. In wartime, with all the chaos of Dunkirk, the fall of France and "standing alone" against the Nazis, it was a marathon. It was a case of getting on any train going away from Pembroke, then consulting the Railway Transport Officer on whichever station I found myself hoping that, in the end, I could shuttle myself in the right direction.

All trains were crowded to bursting point. Very seldom did one manage to get a seat. The toilets in each carriage were either permanently in use or were providing additional carriage accommodation. After dark, only faint blue lights illuminated the compartments and corridors. Stations were in darkness and all sign boards had been removed so that one never knew the name of a place except by leaving the train to ask. A train could rattle along merrily then, for no explained reason, stop and rattle merrily back the way it had just come.

That phrase I saw hanging in the sergeants' mess at Yarm came to mind: "By patience and perseverance, and a bottle of sweet oil, the snail, at length, reached Jerusalem." Only now did it have some significance; by substituting South Shields for Jerusalem I recognised a connection.

"By Patience and Perseverance, and a Bottle of Sweet Oil"

Grandpa`s War

Part 2

233 Field Company, Royal Engineers, Timsbury Manor. 1941.

THE INTERVAL

Between each major campaign in which I was involved during the Second World War there was an interval. This break served to regroup, reinforce, retrain and, to some extent, relax all of us.

After Dunkirk, the interval lasted from June 1940 until March 1941, during that period when Britain could so easily have been invaded by the largely untouched and undamaged German forces. We felt pretty certain, and history has confirmed it, that there was very little to stop such an invasion except perhaps a grim determination by the British people not to give in without a fight. The Local Defence Volunteers, or Home Guard as they became later, were recruited in every village, town and city throughout the land. They trained and were prepared for defence to the death. Knowing what we had learned so bitterly about Blitzkrieg war, it might well have come to that.

Near Pembroke in south Wales, where I eventually got off the train after Dunkirk, we rested and re-clothed. Such new equipment as there was amounted to no more than new webbing to carry replacement packs, a little ammunition, and office typewriters, paper, etc., without which no army can operate!

From Pembroke we were sent to a tented camp just outside Taunton. We enjoyed the local cider and hot summer days doing virtually nothing. The strength of rough cider, "scrumpy," was something everyone misjudged, even hardened beer drinkers from the Tyne shipyards: an innocent brew to drink but with a kick like a mule and a lengthy recovery period.

The little country pubs to which we made our off-duty way offered two new games in addition to the ever-popular darts. One was Shove Ha`penny, not actually played with ha`pennies but with highly polished metal discs. It was a much more skilful game than one would expect. The other pastime was skittles, played on a dried earthen "rink." As the rink was hard and uneven it wasn`t possible to bowl, throw or bounce the ball with any accuracy, but we had hours of good fun trying.

The unit as a whole was still a mixed body of troops and we couldn`t help wondering how many of the rest had survived because, as yet, we`d neither seen nor heard news of the others. Our particular section, however, had gradually been gathered back together and was now complete, so we relaxed, sun-bathed and waited.

In time, orders came to move again. It was said, unofficially, that the remainder of our Unit had got back to England and we were going to join them at a collecting point for all the Division's Engineers, Scraesdon Fort, on top of a hill overlooking the English Channel in Cornwall.

75% of the fortress was underground, reached by long, wide staircases which disappeared into the dark, damp hell beneath our feet. It provided absolute security from bombing, but seemed a useless sort of place in this modern age of blitzkrieg warfare, even defensively.

The only weapons we possessed were the rifles our section sergeant had insisted we brought back from Dunkirk. Those few rifles were kept solely for anyone on guard duty.

Scraesdon Fort was a long way from Plymouth, including a ferry crossing. Only once was a "liberty" vehicle, a locally hired bus, laid on to give us a change of scene, and that was about all it amounted to. We hadn't been paid since our arrival at the Fort so we had finally exhausted the small sub given out at Taunton, and so far, I'd found no-one who wanted to change my French francs for sterling!

This early in the war, food was still plentiful, and we were allowed a ration of beer and cigarettes daily. We understood that the beer and cigarettes were paid for by the CO himself and, although there was no way of proving this, I would be quite prepared to believe it: he was that sort of man.

Over the first few days at the fortress men arrived from other parts of Britain in dribs and drabs, and when a final roll call was taken a mere handful of the Company was missing. Of these, only two turned out to have been killed, the remainder having been taken prisoner. We were lucky, and there were many exciting tales told of escape and near misses. It was amazing to realise that, despite our difficult exit from France, almost at the last minute, nearly everyone had got out unscathed.

Even we small cogs in the big wheel couldn't understand the lull in hostilities. Knowing what we possessed in the way of weapons or rather what we didn't have, it seemed that the Germans were missing a heaven-sent opportunity by not following us across the Channel. A breathing space was granted for which the British people were eternally grateful. I've read since the war ended that we made full use of this interval to rearrange our puny defences, deploy our depleted forces along the south coast, and prepare against the onslaught of "Sea Lion." This, Intelligence assured us, was being mounted rapidly and imminently.

CHAPTER EIGHTEEN – Life on the South Coast and some Nasty Doings

From Scraesdon we were moved, by rail because army vehicles were non-existent, to a pretty little village called Studland, on the coast of Dorset.

The summer of 1940 was very hot during the day and gloriously calm and warm in the evenings. During daylight hours the sappers worked long and hard laying an extensive minefield along the cliff tops and in the fields which sloped towards the sea shore.

As a driver not involved in the mine laying, life for me was very easy. A motor car and a coal lorry had been commandeered for our use and we drivers took turns driving them. The car was for the officers, and we transported men and mines to and from the cliffs in the coal lorry.

One day, having driven the mines to the unloading point, I walked across to watch the sappers. The sloping field in which they were working fell away steeply to the sandy shore. It was divided into rectangular patches, each bounded by a stretch of barbed wire held taut on angle-iron posts sticking out of the ground. As each patch was laid, the sergeant in charge put the detonators into the mines before erecting a warning notice saying, "Live Minefield." Both our side and the enemy did this. It may seem stupid to advertise the presence of a minefield, but minefields were seldom breached before first being swept. The trick was that they were all labelled, "Live Minefield" but some had no mines in at all. These also had to be carefully swept and, as a delaying tactic, they were just as successful as the real thing.

Two fields had been completed and labelled after arming, and the sappers were preparing the third one. Just as a sapper reached the edge of the new area for mining, he stumbled and the plate-sized mine under his arm slipped. Before he could stop it, the mine rolled on its edge into the recently completed field. We, horrified, all shouted at the tops of our voices to get clear or take whatever cover there was, hoping that the loose mine would roll between those already laid. It wasn`t to be. With a horrendous crash the first mine to be touched by the now rapidly moving rogue blew up.

Sensitive mines and certain types of explosive are activated by shock or pressure waves. These mines were subject to both. In seconds, with an almighty roar, most of the nearest minefield went up as each mine exploded in "sympathetic detonation."

The sappers near or not yet far enough away from the explosion were tossed around like rag dolls. When the smoke cleared sufficiently for us to reach them, they looked like broken puppets.

Four men were killed outright. Two were so badly injured with burns and broken bones that they died later. One young lad, very recently joined as a reinforcement, would never be much use again, he was so shocked.

My luck had held. Although I was as near as any of those killed, I was on the cliff top above the minefield and the blast and shrapnel flew over me when I threw myself flat.

We were all upset and shaken by the sudden and tragic way it had happened and having to pick up the pieces. The sadness of this awful accident was that the men killed had all struggled back through Dunkirk only to die so horribly on their own shores.

I don't need to describe the state of the sapper who had dropped the mine. He wasn't physically hurt but it was a long time before he was stable enough to cope with the kindness of a transfer to a base unit.

It took a while to complete the mining of Studland Bay. When it was finished, news filtered down that someone had either forgotten to plot the fields as they laid them, or they didn't have a surveyor amongst the officers who was capable of doing it.

I was in the habit of sketching in my spare time and during the course of my war years I drew quite a number of pictures which didn't come home with me. I also painted murals on the walls of the several messes we occupied for any length of time.

It seemed that my artistic efforts had not passed unnoticed. I was sent for by the CO who asked me to draw the cliffs at Studland Bay and, with as much accuracy as possible, plot in the mines. Ye gods! How does one draw a bay over a mile long with all its nooks and crannies, humps and bumps, overhangs and boulders, and plot in hundreds of buried mines with any accuracy?

Obviously, I couldn't go into the minefields myself to measure and mathematically fix each mine, and no-one could, or would, help me. So, armed with the most high-powered binoculars the CO could get me, an enormous roll of wide paper bought in a Bournemouth art shop, a box of coloured pencils and a 66 foot tape measure, I set to. It took me a week, out in the heat all day, but it was really a very pleasant occupation.

I had to draw what I could see with the naked eye and spot the mines through binoculars, pacing off distances and measuring with the tape. Only the CO came near me and his encouragement and kindness gave me the motivation to complete the job for his sake, at least. It was anything but easy: the picture must be absolutely accurate.

At times I felt sure there were mines I couldn`t see even with the binoculars and I confess I did a silly thing; I tip-toed into the minefield to have a closer look! I worked on the theory that a mine should be there if the sappers had measured accurately from the last one. Usually it was. When it wasn`t, I marked it on my chart anyway, as a measured guess, consoling myself that if there was no mine where I`d put a cross at least no-one could be blown up by a flourish on a piece of paper.

When I`d finally finished my masterpiece, which would have done justice to Michelangelo even if I say so myself, I still had to make a copy of it. I understood that one version was sent to the War Office for records and the other kept by the Unit for future reference. Later in the war all our papers were lost in retreat but perhaps somewhere in the archives of Whitehall I have a picture preserved for posterity. I only hope that whoever cleared that minefield at Studland found it was of some use because my artistic, and I repeat "artistic," plan had nothing technical about it.

In the evenings after our meal, usually stew because our blacksmith cook had got out of Dunkirk too, most of us made our way up and over a footpath which cut across the heath of the headland. It was a couple of miles or more over to Swanage, a sizeable town. The aim of the other ranks was food, drink and girls, or any permutation of those three. The food and drink were usually readily available, but the girls were a different proposition. Those of the fair sex who were prepared to meet the "licentious soldiery" were, in effect, licentious themselves and only attractive to a very few. The "nice" girls, to use a very un-descriptive label, seldom showed themselves. We always hoped that somewhere we might meet girlfriends in the "nice" category but it was hardly likely we would find them unaccompanied in a pub. Good girls didn`t wander around the streets late in the evening or after dark, and they had no reason to go into cafés or restaurants of the price bracket we had to use. The sum total of all this was that girls of the flirty type – the kindest description – could be found, but there were too few of the "nice" kind to go round the majority of young men in our Unit.

We heard that a dance had been arranged and admittance was by ticket only. This looked promising and our little group promptly bought tickets.

The dance hall was a very tasteful, well lit place, not too large, and the band was quite good. It was in a respectable area of the town and, usefully, a pub of somewhat higher than usual standard was nearby.

We had a drink first, cider of course. A glass of something before a dance was a great boon to me as I found it extremely difficult to walk up to a girl and ask her to dance.

Before the war, shortly after I started work, I took a course of dancing lessons at a local academy. My attendance at this dancing school had to be of a clandestine nature as my parents would have considered me to be on the slippery slope to perdition had they known what I was up to. The lessons had taught me the basic steps of a few modern dances but not the ability to overcome my shyness. However, surrounded by friends without any inhibitions and with cider for courage I handed in my ticket and sallied forth.

Faced with a sea of female faces propping up the walls of the dance hall I'm afraid that my resolve weakened rapidly. It took the Paul Jones and a mighty shove from someone to get me on to the floor. I've never known who Paul Jones was, nor how he came to invent the dance, but it is the answer to a maiden's prayer, I suppose. By the end of that dance the ice had been broken and a little group had been formed of which I was, happily, one. The girl with whom I'd finished the dance was pleased to continue with me for the rest of the evening, the way I like to have a dancing partner, although I know it's not the done thing.

The girls in our group were even prepared to accept a drink – gentle strength – and we had a merry evening. Everyone made a date for the next weekend, same place and same time. My friends and I walked home over Studland Headland in a very jolly frame of mind. War or no war, mines or no mines, future or no future, the air was full of romance and we looked back over the moonlit bay of Swanage with starry eyes. Things weren't so bad after all: the war was far away, the nastiness of Dunkirk was fading, and everyone was friendly – with a few exceptions. Our horror of a Lance Sergeant was still as vindictive as ever but I did my best to keep out of his way. That fly in the ointment apart, we had something to look forward to - a pleasant summer evening walk over to Swanage next weekend, a thirst-quenching cider or two after the heat of the day, the pleasure of a dance, and we had found the good company of nice girls.

Next day there was a long march to church parade in Swanage. When we came out of the service and lined up for the return journey, the CO announced that he was sure we`d be pleased to hear we were moving! The march back for some of us was pretty miserable, overwhelmed with disappointment as we were. Before the week was out, we`d packed up and moved to Christchurch.

Christchurch was another pretty little south coast town. It boasted a good deal of private housing but the part where we were billeted was small and compact. A coolness developed between the local populace and us poor souls in the army. Not open hostility; rather a reluctance to co-operate with the urgency to prepare for the invasion which the rest of Britain knew was coming. This lack of co-operation occasionally became obstructive.

Large concrete blocks were being strategically positioned to prevent the landing of tanks, whole barriers being required to make an effective defence. One of our immediate tasks on arrival in Christchurch was to begin constructing these obstacles.

Christchurch front is very flat and rather long. To deter an enemy landing here, our CO had carte blanche to erect the blocks across whatever land he saw fit. The barriers were first marked on a map of the area, then each surveyed position was passed to his engineer sections to carry out the work. In 1940 particularly, the emergency was sufficiently urgent to be ruthless.

All went well to begin with, but one day an unholy row broke out when a householder flatly refused to allow a block to be positioned in one corner of his garden. It wasn`t just an isolated construction: the block was part of a straight, planned, defensive line and could not be left out. Arguments, reasoning and threats were all dismissed out of hand: no block was being stuck in his garden the owner insisted.

I thought our CO was extremely patient and diplomatic. He even offered to move the other blocks in the line slightly as they hadn`t been started yet, so that the householder could have his concrete block camouflaged by existing shrubbery, but he was met with an adamant refusal. There was only one answer to which the army had recourse. Either the householder ceased to be obstructive and physically removed his presence or he would be arrested by the civilian police under wartime powers. He was arrested, or rather detained, while a concrete tank obstruction was built in his shrubbery.

Naturally, the owner occupier grumbled unmercifully about the havoc wrought in his garden. Constructing a large concrete cube is, admittedly, messy and I could understand why the man felt annoyed. At the same time, we were preparing to fight a ruthless enemy for our very survival. We knew from bitter experience that every means of defence and speed of erecting it was vital. There was no alternative than for our CO to be firm about complaints.

As it happened the defences were never put to the test, but such a gap might very well have allowed the further advance of a German tank if "Sealion" had been mounted by Hitler.

This incident was the first of a long list of situations where people living in what we expected to be the front line failed to co-operate or appreciate the urgency of our preparations.

We discovered standing in the corner of the lido, which had closed down for the duration, a very large and luxurious American limousine. It had been propped up on wooden chocks to take the weight off the tyres and springs. We were pathetically short of transport, having had no reissue of army vehicles to replace those we`d lost in France. All army units at that time had powers to "impress" vehicles which were not in immediate use. Civilians knew this, of course, and anyone who had such a vehicle usually made quite certain the army didn`t see it. Needless to say, the decision was very soon made to commandeer the Packard.

The tyres were pumped up, it was lowered from its wooden blocks, petrol filled its tank and, with the first press of the starter, the six great cylinders roared into life. What glorious power and luxury. No-one had ever before ridden in such a car and there was great competition both to ride and to drive it. I counted myself very fortunate to get my turn at the wheel before the vehicle was moved permanently to the officers` quarters. I often wondered if anyone finally returned it to its original resting place on the wooden blocks. Certainly none of our Unit`s transport staff ever did!

Our mode of transport for all essential purposes was another impressed vehicle, a Morris Cowley baker`s van, the bull-nose model. Once, in an episode of the television series "Dad`s Army" many years later, an exact double of this van appeared. Everyone laughed at the sight of the old crock but, believe me, although I laughed along with the rest, it was a true gem from my past.

I was driving this van one day on our way to drop off an officer at a job when, to my surprise, I was overtaken by a wheel. It bowled past my window and eventually wobbled into a ditch. At the moment of its disappearance my van tipped sideways and ground to a shuddering halt. It was my wheel! After that we felt it was necessary to carry spare wheel nuts with us because the wheels often came off our little van, sometimes at embarrassing moments.

There was nothing to make life exciting after duty in our small backwater of Christchurch so Bert Walker, Robbo and I, who had stuck together for some time now, went into Bournemouth for entertainment. Fortuitously, the Bournemouth and District Corporation had declared free travel on all public transport for members of HM Forces, a concession which they later withdrew.

Bournemouth had practically everything to please all tastes from culture to lechery. Lechery seemed to be going a bit far for me. I was rather glad to be surrounded by friends who were strong enough to withstand the many attractive temptresses who constantly offered "creature comforts" in a most charmingly innocent way. Perhaps my friends looked upon me as the one to keep them out of trouble, but that was the way I looked upon them! We found other things to do which passed our evenings and days off very happily.

At this stage of the war the shops were still well stocked and interesting to look at, and there was any number of cinemas, theatres, and dance halls to enjoy, although the dances were too large and saturated with young people ever to allow us to strike up a relationship that was at all personal or permanent.

The idea of culture was off-putting, too, in a different sort of way. Nevertheless, one evening I booked a seat for a Bournemouth Symphony Orchestra concert. Up till then I'd never taken much interest in classical music but I enjoyed that concert so much that it initiated one of the great loves of my life and I regularly booked a seat for concerts during the whole of the period I was at Christchurch. Unfortunately, neither Bert nor Robbo could be persuaded to accompany me and I always had to go alone, though I usually joined them for a drink in some pub afterwards before dashing for the bus back to our billet.

Aerial photos and intelligence reports flooded in daily detailing German preparations on the other side of the Channel. I cannot remember now whether much of this official and disturbing information was made public but it seemed that the community was not nearly as concerned as we felt they ought to be.

We'd laid minefields and we'd built tank obstacles. At this time there were a lot of boffins inventing various peculiar "nasties," some of which were more dangerous to the operator than to the enemy. Our Colonel Royal Engineers came up with a wonderful invention which would make sure that if any German reached our shoreline he'd either burn on the way in or fry on the way out.

On the cliff tops overlooking a beautiful sandy stretch of beach somewhere on the Hampshire coast, our sappers dug a very large pit, removing clay and boulders, and shoring up the sides to prevent the cavity collapsing upon them. An even more difficult task then faced the officers directing operations: how to lower a huge empty petrol tank into the hole? There were no cranes in the area. Even if there had been one, the hole was dug in a most inaccessible place across fields. So it was done by brute force, man power, rolling ramps, ropes, ingenuity and a great deal of puffing and blowing.

A pumping engine and control valves were installed near the tank. From this reservoir, pipes ran up hill, down dale, through woods and copses, over the cliffs, and under the beach, coming up 100 yards out to sea with only a six inch nozzle showing above the waves to indicate there was anything unusual there. To each nozzle was attached the mechanism of a cigarette lighter. These lighters were actually purchased from the local tobacconist, the excuse for buying so many being that the Brigadier needed to make some presentations to his staff. Each cigarette lighter had a thin wire running from it under the water to a hidden position inshore.

The procedure to activate this contraption was:-

1. As the enemy landing craft approached the shore, a sentry would pass a signal to the operator standing by the petrol tank inland who would turn the valves and start the pump. Petrol/oil would then flow down and spread out onto the sea through the nozzles 100 yards out. The German landing craft should, by then, be right in this flammable zone.

2. Another operator hidden nearer the shore would pull the wire and the cigarette lighter on each nozzle would ignite the quickly spreading petrol/oil. The enemy would be caught in the inferno or would have to escape landward and be shot down. In addition, the oil mixed with sea water would create a very effective smoke screen to hide the happenings from any enemy forces following up.

The great day came when all the boffins and high-ups stood on the cliff tops for the first demonstration of Britain's latest secret weapon. We, too, were caught up in the excitement of the event and everyone, cooks, drivers, storemen, even my mortal enemy the Lance Sergeant, turned out to watch. He was the world's greatest cynic. He believed in nothing but himself and announced to all and sundry in no uncertain terms that we were all wasting our time because none of our "bloody officers" had enough sense to invent a fly paper.

With great ceremony, the order, "Fire!" was called by the Brigadier, no less; a well-chosen word, I had to admit. The pumps began and the wires were pulled ... and pulled, and pulled, but not the smallest flicker of a flame appeared, although the sea was an oily mess. The Lance Sergeant smirked, "Told you so."

The fault lay in the fact that the nozzle and its mechanism were saturated with sea water, so there was simply no ignition. Adjustments were made. The great brains of the Royal Engineers, after some sleepless nights, came up with a method of "keeping the powder dry".

An officer, a 2nd lieutenant I'm sure, was sent to Bournemouth, Christchurch and everywhere else locally to buy up the entire stock of rubber sheath condoms from any shop which had them! In that age of under-the-counter sales of such merchandise there would be many a blush and a stammer, no doubt, not to mention numerous eyebrows raised at the request for such quantity. The Brain who thought of this brilliant solution earned the eternal gratitude of Churchill. I do feel, however, that the poor officer who was despatched to purchase the goods deserved a decoration, perhaps the Croix de Guerre because of its French connection!

The nozzles were now suitably protected. We gathered again for the great display. The pumps pumped, the wires were pulled, the letters were delivered of their responsibility and, with an enormous bang, the spreading fuel flashed into blinding light, burning off in thick choking smoke. A great cheer went up. We all felt that little bit more secure to see this wall of flame waiting for any Jerry silly enough to try it on. Rubber melts in heat so there could be no more rehearsals because all supplies had now gone. I often wonder if there was a population explosion around this time, as well as a military explosion.

There is a tail piece to this story.

Being a weapon still very much on the secret list, no-one other than us knew a thing about it and it was policy not to inform the local authorities of our "goings on." In all towns and villages on the south coast someone was always ready, alert and vigilant for anything unusual. The great bank of smoke which rose from our piece of nastiness caused an immediate and rapid reaction: Fire Brigades for miles around were alerted. Our first inkling of this intrusion was the clamour of many fire bells as the engines tore down country lanes, converging on us. They were not at all pleased, nor understanding, when stopped at road blocks and refused further access.

It took some days, and probably a few bottles of whiskey, before the local authorities were mollified by our staff officers.

CHAPTER NINETEEN – Not Quite the Dunkirk Spirit

I cannot really emphasise too strongly how frantic this preparation was to ensure that there would be some resistance to any German landing.

One day when I went to the Company Office, the Chief Clerk showed me some aerial photos which had just come in from across the Channel. We could see clearly row upon row of barges collected from the canals of France and Belgium. There were even some close ups, taken by low flying aircraft, of German troops marching onto or off these landing craft. The build up for an invasion was certainly under way and we all felt that very shortly our country was going to be a battle ground. Had this ever happened, I feel sure we would have fought tooth and nail and the Germans would never have had the walk-over they got in France.

There was even a rumour about some fully equipped German troops being washed up, dead of course, near Weymouth which was not far away. I never saw them nor did I know of anyone who did, but the truth of it wouldn`t have surprised me.

Along this part of the south coast it was disheartening to experience the apathy of a fairly large section of the community and, even worse, to come up against open obstruction. A distinctly unpleasant relationship was developing between the troops and the residents.

The Royal Artillery was being re-equipped with guns, the effective 25 pounder which had been so useful in France, and batteries were being dug in along the coastline so there could be a continuous barrage covering the beaches and open stretches of land.

One of these open stretches was to the east of Bournemouth. Unfortunately, the artillery`s field of fire was obstructed by some lines of beach huts, locally owned. Nuisance though it was, these beach huts had to be removed. The first step was to announce in the press and by posters that the owners were requested, in the interests of the National Emergency, to remove all their belongings from the huts. The army, us, would then carefully dismantle the wooden chalets and huts and arrange for them to be stored safely for the duration.

Absolutely nothing happened. The police were asked to tour local towns with loud hailers repeating the request and a very few owners complied. A further announcement through the press and posters was circulated as an urgent order because this was vital.

The lack of response put our side in a quandary. The huts had to be moved, that was certain, but they contained so much in the way of personal possessions, they presented a problem. What might have happened is anyone's guess, but in the end, the impasse was solved by nature.

After the beautiful summer weather we'd enjoyed, the wind suddenly sprang up, the rain lashed down, the Channel was whipped into a rage, and the exceptionally high tides which followed this bad weather crashed upon the beach huts and reduced most of them to matchwood. Even those still left standing were no longer habitable. The possessions were either scattered over a wide area or left in a jumbled, mangled heap. Our job was merely to collect together everything we could find. The owners appeared rather sheepishly, and had the unhappy task of trying to sort out their own belongings from the heap. The wood from the wrecked beach huts and chalets was there for the taking and, by the grace of God, the Artillery had their uninterrupted field of fire.

The attitude of the locals to the army and its efforts to erect defences along the south coast hardened, impossible though it may seem. Each day the national news announced further failures, defeats, and collapses both of our own and our allies' battles on land and sea. Yet somehow these people along the south coast hadn't come to terms with the fact that our backs were being pushed further and further towards the wall.

Quite a number of men in our Unit couldn't have cared less about this attitude. Their only concern, to be quite blunt, was beer, baccy and women, and to hell with the future, understandable when there didn't really seem to be much future to look forward to. There were others of us, however, and I was one, who examined the situation in depth. Perhaps our ability to reason out the worsening situation disturbed us to the extent that discussion acted as a release valve and a way of escaping the stark reality. In spare moments and over a drink in the local we'd spend hours "putting the world to rights" and getting nowhere. We had no influence whatsoever on war strategy generally, nor the work of our Unit in particular. I sometimes wondered if the ordinary soldiers of the German army ever discussed matters the way we did, or whether it was more in the nature of German servicemen to obey orders blindly without questioning. At least, the work of our Unit, distasteful though it may have been to the local people, did them no harm and the overall plan which we were trying to implement was for the good of everyone living in our country.

The next job was in Bournemouth itself. The sea front and promenades are below the level of the town, and the cliffs gently slope down to them. Here and there chines or valleys run inland, some with streams and some dry. There are steps and zig-zag paths from one level to another. Along the promenade is a railing to prevent anyone falling the twelve feet or so onto the gravelly beach, and on the landward side of this concrete walk stood a long row of beach huts, shoulder to shoulder.

Where the promenade met a wide road from the town, an open space led to Bournemouth pier. This long wooden structure, one of many piers to be found along the coast of southern England, ended in a Pavilion Theatre where concerts and variety shows were presented nightly during the summer season. It was the summer season now, but the shows were not being put on with their usual regularity, perhaps because the actors had been called up, or perhaps just due to wartime conservancy.

The orders for an extension to the defences of this area were something like:

a. the cliffs, walks, chines and shrubberies would be laced with barbed wire obstructions

b. the beach huts would be closed for the duration and owners should remove belongings for safe keeping

c. the beaches and promenade would be lined with triple Danert barbed wire fences

d. souvenir and sweet shops along the sea front would be closed and the owners should remove stock for safe keeping

e. (*and this was the "knotty" one*) the owners of the Pavilion at the end of the pier would be asked to remove all valuable equipment, pianos, musical instruments, stage lighting and props, even the plush seating, etc.

A hole had to be blown in the centre of the pier. It had been decided that if the Germans invaded, the pier could be used as a landing quay just as we'd used the structure of Dunkirk Mole, even though neither structure had been constructed for ships to dock against them.

All this, as a plan of defence against a full scale enemy landing, seemed quite reasonable to the High Command and no less to us as the troops who had to do the job. Not so the civilian population, however, who had interests or property on the sea front at Bournemouth. It seemed that everyone objected to our efforts, and they were forever trying to hinder our work. Possibly there were people who were sympathetic to us and even objected to those who were being obstructive, but I think I can say, in all honesty, that they made no effort to show their support in voice or deed.

After the deadline date had been announced, our three engineering sections moved down onto the promenade to begin work on the defences. One party began laying barbed wire in the chines and along the cliffs. Another set to work on the promenade with pneumatic drills. They sank holes for tank traps, and lengths of sharpened railway track were set at an angle to damage any armoured vehicle coming up from the sea. Another section began laying down loops of triple Danert barbed wire along the beach and round the promenade railings. The third section had to convert various innocent looking souvenir stalls and even a public lavatory into pill boxes for machine guns. Meanwhile, the specialist job of blowing a hole in the pier was surveyed by the 2i/c.

It is difficult to believe what happened over the next few weeks. To begin with there were no obvious signs that the beach hut owners were preparing to close down their holiday establishments. Until the announcement of closure, not many had appeared to be occupied even. Then suddenly, every day, the owners were there, on deckchairs outside their huts, sunning themselves in scanty dress, while we slaved at our tasks. Few went home before we departed, but as soon as our tools were packed into our vehicles and they were sure the day's work was done, the locals left, too. Next morning, as we arrived so did they but, without fail, any barbed wire we'd already erected along the shore had been cut in many places, and strong cutters must have been used, too. The hut occupants came and went through the gaps in the wire to splash around at the water's edge. Barbed wire in the chines and along the cliffs suffered similar damage and removal.

The tank trap preparations were tedious, complicated and heavy going for the sappers, digging and working with pneumatic drills. Their tempers were sorely tried by a local who had a souvenir shop on the promenade. He could have cleared his shop in one trip, but he made our lives a misery by going back and forth for "loads." Each time the sappers had to stop and clear a path for him, moving pipes, machinery, etc., to let him pass. How we obeyed orders to be patient, diplomatic and co-operative I'll never know.

When that job was completed and the steel rails slotted into their holders, every single one disappeared overnight and the holes where they had been were filled with cement! This couldn't go on, of course, and the police were called in. They didn't arrest anyone but the nonsense stopped—almost!

The beach huts were closed. The wiring of the beach, promenade, cliffs and chines was completed. The tank traps were in place and all the souvenir shops were emptied and closed – except one. At the landward end of Bournemouth pier a man kept a stall which sold postcards, maps of the area, key rings, pencils with pictures of the sea front, newspapers, magazines and the usual sort of things visitors would want to buy in the halcyon days of peace. But this was war and he`d been told, both for his own safety and the security of his stock, to close down and clear away anything of value because there would eventually be quite an explosion. He took no action and each morning opened up as usual.

In addition, despite continual pleas and the obvious fact that their pier was being prepared for partial demolition, the owners of the Pavilion had made little, if any, attempt to remove their possessions from the theatre. A final warning had been issued and a deadline set, again by press announcement, posters and the efforts of the police. Everyone in Bournemouth must have been fully aware that part of their pier was to be blown up at a certain time on a certain day. Visits were made to the owners and residents of businesses and houses near the pier approach, who were told that it would be sensible to leave their windows open slightly and keep away from the glass at the time of the explosion.

The day came for the last act in this saga. Those of us who were able to be there found suitably safe vantage points overlooking the pier and its approach. The Top Brass came to watch, and a surprising number of Bournemouth citizens crowded behind the barrier at the top of the road leading to the town. The approaches were cleared, and last minute electrical connections checked. The atmosphere resembled that moment before the teams run out onto the field at Wembley: not hushed, just a murmur of expectancy.

As we waited, the elderly gentleman walked across to his kiosk at the end of the pier and began setting out the postcards, souvenirs, magazines, etc. Our CO ran over and it was obvious that he was telling the old boy in no uncertain terms to move, at the double, but he didn`t.

Another party arrived to argue with the CO. These were the owners of the Pavilion Theatre. They wanted, at this last minute, to remove all their valuable heavy equipment from the pier end. More than likely they hadn`t believed we really intended to destroy part of the structure, but they`d carried their bluff too far.

Finally, with the help of the civilian police, both the stall holder and the pier owners were removed from the danger area, still protesting like mad, and after a short interval, one of our officers pressed the plunger. There was a suitably impressive crash and a large chunk of Bournemouth pier shot skywards and splashed back into the English Channel. It was a successful demolition which would have been a considerable nuisance to any German landing.

Pier debris wasn't the only thing falling from the sky. Like snowflakes on a wintry day a cloud of postcards, papers, magazines and sundry knick-knacks slowly fluttered down upon the pier approach. The explosion was also followed by much tinkling of glass from most of the hotel windows nearby because the occupants hadn't take the precaution of opening them. There were even reports later of one or two injuries to people sitting at their windows to watch.

Of course, a number of days were subsequently spent by a section of sappers in bringing ashore all the equipment from the pier end Pavilion, an unnecessary, difficult and heavy task. It all had to come over the blown gap on a steel cable stretched between sheer legs erected on either side of the hole. What a fiasco.

A little later there was a meeting of General Montgomery, Commander of 3rd Division, who, at the time, was the king pin of our defending force, and Winston Churchill. The lavatory on the corner of the pier approach had been converted by some of our people into a pill box, although to outward appearances it looked exactly as it had always done.

Montgomery took Winston into the pill box / loo to show him what had been done, I suppose. Some years later they met again in a similarly camouflaged position and it is reputed that Churchill remarked, "I haven't seen you since that day we stood together in the gentleman's lavatory in Bournemouth, General!" It was the sort of Churchillian risqué remark the Prime Minister might make, but members of Monty's staff suggested that the General didn't chuckle along with his leader.

One day, Bert, Robbo and I were just coming out of Bournemouth's Woolworths when the air raid sirens wailed. There were shelters but we didn't feel inclined to bury our heads in the sand so we found a clear space where we could watch which might happen. Sure enough, a flight of planes, silver in the sunlight, soared overhead, and almost at the same moment the RAF tore into them. Within minutes they had scattered so wide there was little to see. A few explosions indicated they might have bombed something, but, on the other hand, it could just as easily have been the planes hitting the ground after being shot down.

Later, we learned that this raid had been made by the Italian air force. Apparently, Mussolini wanted to be able to say that his all-powerful, brave pilots had penetrated the British defences and destroyed this and that. Goodness knows why the flight came in over Bournemouth. Unfortunately for Musso, he didn`t get the propaganda material he`d hoped for as no damage had been caused.

CHAPTER TWENTY – The Stately Home and Clerk i/c

I can't say that I enjoyed our stay in Christchurch to any great extent. There had been moments of interest and excitement, especially watching the dog fights as the RAF intercepted enemy aircraft when they came over from France. More than once I saw these tests of skill. It was rather like watching knights of old jousting to the death. Now, as then, it was man against man but with the loser crashing into the English Channel, a huge plume of water marking the end of the contest. Sometimes the pilot floated gently down on his parachute and the RAF rescue service was never far away. Sometimes, the falling plane took its brave pilot, from our side or theirs, to the bottom of the sea.

We had worked long hard hours and hadn't had a great deal of spare time except at the weekends. When we went into town the only company was almost always that of our own forces personnel. It could never be said that the people of the area took us to their hearts, and I felt very much like an interloper. I was quite happy to be moving on.

The logistics of making a move was, by now, somewhat easier as we'd been issued with some brand new army vehicles. Instead of the pre-Dunkirk Morris 15 cwt trucks and those difficult and temperamental Ford PUs, American lend-lease exchange meant we could have Ford 15 cwts, powerful and updated vehicles. In addition, there was a small Austin car for the officer in each section and a very business like Humber staff car for the CO. All vehicles were painted in a dull matt camouflage.

It was autumn when we moved to Timsbury near Bath.

In the course of my "Cook's Tour" provided by His Majesty between 1939 and 1946 I lived in some strange places but none was more stylish than that at Timsbury. Not many people can say that they've lived in a stately home.

Timsbury is a little village about seven miles from Bath, comprising two or three pubs, a Post Office, a butcher, a general store, a garage, a sweet shop and a very old and beautiful church. It didn't take the locals long to make it known that the vicar was the brother of the great stage personality Clarkson Rose. I had to confess that I'd never heard of Clarkson, or a Rose by any other name for that matter.

An army unit moving into a small village community of this sort created many and varied problems: administrative, social and, unfortunately, moral. The simple, ordinary, kindly folk of Timsbury must have been overwhelmed by the two hundred and fifty boisterous young men of our Unit swamping their little community, not to mention the many comings and goings of army vehicles along the narrow main street.

All the vehicles required petrol, maintenance and repair. Either by negotiation or official command, the local garage became the Transport Centre for everything we needed. One of the two petrol pumps provided fuel solely for our needs and the workshop was staffed by our mechanics. The garage proprietor and the young workmen who were still with him continued to function in their private capacity, but petrol restrictions and the shortages of wartime had dulled their business. Our arrival was probably a considerable financial advantage to the cheerful owner.

The village was too small to house the whole Unit, so each of the three sections moved into large farmhouses or suitable buildings within a mile or two of Timsbury. I couldn't say whether these houses were already empty or whether the occupiers were moved elsewhere by the War Office.

Our section's accommodation was both unoccupied and intriguing. To the right of the church lych-gate was an impressive gateway. Passing through the gates and up the gravel drive one came to a wide sweep of forecourt beyond which stood the most imposing Elizabethan manor house, with a decorated and canopied porch over the entrance, and above, clustered angular chimneys, gargoyles and mullioned windows just as one would see in the pages of a history book.

Every time I entered that glorious building, so old and steeped in the past, I marvelled that the war had brought me to live in it, though not many felt as I did. Back home most of the Jarrovians happily enjoyed two roomed flats with a netty at the bottom of the back yard – specialised type of living conditions - and this place was an abomination to all the politics of their upbringing. Not that I had any "blue blood" in my veins, but I couldn't help admiring the architecture of this manor house, so unique and so beautiful and so definitely part of that heritage for which we were fighting this war. As expected, it wasn't long before we learned from the locals that Queen Elizabeth had slept there!

Timsbury Manor was owned by the Sambourne family and I was led to believe that the last of the line was now very old and living alone in Poole, Dorset. The house, being empty, had been taken over by the War Office.

The previous occupants, who had recently moved out, were a Guards company. Apparently, just before our arrival, assessors had been through the house to calculate the damage caused by these "gentlemen." Even to us there seemed quite a lot.

A very lovely and large stained glass window on the vast half landing of the stairs was smashed. It may have been repairable but the stained glass was old and it would be unlikely that even experts could ever have restored it to its original condition.

Another act of needless destruction was the emptying of the wine cellar. It had been padlocked but that hadn`t stopped someone breaking in. The cellar had held a large stock of vintage port, sherry and table wines including champagne, and the value of such a cellar must have run into thousands of pounds. Dozens of shattered bottles littered the floor. There were stories amongst the locals that troops were drinking these irreplaceable wines out of tea mugs and pint pots then throwing over each other what they didn`t like. Not a bottle of anything remained to tempt us.

It says something for the "rough nuts" in our Unit of Northerners, and we had plenty, that none of the many porcelain and metal wine labels which hung from chains on the now empty wine racks, was ever touched, although they were there for the taking as souvenirs.

When I had time to explore the house which, as one might expect, was a building of corridors, landings and odd little rooms in the most unlikely places, I found an attic full of objets d`art which had most certainly been stacked there for safety. Once again, the owners` trust that their valuables would be respected had been betrayed. Someone had rummaged without regard for the value and delicate nature of the things stored there and many fine-looking and possibly priceless articles lay strewn and broken in jumbled heaps.

One huge painting, which seemed to be of a battle at the time of Wellington, must have attracted the attention of a vandal. He had used it as a dartboard. Jagged rips in the canvas evidence of wanton damage which could never be repaired.

A pile of smouldering personal papers, books and documents in the garden made me wonder why there are some amongst us who have so little regard for the possessions of others. The whole episode left a bad taste. If the information of the local people was accurate, all this vandalism was by the troops who had occupied the house.

I returned long after the war to show my family Timsbury Manor. Incredibly, it had vanished. Not one solitary stone remained to indicate where this glorious house had once stood. As I looked at the spot, quite speechless, I couldn`t help but ponder whether there was now anything left to remind the world that the long line of Sambournes had ever existed.[2]

To return to 1940.

We moved in. At Timsbury Manor there were dozens of bedrooms in which to spread ourselves. There were no beds, of course, but we`d all become used to sleeping on hard floors by now.

One of the great panelled rooms downstairs was the Officers` Mess and a similar one opposite, with deep leather armchairs, was their lounge.

We had one of the rooms at the back for our Mess. It wasn`t panelled: instead, some rather clinical tiles lined the walls from floor to ceiling. This was the servants` quarters: most appropriate for our humble station.

The large, old-fashioned kitchens with their huge, coal-burning cookers and massive pans, served both officers and men. The quality and quantity of cooking facilities mattered little to our blacksmith-cum-cook`s versatility. He could just as easily ruin his eternal stew in an ancient setting as a modern one.

A mound in the garden suggested there was something underneath. A large flat stone topped the mound. With Bert`s help I moved the stone and we found we were looking down into the damp, dingy depths of an ice house. It was broad at the bottom but only wide enough at the top to push snow through. The smooth interior would have been packed tight and being windowless, without light or ventilation, the resulting ice would have lasted a long time.

With the reorganisation of the Unit and of Section 1, in particular, my clerical and administrative capabilities were called upon once more. In France and Dunkirk and since our return to Britain, I`d been just another driver, the rank in which I`d mustered. That I accepted: I had no responsibility, extra duties or worry. I only had to think about a warm, dry billet, a comfortable bed and food to eat. Sometimes I had driving to do as and when vehicles became available. Otherwise I lived a sort of "dogsbody" existence.

Once we`d settled into Timsbury Manor changes gradually began to take place. The British Army`s love of form-filling and writing letters in quadruplicate was restored.

Our section had stuck together all through the Dunkirk emergency and up to now we had been under the very capable guidance of our elderly

2 EC – the manor house was demolished in 1961

sergeant. He was essentially a practical man but I doubt if there was a better sergeant in any territorial unit anywhere.

Our sergeant had one pet hate and that was "bumph," a very expressive word which can best be translated as "toilet paper." Not a man of high academic qualifications, he'd left school to go into the Jarrow shipyards at fourteen. He loathed paperwork and, because I think it rather frightened him, he completely ignored it.

The old boy was quite unrepentant about his attitude to forms, returns and written directions but, because of his terrific value within the Unit, this idiosyncrasy was tolerated up to a point. Someone, probably our very diplomatic and gentlemanly CO, must have advised him that if he couldn't deal with the administration he'd have to find someone who would, and establish a Section Office. You know who got the job!

This new occupation suited me fine. The "perks" of the job by far outweighed its problems. The greatest advantage was that the telephone had to be constantly manned for emergencies, though I can't honestly remember any, so I had to be always in the office. Being always in the office meant that I couldn't attend morning parade nor be part of the eternal, boring and, to my way of thinking, useless squad drills which occupied the whole of most mornings.

My working hours were long but not particularly arduous. I could only leave the office for meals when relieved, usually by the sergeant himself. This, again, was an advantage because the cooks were always "canny" about serving the first sitting, made up of the bulk of the section. The principle was that there had to be more than enough left for the second sitting – themselves, an occasional driver or sapper out on late duty, and me. I never failed to get a large helping of everything. Not that it was Cordon Bleu, but it was nice to have plenty.

Organising the office was left entirely to me. There were orders coming in from Company Office which had to be acted upon, numerous inventories to be tabulated, and requisitions to be made for stores, and as a result of the chaos of our return to Britain every man's service record had to be checked and brought up to date, as well as many other jobs much loved by officialdom. Most of the work was "self inflicted," a lot of it was paper chase material, and a little of it was vital. As far as I was concerned everything was "useful." I'd invented it, nourished it and filed it. I made quite certain that I alone could handle it and thereby became an indispensable "king pin." My boss was quite content to leave things in my hands while he concentrated on practical matters. The CSM in Company Office was happy because he could always get an immediate and accurate answer to questions when he phoned or called in. The Section Officer left me alone because a) he relied too much on my sergeant to upset the man by ruffling the feathers of his clerk, and b) he knew little of the section`s administrative side and I`d quickly learned how to "baffle him with science" if he asked awkward questions.

There were those who were jealous of my position, however, because I held quite a few trump cards but no rank. No-one in the army is happy with having to take orders from, or being dependent upon anyone of lower rank. I had three potential enemies. One was the Quartermaster. He`d been in this exalted position since TA days although he was still quite young. In civilian life, he`d been in the office of a Tyneside shipyard, he had some early accounting qualifications and he acted like a Town Clerk. I had to admit that he was very much on top of his job and knew every last article in his stores. Unfortunately, to get anything out him was like getting blood out of a stone. We were completely cleared out of stores after Dunkirk but for years afterwards the QM would fight tooth and nail before he would issue as much as a new button. It was said that one could get a new pair of socks when there were only the holes of the old ones left to hand in.

The QM didn`t take kindly to me at all, partly because I was more than his civilian life equal. He also held the opinion that no-one without rank should be in a position of responsibility like mine. Equally, those holding rank should not even speak to those of lower status. He carried this to ridiculous lengths by "speaking" to me, which he often had to do in the course of our work, through his Lance Corporal. Needless to say, much time was wasted because of this stupidity, not to mention confusion because his Lance Corporal was not the brightest of individuals and I used to confuse him deliberately to add to the QM`s discomfiture!

Another enemy was the current holder of the SgtMT`s position, he who had taken over in France from the illiterate character who was moved elsewhere in somewhat mysterious circumstances. The SgtMt had no objections to speaking to me. On the contrary, he spoke to me on every possible occasion and was at great pains to assure me that I was an upstart of the most objectionable kind, that I had neither the right nor the qualification to be where I was, that I was a driver not a clerk, and as soon as he could arrange it I would be returned to the ranks TO DRIVE. And then, pity help me – he would make certain of that!

At any other time such threats might have worried me. I knew, however, that I was far more useful as a Section Office Clerk than I would be as a driver of a non-existent truck. The Unit was still far below its full complement of vehicles as yet.

It would have been folly to cross the SgtMT: he would cheerfully have charged me with insubordination. As a Local Government Officer in civilian life and a L/Sgt in the army, he`d tasted the power of both worlds and intended to make everyone "sit up and beg." Having said that, after he`d taken over in France and we were on our way back, he`d been conspicuous by his absence whenever a sticky situation developed. The leadership expected of the rank he flaunted now in the safety and security of England, had been utterly lacking when we were so hard pressed on the continent. It had been noted with considerable disgust that his behaviour in the sand dunes at Dunkirk had been, to say the least, "lacking in moral fibre." An ostrich buries its head in the sand at the thought of danger: a human makes a pretty pathetic picture emulating this stupid bird. We were all scared to death on the Dunkirk beaches, but most of us tried to not to show our fear. With this one exception, those who carried NCO or commissioned rank made at least a pretence of displaying confidence to men without stripes or pips, rather than appear foolish. All that, it seemed, had been forgotten, and buried with those who were left behind. Here in Britain, discipline and obedience to higher authority had returned. We were back to normal.

My third enemy was, of course, the MT Lance Sergeant who had maintained his venomous attitude to my very existence since territorial days. He still leered his brown toothed, twisted smile at me whenever we met and never missed an opportunity to threaten me with every charge in King`s Regulations as soon as the opportunity presented itself. Fortunately, his section was far enough away to keep us well apart for most of the time. When he was around I used all my guile to keep away from his clutches, but the war might not last long enough and I began to think my luck would run out one day.

CHAPTER TWENTY ONE – Local Relations

It never seemed to take most of the men in our Unit much time to settle down and "get their feet under the table", an expression which could be rewritten as "getting into a well warmed bed."

Timsbury, a very rural, out of the way, quiet, unexciting little village, was suddenly swamped with virile lusty young men, hungry for food and more. The uncertainty of war, the false life of few responsibilities, the freedom from home ties and the mutual attraction that seemed to flow between the young people of the village and our troops was quite amazing. I`m sure the older residents of Timsbury found it startling. Sadly, some of the married women, not all young ones either, having offered one bite of the apple, were devoured willingly to the core.

Our little group stuck together, unattached. The idea of being enmeshed in village intrigue was both scary and hazardous. Situations became explosive when husbands returned unexpectedly on leave, or parents discovered how far their daughters had gone. So we met in the pub, drank our cider and played darts.

Because I used the telephone frequently, after a while I became on speaking terms with the operator. She had very quiet, slow speech and I promised myself I`d call in at the Post Office one day and meet the girl behind the voice. Such a day came.

It`s funny how a voice so seldom matches one`s image of its owner. The girl who worked behind the counter in the Post Office and doubled on the switchboard, was "canny," a Geordie expression for "pleasant enough but ordinary, naive, wouldn`t be noticed in a crowd", and no more than that. She had the most ruddy complexion I`d seen outside a pot of jam, the broadest of Somerset accents away from the telephone, and a beam and bosom to match. Frankly, she would have made two of me, because at that time I was very slim. It was a bit of a shock to find something other than I`d expected, but most astounding of all was that she turned out to be only sixteen!

I was left with the problem of wriggling out of a situation I`d created for myself, albeit unwittingly, but I certainly wasn`t going to make any progress there anyway. Within seconds the Postmistress, an elderly dumpy grey-haired little woman of dynamic personality, thrust herself in front of the girl behind the counter and dealt swiftly with my trivial reason for being in the Post Office. I got the impression that my presence was looked upon more as a hold up than the purchase of half a dozen penny stamps. Mind you, it would have taken a brave robber to hold up that Post Office, and the deterrent protecting the counter wasn`t the iron grille!

Later in the week I had a legitimate reason to go into the Post Office. As I crossed the threshold I could almost hear the shutters clang and the safe locks clicking. The assistant was pushed into the back to dust the switchboard, and every inch of space behind the counter appeared to be fully covered by the person of the Post Mistress who asked for my purpose. Of course, she was just being protective towards her assistant. She might have had good reason to adopt this attitude with some of our lechers, but frankly I`d lost interest at my first visit. I wasn`t very old myself at the time, twenty to be exact, but sixteen almost seemed like baby snatching. Not that the young lady in question looked a day younger than twenty five. Nevertheless, Mrs Cook, the Post Mistress was making quite sure there was going to be no "hanky panky."

When, after a few visits and some chat, the lady in charge realised that my motives were not ulterior, she began to mellow. She mellowed so much that, before very long, Bert and I were invited for tea on Sunday.

That small beginning was the start of a very happy association with that dear lady who, after such a frosty beginning, mothered us, or should I say smothered us, with every home comfort money and ingenuity could provide in wartime. Bert and I spent most Sundays in the warmth and comfort of the living room behind the Post Office.

We usually went down to Bath after duty on a Saturday. We`d have a look around the shops, sometimes before going to the cinema, sometimes after. Then we`d find a good place for a meal, and there were lots of cafes and restaurants for this. Even the YMCA provided good meals, basic but big and cheap. We`d finish off with a drink somewhere then catch the "liberty" truck back at about 10.30 pm.

Bert, Robbo and I needed to find three girls with tastes like ours who would make up a party of six, and none of us felt sufficiently attracted by any particular one to split up our group. Sometimes it happened that we`d share a table in a pub or cafe with the same number of girls. We`d laugh, chat, exchange experiences but they didn`t want to separate and neither did we so we`d eventually go our own ways.

On only a couple of times did we form a gang. Six of us went to a dance the first time and to a cinema on a second occasion, with a meal and a drink afterwards. The girls probably had an even lower income than us and there was no offer to stand their turn when it came to paying for the dance or the cinema, nor did they make any determined effort to contribute towards what we ate and drank. The hole in our finances after those two occasions confirmed that female company was too expensive, pleasant though it might be at the time.

Many men and women in the forces seemed to be motivated by sex when looking for company. It was almost as if it were expected that the ultimate reason for meeting up with a partner was to satisfy the urge. Healthy young people all had that urge but, thank goodness, not all allowed their will power to weaken. The reasons for resisting were quite a few, not least of which were warnings of disease, but we also had no intention of being put in a position of having to marry a virtual stranger for whom we had no love.

I enjoyed Bath. It was a beautiful town with lots to see. There were some wonderful little second hand and antique shops. In one of these I bought an old violin for ten shillings, complete with bow and case. I couldn't play the instrument but it still looked good. I kept that violin for years and my daughter, who took a music degree, eventually made very good use of it.[3]

Back at the Post Office, we enjoyed Sunday's roast, Yorkshire pudding and three veg.

I cannot speak highly enough of Mrs Cook's efforts to make her home ours for a short period each week. The Post Office was open six days and we were fully occupied during the week, but every Sunday, except when on guard duty, which was only to satisfy army regulations because there was absolutely nothing to guard, we made our way down after morning parade, to relax in the comfort of an armchair and be waited upon hand and foot. Those were the days of ITMA and Workers' Playtime and somehow there was always something to talk about. At the same time, we did have to accept the gushing, forceful and, at times, overwhelming personality of the Post Mistress.

She was a very well educated woman who had fallen on hard times when her husband was killed in the First World War. She had suddenly been left to bring up two very small children. The Post Office, needlework and a small annuity left by her parents had supplied a very basic income, but she

3 EC – I still have it and played it throughout my childhood and adult life, although I did eventually invest in both a new bow and a new case.

wasn`t afraid to work hard. The Post Office also housed the telephone switchboard through which a great deal of communication passed to a wide area. The bell was always ringing and it had to be answered immediately, night and day. This inconvenience, which Mrs Cook accepted philosophically, was probably the major source of her income, but she also sold sweets and stationery in the Post Office itself.

The time came when we met her daughters. The elder one, Jane, who was about five years my senior, was married to a civil engineer and lived in Staffordshire. We only saw her and her husband twice as distance and petrol rationing governed their visits. I never really got to know her. She was pleasant but cool, and I had the feeling she resented the way we were "at home" in her mother`s house. I`m sure she thought we had personally arranged it, but this was far from the case, although I would not deny we enjoyed the privilege.

The younger daughter, Dorothy, was two years older than me, but years ahead in maturity. She lived in London, had her own flat, and was actually one of Winston Churchill`s secretaries. She spent a good deal of her time in the bunker he had had built for himself, the famous "War Room," and although she would say very little about her work, which certainly was most secret, she did admit to helping to write Churchill`s speeches. I wondered if she meant "write" or "type" but didn`t dare ask because she was very like her mother, without the sense of humour. Perhaps the daughters had talked to one another because it seemed that Dorothy agreed with her sister when it came to her attitude towards Bert and me (Robbo didn`t come with us on a Sunday. By a number of misfortunes he had always been on duty). Dorothy`s visits home were more frequent possibly because when the bombing of London started, her office insisted that she come home to Timsbury every other week or so to preserve her sanity. Not that I would have expected her to be upset by such a triviality as a few bombs dropping too close. Dorothy was, indeed, a very cool customer and one who could sometimes be brutally frank.

One of these brutally frank moments led to an unpleasant argument I had with her. She was pointing out, in no uncertain terms, that we uncouth soldiers (by that she meant anyone who did not hold a commission) had taken over a small village like Timsbury, raped the girls, indulged in drunken orgies and preyed upon elderly widows in parasitic fashion. Admittedly, she was intending her remarks to be general rather than specific but the inference was more than clear, so it wasn`t surprising that I "saw red." In equally not uncertain terms, I called upon my very best English vocabulary to assure her that I had neither raped nor preyed, nor had I any wish to do so. I agreed that there were elements of our forces who misbehaved, but that was only a small percentage doing what soldiers had always done since time immemorial, and it didn`t follow that everyone in uniform was a sex maniac. I also pointed out that some of the worst offenders wore pips, even in bed. I went on to say that as for her dear mother, she could very well take care of herself and would be the first to boot anyone who preyed on her the length of the village. I concluded that in the not too distant future all our lecherous soldiery would be drafted many miles away from Timsbury because we were a fighting unit, and she could rest assured that few would return to continue the rape and pillage she imagined. When we left, I snapped, it might be that the village would find the resulting vacuum hard to take. I was prophetically and tragically right on both counts but, at least, it shut Dorothy up once and for all. I think it was the only time I saw her speechless because my attack was so unexpected.

I got on with Mrs Cook`s younger daughter rather better after that in a sort of older sister kind of way. I think, perhaps, I would rather have liked to have her as a sister.

One weekend she brought a friend back from London. Joyce lived further north and couldn`t get home. She was younger than Dorothy and married to a pilot in the RAF. I felt sorry for her because the danger her husband faced daily obviously filled her mind and left her a bundle of nerves.

I think it must have been about Christmas because being two couples we must have agreed (and that was a miracle in itself) to have a night out in Bath. Dorothy arranged to borrow her brother-in-law`s car as he and Jane were also down for the weekend. Bert and I put on our best uniforms – the same ones, which were all we had!

We`d booked a table in the restaurant of the best hotel in Bath for a dinner dance. I can`t remember many of the details now except that we ordinary ranks were in an absolute minority. Not that we cared about that, but we did get some disdainful looks from the Brigadiers, Wing Commanders and masses of Naval gold that seemed to fill the place. Surprisingly, I honestly felt that the two girls enjoyed the novelty of the situation, because they were so used to mixing with Top Brass in their everyday work. We didn`t disgrace ourselves and it was both a pleasant and interesting occasion which, incidentally, left us stony broke for weeks.

At the dance there were a number of men and women who didn`t display any rank on their uniforms at all, although they did have the word "Intelligence" on their shoulder flashes. I learned many years later that near Bristol was a training establishment for overseas agents. These must have been some of the very brave folk who went back to the continental countries to carry on the underground war and, perhaps die as so many did under torture or in the concentration camps of the Third Reich. How ordinary and commonplace they looked, and how much they were enjoying themselves.

Later in the war Dorothy married a Wing Commander. Sadly, we heard that Joyce`s fighter pilot husband was shot down and badly burned towards the end of our short stay in Timsbury.

It was in Timsbury that I first saw the Home Guard. There was a local group – the butcher, the baker, the candlestick maker – who were commanded by a gentleman farmer. They were so very similar to that famous TV cast who played "Dad`s Army." Many of the antics on television which had Britain laughing so uproariously were carried out in all seriousness by the Home Guard on our doorstep. It wasn`t funny then and I`m quite sure those old and young men who made up the platoon would have died for their country, fighting to the last with pitchforks and broomsticks, had Hitler and his armies invaded.

CHAPTER TWENTY TWO – Bristol Bombed

For weeks we had read in the papers and heard on the radio horrific stories about the bombing of London. Dorothy Cook was able to confirm the reports of destruction and the trials of the people who continued to stick it out, sleeping in shelters and tube stations each night. I think we all felt a bit guilty that we soldiers, who should be at grips with the enemy, were comfortably insulated from the blood and tears of war, living a gentle routine in our little country village where no louder noise than a motor cycle engine ever disturbed the peace.

Then the Germans switched their targets to other cities, and one of the first to be selected was Bristol, the mere flight of a crow from Timsbury.

One night, shortly after darkness fell, the sky seemed to fill with the sound of droning aircraft. The Luftwaffe had arrived. We knew only too well that the planes were not ours. German planes were de-synchronised, which meant that their aero engines ran unmatched with one another, producing a very distinctive undulating, moaning noise, instantly recognisable as a Heinkel or a Junkers or a Dornier. That night, even without the droning, we were fully aware that something big was on. Searchlights and anti-aircraft fire lit the heavens, the beams and flashes turning night into day.

Our own air raid warning sounded for the first time. We had no shelters, other than the ice house which would only have held two at a pinch! Everyone put on their tin hats, grabbed their gas masks and rifles, and stepped outside to watch. Apart from the pyrotechnic display, we all wanted to see a plane shot down and learn what might be the target. We hoped it wouldn`t be us.

When lots of hot exploding metal is whizzing around in the sky, anyone in an aircraft, with very little more than thin fabric or Perspex between himself and destruction, must consider taking the easy alternative of getting rid of the bomb load quickly and heading for home. The first aircraft to do this sent a shower of incendiaries cascading down around our ears in Timsbury. Fortunately, none landed on the Manor: we could never have got at fires in a house of this age and that would have meant its end. A considerable number landed in the garden, however, and burst into brilliant candles of incandescence. We had the means to douse them but, being widely scattered around the garden, this took time. Most of us, drawing on experiences in France, knew that if we didn`t extinguish those tell-tale beacons of light, some other aircraft would drop a more lethal load on them in sympathy. Just as the remaining few incendiaries were fizzling their last, some "eager beaver" flier up above did just what we feared. A stick of bombs screamed down. We had had enough practice to be prone before the first bomb exploded and, by good fortune, no one suffered injury. Two outhouses and a lorry were destroyed, not to mention lots of windows and daisies, while some sleeping birds never knew what hit them. Quite likely, some brave German pilot in his debriefing proudly boasted he`d destroyed a Bristol aircraft factory.[4]

For the rest of the night the bombers droned over and unloaded their bombs onto the unfortunate city of Bristol. We suffered no more than numerous anti-aircraft shell nose caps which at times pattered down like hailstones.

One or two German aircraft were hit and fell in flaming streaks to crash somewhere over the horizon.

Meanwhile, a red-orange glow spread across the sky to the north as the deadly incendiaries did their work. A city dying is a sad and tragic sight. It wasn`t the first time we`d seen one, nor was it to be the last.

Knowing how close we were to Bristol, it was no surprise when, during the night, an emergency call for assistance arrived. We were warned to stand by to move into the city at dawn for rescue and demolition work.

By first light everyone in the Unit who could be spared had dressed and been loaded onto our transport for the short journey to the target area. This was the first time anyone had experienced or seen what was later to become known as "carpet bombing," a polite phrase for indiscriminate saturation. The docks were, admittedly, legitimate targets, factories likewise, but it seemed as though most of the high explosive had fallen on the commercial buildings, shops and houses of central Bristol.

Soon we were digging out the buried. Amazingly, many were still alive, more shocked than injured, but we brought out those killed too. It was very sad to see an elderly person or a child taken, dead, from some ruined building, looking like a rag doll, covered in dust, arms and legs flopping loosely, quite lifeless.

Identification was a problem. Few casualties, alive or dead, carried anything on them indicating their names or addresses and, as often as not,

4 EC – In April 2018 we discovered that there had been a Starfish site near Timsbury, a top secret area where braziers were lit by local volunteers to imitate fires which might have been caused by the incendiaries dropping on targets, so that the bombers following up dropped their full loads in places where they could do little harm. This might account for the dropping of some bombs on Timsbury, short of Bristol.

the building and its contents were so mangled and jumbled together it wasn't possible to extract much information from the wreckage either.

The first day was spent in non-stop rescue work. At the time there were none of the large machines we had later for lifting and scooping heaped masonry and splintered timber beams. It all had to be done by hand or with picks and shovels and it was hard, back-breaking work.

We had brought our cooks and food with us to supply the main meals but I still have grateful memories of the devotion shown by the Salvation Army. They were quickly on the scene with vans, dishing out endless cups of tea, biscuits and cigarettes. This to me was practical Christianity at work and I have never lost my admiration for the work of the Salvation Army.

Sappers working in the ruins of Bristol after it was bombed. 1941.

THIS WAS TAKEN IN THE RUINS OF BRISTOL. YOU CAN'T SEE THEM BECAUSE I HAD MY BACK TO THEM. THE TWO MEN IN STEEL HELMETS ARE PREPARING EXPLOSIVES TO DEMOLISH THE WALL BEHIND ME. SGT. VARLEY IS THE ONE WEARING THE GLENGARRY AND WITHOUT THE TOP COAT.

Reverse.

Looting started, something I would never have expected at all. An example of this was when we had to deal with a public house.

The pubs that had "caught it" were either blown apart or suffered fire damage. Sometimes the publican and his family lived on the premises but in most cases, because the raid had taken place during the night, the pubs were unoccupied. It was our job to search the rubble for survivors or, more often, demolish dangerous structures which remained.

Amongst the rubble or below in the cellars were barrels of beer and boxes and crates of bottled beer and spirits. Some were fire damaged or broken, of course, spirits having added to the intensity of the conflagration. A good deal did survive, however, witnessed only by our party, working in the ruins. Seldom did any owner or publican appear to lay claim to the goods left behind, and the police were too few and too busy to bother about such matters, so the choice was that either we "rescued" what had survived or we left it lying for someone else to help themselves. All Messes of the Units involved were well stocked with drinks and cigarettes for weeks. Not only licentious, but now thieving and drunken soldiery!

There were many other things lying around for the taking from the many wrecked shops. Strangely enough, I can only remember one or two in the Unit helping themselves to anything other than "hooch." Those who did indulge in this rather blatant form of looting were, I must admit, the ones I would have expected anyway. Included were my favourite Lance Sergeant who had no scruples, and the "Sanitary Wallah" whose morals, attitudes to others and language never rose above the level of the sewer.

For obvious reasons this character was known as "Dan, Dan, the S***house Man" and everything about him betrayed his occupation. He helped himself to everything available and one day was caught. He nonchalantly accepted being caught at all his nefarious activities and had the most subservient, apologetic and open method of acknowledging his crimes. Most of the officers who had to deal with him usually gave the lightest of sentence or even exonerated Dan for his "honesty." He`d perfected this method of crime-and-excuse long before he joined the Territorial Army, of course. He drank a lot and after a drink was a demon and unbelievably violent towards anyone. Before the war he`d spent a lot of time in fairground boxing booths and could, therefore, be described as pugilistic, but he didn`t look upon fighting as a sport. Far from it. His cauliflower ear and punch-drunkenness betrayed only too clearly the sort of yob he really was. Yet when sober it seemed that butter wouldn`t melt in his mouth.

There was quite a number of unexploded bombs to deal with in Bristol. After they`d been dug out of sometimes quite deep craters, it was the job of us transport drivers to rush them to a piece of marshland where they were blown up with a slab of gun cotton and a primer. For transport we had a 15 cwt truck splashed liberally all over with red paint, and large notices reading "Unexploded Bomb – Absolute Priority" were prominently displayed back and front. In the back of the truck was a coffin-like cradle to hold the bomb steady. Once it was lifted into place the driver – quite often me – was detailed to get it over to the waste land double quick, "before it went off." No-one ever told me how long I had! As I`m here to tell the tale I must have beaten the clock every time. It was great fun, however, tearing through the streets of Bristol with a bomb on the back. All traffic was stopped by the police and even where there wasn`t a policeman our notices and red patches deterred any vehicle from arguing about our priority. We could drive flat out, race track fashion, without hindrance. Only once in a narrow street did I meet an officious type in black pinstripe suit and Homburg hat who refused to allow his driver to give way to us.

I got out of my driving seat, stuck my head through the window of his limousine and yelled, "This bl***y thing has stopped ticking. If you want to sit here that's fine. I'm off!"

The black pinstripe and his chauffeur shot up a side street, leaving their car to be blown up with us. The bomb wasn't ticking: it had never started because the fuse had been removed. We edged past the car and went merrily on our way, waving to the two brave gents who were lying flat on their faces round the corner.

Our sappers had a good deal of demolition to do especially down by the docks where warehouses and buildings leaned over like grotesque skeletons. There was considerable damage but not really of the type to have much effect on the war effort, though the cost of rebuilding would, no doubt, hit the country hard at a later date.

The hard, dirty and often dangerous work eventually came to an end. The streets of Bristol were re-opened, although mountains of rubble remained to tell the tale of the city's trials. Much worse was to befall other urban centres before the war was over.

CHAPTER TWENTY THREE – Promotion

It was something of a shock when a message came one day from the CSM personally, to say that the CO was waiting in his office to see me. I ventured to make a casual enquiry as to the nature of this summons from a person of such importance because the CO held a position of unapproachable omnipotence. The Company Sergeant Major was giving nothing away, but there was something unusual about his refusal to divulge the reason. I just had to make my way down to see what was the matter. One always assumes the worst, of course, and I puzzled over all the things that might have gone wrong. Had I failed to fill in some form? Had I exceeded my authority in the lowly capacity of driver (I frequently did that)? Perhaps one of the people I`ve mentioned, who would be only too happy to "shop" me, had finally spotted a chance. I couldn`t recall having made any serious mistakes, at least not the sort which would require the Commanding Officer to be involved.

The top man was waiting to see me and I was ushered in immediately. It was quite a shock to have him say, "Take a seat, Driver," after I had given him the smartest salute I could produce.

"You`ll be wondering why I sent for you," he went on, and I thought, "How right you are!"

"It`ll not be long before we will be moving on from here to more active service and I need to make some changes."

At this point I felt I knew why I was here and why I was sitting down. The CO, thoughtful man that he was, was about to break it to me gently that I was one of those to be cleared out, transferred, moved, so that he`d have just the right people in his company for active service.

He went on.

"I`ve decided, having watched your approach to life and examined your pre-war qualifications and achievements, to promote you to full sergeant."

I was very glad indeed that I was seated as I was given this piece of news. To say you could have knocked me down with a feather would be the greatest understatement. Promotion from Driver to Full Sergeant was unheard of. No-one had ever made this jump to my knowledge.

"No-one has ever made the jump from Driver to Sergeant, you`ll understand," said the Major, "but I`m backing my judgement that you can do it. Do you agree with me?"

I would have been a fool to say No, for more reasons than one. If an officer of such high calibre as our CO was prepared to gamble on me, I was quite certain his gamble would pay off. With that one sentence he gave me the confidence to be a success.

The CO then explained that Army Regulations required that my promotion had to go through the stages of Corporal and Lance Sergeant before reaching Full Sergeant. This would be done in the matter of a fortnight or so while I was on a MT crash course, learning the basics of the job. As from that moment I should put up my corporal's stripes and pack to go to Minehead.

I had to say that I couldn't very well leave my section sergeant in the air without a clerk.

"That's all taken care of. He knows what I'm telling you now and fully approves."

It seemed that a lot had been discussed in secret!

"You will have problems," said the CO. "There will be a few NCOs both in your transport section and among the older and more experienced sapper sergeants, who are not going to take kindly to authority so rapidly achieved. Do you think you can cope with that difficulty as well as everything else?"

Again, what could I say? To be frank, when the boss began to tell me what he wanted me to do, my first thought was that several people were not going to like this one little bit. My reply was that I'd let the situations arise first before worrying about them, then take action on the strength of what happened at the time.

The Major went on to explain that the division was being prepared as a "crack" fighting unit to go overseas and that I was going to have to start from scratch to build up the Transport Section in vehicles, efficiency and discipline, a daunting task even for one with more experience and service. I had no experience and two years service, of a sort.

It wasn't until I left the office, floating on air, that I realised what had been done. It was frightening. For a moment I was so terrified at the prospect that I felt like going back to the CO and resigning. But one doesn't resign in the army in wartime or at any other time and I knew that I couldn't rebuff his confidence in me. Somehow or other it would work out – I hoped.

From the moment I sewed on my corporal's stripes life became an absolute whirl. My own section sergeant was delighted and couldn't have been kinder, but I soon learned something of what to expect, not by what others said but by what they didn't say. It was perhaps a good thing that within 48 hours I was packed and on my way to Minehead on the north coast of Devon to join the crash MT course which was supposed to turn me from a Driver who knew nothing into a Sergeant RE who knew everything!

Minehead is one of those pretty little holiday villages, so attractive in peacetime, but the weather, late in the year, was wet and windy, so the beauty of the place was lost on me.

A large boarding house just off the sea front had been taken over as our living quarters. Another house a few minutes' walk away was the Mess, and various halls around the town served as our lecture rooms.

For the next fortnight we marched and drilled, attended lectures on every aspect of the internal combustion engine, and worked in a local garage taking engines and cars to pieces and putting them back together again.

Other than a cinema there was virtually no social life and such spare time as we had was occupied in interminable games of chess in the NAAFI where good cheap meals were available.

Towards the end of the fortnight a convoy motored onto Exmoor and each member of the course in turn had to be in charge and lead the map reading. That wasn't difficult.

Another exercise was when the instructors deliberately overturned three trucks in ditches. Small parties of four had to get them back on the road. I wasn't so good at that. All the vehicles I'd seen ditched previously had been left for the Germans to put back into operation! Luckily, in my group was an experienced Lance Sergeant who had been sent on this course to gain his "bomb," the little brass grenade worn above the three stripes which indicates the rank of Full Sergeant RE. He knew exactly what to do and we completed our task in no time with ropes, iron

Promotion to Full Sergeant. Timsbury. April 1941.

stakes and the minimum of physical effort. I learned a great deal from this fellow.

At the end of the fortnight we all sat an examination and returned to our units. I found my name on Company orders when I got back to Timsbury. I'd made the step up the promotion ladder to Lance Sergeant. My pay, too, had risen to something in the region of £2 a week, a considerable increase from fourteen shillings.

CHAPTER TWENTY FOUR –
An Unpleasant Incident

As a result of my promotion, the deputy SgtMT who had been put in charge in France before Dunkirk was moved to another section to allow me to take over. The CO told me at my interview that this would happen because the man had not conducted himself in a manner befitting his position and responsibility, both before and at Dunkirk. I wasn`t aware of what this meant exactly except that immediately after his return to England he was extremely "bomb happy." We`d all suffered harrowing and frightening experiences, but when one holds rank and there are men depending upon one`s ability and outward confidence, it`s not done to bury one`s head in the sand, so to speak.

He wasn`t demoted because he`d never gained the "bomb" to his three stripes, but he knew that he was finished in the Unit and made no effort to hide his extreme anger at my promotion. I decided that it would be best to see as little of him as possible for the time being, managing to do most of my work with his section at a distance, either by phone or through his other NCOs with whom I was on better terms. It wasn`t long before he was transferred to another Engineer unit and I heard, years later, that this unit had been home based for the rest of the war, eventually being sent to take over from the Germans in the Channel Islands when they capitulated.

I still had problems, however. First, my driver friends were now my "men" and I was their sergeant. To me this didn`t matter: a friend is a friend, but I`m afraid I found out, rather unpleasantly in some cases, who my real friends were. Bert and Robbo remained staunch and loyal as ever. Larry Sanderson, too, declared he was happy with the situation, but some of the others cut me dead. They were having nothing to do with any sergeant. Such difficulties were exacerbated by the fact that there were rules about the different levels of rank, a sort of class distinction. The army said that NCOs shall not fraternise with anyone below their own rank, and officers will, likewise, only consort with officers. I found it hard to be forced into thus distancing myself from my friends.

Most of the friends I`d made were sincere and sensible enough not to consider taking any advantage of our previous association, accepting that old army maxim, "On parade – on parade: off parade – off parade." In other words, what you said on parade and how you said it was only for the benefit of the observer, usually the officers, but once you'd come off parade you could forget everything. That suited me and my closest friends, but there were others who were resentful and took my every word and deed as a personal and vindictive act directed at them. I might be a lot of horrible things but I am not spiteful and I do value friendship.

Needless to say, I had a serious problem with the uncouth, loud mouthed, Lance Sergeant who had been moved out to the other section as well. He was aware of how far he could go without overstepping the mark and he took full advantage of that knowledge. Everything he did was designed to be awkward, obstructive, malicious, or just plain nasty. How he ever gained three stripes was a mystery because he was abysmally inefficient in all matters other than Squad Drill. Perhaps because of its repetitiveness and mind-numbing uselessness he was good at marching, halting, shouldering arms, porting arms, standing at ease, and so on. Being good at this himself gave him great scope to be sarcastic, scathing and insulting towards the poor drivers and sappers who found the movements difficult to master. He cursed and swore at men in his section, calling them names which any civilised human being would find difficult to utter or even understand, and the badge of authority he carried on each arm gave him the protection he needed because no-one could answer back.

Sooner or later I knew there was going to be a show-down between him and me and it was a worry. Meanwhile, I thought that, as relations between us couldn't be poorer, it would not make matters worse if I expressed an opinion, backed by my higher authority.

One morning I had to visit Section Three where the L/Sgt would, I knew, be drilling his men. This was a normal daily task in all sections, with most NCOs spending about half an hour or so on it. Our friend could easily make it last a couple of hours until his men were just about dropping. At the same time, his vehicle maintenance was well below standard and he had no idea how to keep his paperwork in order.

After completing the task I'd come to do, I stopped to watch his drill. I was no expert by any means: I knew I couldn't fault him and he knew it, too. Being the show-off that he was, he started the drill again especially for my benefit. The language, the threats, the insults reached new heights and I had to stop him.

"Dismiss the section, Sergeant! I want a word with you," was my order. Nobody had ever said that to him before, for starters.

"We haven't finished yet, Sergeant. This lot are hopeless!" was his reply.

I`d never in my life, much less in the army, had to impress myself on anyone and I didn`t know whether or not I could do it, but I had to try. It was now or never.

"Dismiss the section, Sergeant, as I`ve told you. If they`re hopeless you are not going to cure them this morning."

"Bugger this!" was his expected reply, but I`d prepared for it.

"I have a bit of a cold this morning, Sergeant, and I don`t think I heard that remark clearly, as I`m sure you muttered it to yourself. I`ve watched your drill and it is excellent. The men have obviously benefited from the time they`ve spent on it. You most certainly have them at your command and I`m very pleased about that. However, now that you`ve worked your section up to this peak of perfection I want you to concentrate on the other side of your work. When we eventually leave here and take our places with the rest of the Division on active service, the sappers and drivers in your section are not going to march into action in columns of three carrying their drills, explosives and barbed wire on their shoulders at the slope. Every Man Jack of them will have a place in one of the vehicles in your charge, together with all their stores and equipment. It is our job as the Transport Section of 233rd Field Company to transport – carry on wheels – this Unit and its equipment. I have looked at the maintenance of your vehicles and, quite frankly, I doubt if half of your section will reach the port of embarkation without serious breakdown. From tomorrow, your working day will consist of only half an hour`s squad drill, and the rest will be oiling, checking, repairing and cleaning your vehicles until every last nut and bolt is in as good condition as the barrels of your men`s rifles, and shines as brightly as the toecaps of their boots. I admit it is vital for men to know how to carry out drill to perfection. I agree that their rifles should be in tip-top condition, and I would be very critical if they were not smartly turned out. You have carried out that part of your job admirably but, understand this, you have failed miserably to justify your existence as the NCO in charge of this section`s transport and that, in my book, is your greatest responsibility. See to it that as from tomorrow you devote your attentions to the job you`re in the position of Lance Sergeant to do, or one of my first unpleasant tasks will be to take some action which neither of us will like. One further thing before I finish ..."

... and I might say that all the way through this tirade, to which I had warmed considerably once I got going, there were obscene mutterings and oaths being grunted quite loud enough for me to hear ...

"... you are in charge of a group of human beings not animals. Each man who stands before you can be made to look like every other because of the uniform he wears. However, every man is different. Every man has a personality of his own, some have a wife and children or a family back home. You will remember this when you talk to them. I cannot expect you to wipe your mouth clean of all the words and expressions you use. If that had to be done you would be rendered speechless. I suppose you have grown up with a lot of it but, nevertheless, I object to the blasphemy, ..."

...and I had to explain this to him,

"... and many of the obscenities ..."

... and this, too,

"... are quite unnecessary. Swearing and the constant repetition of four letter words beginning with "f" and "s" I suppose I'll get used to in time, but I warn you to moderate your language and speak to your men as human beings or I shall use an Army regulation which is seldom invoked, I imagine, and charge you with "the unnecessary use of foul and obscene language.""

This fellow hadn't been used to anyone telling him what to do. He had himself held my post for a time and had always, since territorial days before the war, enjoyed authority, most of it in the Headquarters Mess in Jarrow drinking with his cronies from the local shipyards or at the Unemployment Exchange when he wasn't in work. Naturally enough, I suppose, he took my intrusion into his life very badly. Perhaps, like me, he had seen this confrontation coming, yet even now he wasn't defeated nor prepared to bow.

"Take you coat off and come round the back of the house and say that again, you bugger!" was his answer.

I knew full well that most arguments in his life had been settled with a fight, and didn't doubt that most of them ended in his favour since there would be no Queensbury Rules involved. I wasn't falling for that one.

"I have no intention of taking off my coat for you or anyone, now or ever. I have been given a job to do and the authority to do it. I intend to do the job to the best of my ability, not only for the war effort but also for the safety of us all. The authority I have, which is superior to yours, I will use swiftly and successfully. It's likely I'm not going to have to look far or wait long for you to provide me with an excuse to "throw the book" at you. If you want to hold onto those three stripes do as I tell you, control your tongue, and get off my back!"

With that I turned and went, half expecting to be jumped on from behind. Nothing happened.

I left the Lance Sergeant alone for over a week, keeping a finger on the pulse of his Section via those I knew in it. There was a change. Not a lot to begin with: he didn`t confine himself to half an hour`s drill, but it wasn`t as long as it had been. More time was certainly spent on the vehicles, which was my main worry, though apparently His Lordship went around all the time muttering threats that he would get me. There was that possibility, but it was a risk I had to accept with my new job.

Whilst these may not have been my exact words, the substance is pretty well accurate, and my memory of the incident is clear because of its importance and the impact it would have on the future.

CHAPTER TWENTY FIVE – Leave, and the Last Few Months in Blighty

Christmas approached and I was disappointed to find myself left off the list of those going on leave. Half the Unit was to go over the Christmas period, and the other half at New Year. It transpired that all the people in the know, the "old sweats" and officers above 2nd Lieutenant, were to go home for Christmas, and the rest for New Year. I hadn`t the pull yet to be one of the "inner circle," and in the event, I found that my disappointment wasn`t nearly as bad as I had anticipated.

With so many being away, all work and parades were cancelled. We ate if and when we could be bothered to drag ourselves to the Mess. The cooks had ordered food for the whole Unit but, as there was only half to eat it, we all got twice as much. And there was another advantage: the regular cook had gone on leave and his deputy (Lance Corporal, unpaid) took over. This meant we were having our meals prepared by a man who was a painter and decorator in civilian life, hence his nickname of "Schicklgruber". The food definitely had a different taste. Long practice at stirring paint meant we now had custard without lumps which tasted more or less like custard. The meat could be cut with the ease of slicing putty rather than having to beat it on an anvil with a hammer to tenderise it. As for the pastry, it was actually flaky and delicate, not at all like the sheet metal covering our pies usually had.

Christmas Day was a real pleasure. We arose at about ten thirty and strolled down to the pub to cleanse the palate ready for our traditional mid-day dinner.

The army custom of officers and NCOs waiting on the men was introduced to many for the first time. Everyone enjoyed the fun of that. It was early in the war and food restrictions weren`t yet biting. Turkey and all the trimmings had been laid on and quite deliciously prepared. Even a luscious Christmas pudding of generous proportions, laced with ample rum, was carried in ceremoniously. Again, our little Schicklgruber had exercised his artistry: the servers found that it was possible to drop a spoonful of Christmas Pud a full six inches without smashing the plate. Had the blacksmith been in charge it would have bent a tin plate and been lethal to the digestion.

Most of those left in Timsbury retired to rest after dinner. Bert and I didn`t, because both Dorothy Cook and Joyce had arrived from London for a couple of days. All four of us went for a lovely walk through the fields round about. It was one of those mild, damp days, not sunny, but just right for walking. We needed some fresh air to work off the meal and disperse the alcohol fumes. We were relaxed and so were the girls. We laughed and chatted about everything under the sun. It was the first and only time I ever heard Dorothy talk at length about London and her work; not that she gave much away, but there was rather more than she was usually prepared to say. For instance, it seemed that Churchill often kept members of the War Council and "Top Brass" up into the small hours sorting out problems until they were dropping with fatigue, while he choked them with foul cigar smoke and breathed brandy fumes all over them, without ever offering anyone else a drop. Next morning, when they needed to consult with him, he wouldn`t be disturbed. Eventually, he`d invite them into his bedroom to discuss matters of high policy from his bed, again with cigar and brandy at hand to concentrate his mind and sharpen his vocabulary. Dorothy did say that the Prime Minister was a difficult man to work for, very exacting and moody.

Despite his idiosyncrasies, Churchill was always most solicitous about the families of his staff. He had a marvellous memory for names and details, and would ask Dorothy about her mother and sister, mentioning the Post Office and her mother`s work in the WVS.

Joyce said next to nothing about her work and I was pretty certain it was of a highly secret nature. Once, after she`d remarked to Dorothy, probably thinking that I wouldn`t hear, that "a number of parcels had failed to arrive," I wondered if she must have been involved in the control of secret agents travelling to and from Occupied Europe. When she made this remark about the parcels she seemed too upset to be talking about brown paper and string, and I knew that "Parcels" was the term used by the organisations who dealt with agents.

Christmas week was very pleasant. We enjoyed sumptuous meals at mid-day on both Christmas and Boxing Days, had pleasant walks in the afternoons, and during both evenings consumed even more lavish meals at the Post Office. We young ones provided the party atmosphere and even wore funny hats, and Mrs Cook, I`m sure, had her rather humdrum life livened up for a short while.

I had a feeling that Mrs Cook was hoping I might look upon her daughter with an eye to marriage, but Dorothy certainly didn`t take that view at all, and neither did I. She was good company for a short time but only when she made a conscious effort to come down to my level. She was usually very stand-offish, distant and uninterested. Over Christmas she did, undoubtedly, relax and try to be nice, but it was only temporary. She was older than me, much more mature and much more highly qualified academically. Dorothy had a career and a future that I certainly didn`t have. Quite apart from all these factors, she wasn`t interested in me as a husband, and the idea of her as a wife would have scared me stiff!

Joyce, who partnered Bert most of the time, was a different proposition. She was much more attractive and feminine. Joyce could have been the girl any man would want to run after but she was happily married. Sadly, the future of her husband was very uncertain but it was obvious that her love for him was absolute. She enjoyed her visits to Timsbury as pleasurable diversions from the tensions of London, and they probably helped to take her mind off the constant dangers her husband faced. Bert was very good and very kind to her, and I did my best for her, too. Anyone could see she was just longing for the day when her marriage would be normal again. She never said where her husband was nor why she couldn`t be near him. I only hope he survived and they lived happily ever after.

Just before New Year I went home on leave. Most of it was spent at Allenheads, the small village in Northumberland where my sister had a cottage. My mother had moved there from South Shields where the shipyards were being bombed, partly for her safety but partly so that she could look after my niece who, at that time, went to the village school. My brother-in-law was a dental surgeon. He had lost a leg in the First World War, left the Royal Navy as a Lieutenant Commander, and qualified as a dentist. He had set up a second practice in Allenheads so that each weekend the whole family could enjoy quietness and safety in the hills of Northumberland.

I enjoyed my leave, being fussed over, eating, sleeping and just doing nothing.

Back in Timsbury there was an obvious change in the pattern of life. Everything seemed to wake up. A few of the older men were transferred but, fortunately, my section sergeant, who was relatively elderly, somehow escaped the purge. Probably he volunteered, or rather demanded, to go wherever we were going, and no-one but a fool would have rejected his services and steadying influence. Some of the "dead wood" also disappeared and we were left with two hundred and forty men who were fully fit, young or young enough, and working hard to reach the peak of training, in theory anyway. Unfortunately, I still had my Lance Sergeant.

I was called with other senior NCOs to a meeting with the CO and all his officers. This was unusual at the time; it was not until General Montgomery's day that the system changed and everyone was put in the picture. Our CO had his own ideas, however, and as far as he was able, he kept us informed of future movements. We weren't allowed to pass this information on any further, of course. Montgomery changed that later, too. He made sure that every man, even of the lowest rank, was fully informed.

The CO told us that we were to go overseas in two or three months. Although he couldn't or wouldn't say where to, he did say that we would have a very busy time preparing for the move. There would be a good deal of paperwork, indenting for materials, recording every last item in our own departments, receiving, checking and servicing every piece of equipment and clothing.

The Transport Section was to hand in its existing vehicles and be issued with a full complement of brand new trucks and motor cycles. There would be a small staff car for each officer, and a large Humber staff car for the CO.

We, the senior NCOs, would have our rifles replaced by revolvers – what a relief – and we were to get some automatic weapons, including Bren guns to replace the outdated Lewis guns. It was all very exciting.

Those months were certainly busy ones. As far as the Transport Section was concerned, we were sent some replacement drivers, called-up men generally, and an NCO to replace the MT Lance Sergeant who was transferred. I would have liked one of our own NCOs to have been promoted to fill this position, but the army, in its wisdom, had its own way. There was nothing I could do about it and I felt sure the CO's hands must have been tied, too.

I was allowed to choose my own MT Clerk to deal with the very exacting paperwork. Arthur James who, in civilian life, worked for a company which supplied pharmaceutical products to firms on Tyneside, was my choice as he was used to handling and tabulating stores. The many spare parts and their complicated numbering system required someone who could do this with a minimum of training. Arthur took to it like a duck to water and received an immediate stripe for doing so. He was a quiet, methodical fellow of about my own age, with undoubted clerical ability. Many junior NCOs were always "on the make", forever looking for an opportunity to jump into someone else's shoes through promotion. Their methods were often ruthless, blatant and morally doubtful. Arthur, however, was quite unambitious and content with his lot. He did his work in the most diplomatic and efficient manner right through the war, under every condition, good and bad. He never got upset, he never flapped, he never annoyed anyone, and I can safely say that I made a correct choice in Arthur James. He took over my office and ran it from the first day as though he'd been born to it. It was the greatest comfort that in my new and difficult position, I never needed to worry about administration.

In time, our old vehicles were driven away and new ones brought back. I had the foresight to go in person to the Vehicle Park from which the new trucks and motorcycles were being issued, taking a small team of mechanics to choose the lorries we wanted. All 30 cwts looked alike in their green camouflage, parked up in straight lines like guards on parade. So did the 15 cwts, the staff cars and even the rather luxurious Humbers, but it was amazing how different they could be when examined closely. It was worth the time and effort making our own choices, and we got good ones.

Everyone then had an issue of new uniform, shirts, underclothes and boots. Even the webbing which held packs, ammunition pouches, etc., was replaced, and we seniors got our revolvers and holsters.

When I examined my new weapon I was quite impressed. It looked a very lethal job, shone a rather attractive shade of gun-metal blue, and came with six rounds of ammunition. I asked what we were to do about the seventh German and was told I could draw a further supply of six rounds from the QM's stores if they were needed! I concluded that the procedure was that when I came face to face with the seventh Hun I was to ask him to hang on while I nipped back to the stores for six more rounds of ammunition.

I found to my horror that the rounds of ammunition supplied had soft-nosed bullets in them. This design was known as "dum-dum" and had been outlawed by the Hague Convention many years before.

Some considerable time later these revolvers, which were .45, the sort cowboys used, were replaced with .38s. The lighter weapons, much easier to handle and considerably more comfortable to carry, came with new ammunition and nickel plated bullets. It was nice to think that it was now legal to kill with a bullet fully approved by all countries that were

159

signatories of the Hague Convention. Any enemy on the receiving end of a shot fired by me would feel relieved that he was being despatched much more tidily and with nice nickel plating, unlikely to inflict nasty big wounds.

Our lives fell into a regular pattern of work and preparation for our departure and future role in a war zone. Only at weekends were we given any time off. I still went with Bert and Robbo into Bath for a cinema show or concert, then a good meal and a few drinks. On Sundays, I usually had some sort of administration to discuss with Arthur in the office, and later I`d go to the Post Office and relax over a meal and "ITMA" or a play on the radio.

Towards the end of February, amidst great excitement, bundles of uniforms arrived for everyone in the Unit, khaki drill uniforms, the sort worn in hot countries. The speculation was that we were almost certainly going to Finland, Russia or Norway because this was the army`s way of baffling the enemy.

We all had to collect shirts and shorts and try them on for fit. The result caused both helpless amusement and embarrassed annoyance. These Khaki Drill uniforms were of "North West Frontier" vintage. By the time we`d donned the shorts (which fell below the knees), the voluminous shirt, and the topee which enveloped the head to the point of total obscurity, one looked like Rudyard Kipling on the Road to Mandalay. The part of the uniform which caused the most frustration and amusement, however, were the puttees.

Each of us was issued with a pair of puttees, rolls of olive-green serge cloth, three or four yards long, with a long tape sewn on one end. Fortunately, we had an ex-guardsman in the Unit who had worn puttees in his pre-war days, and one of the older members of the Sergeants` Mess could remember how his father had put them on in the First World War. Our efforts were anything but elegant but we had to master them somehow.

Years later, after the war, there was a television comedy programme called, "It Ain`t `Alf Hot, Mum." In this, the stooge, Don Estelle, a round little man with a very good singing voice, wore an identical uniform, complete with topee, and whenever he appeared everyone screamed with laughter at his dress. In 1941 we were dressed exactly like him in all seriousness!

Shortly after we got the KD uniforms, an order arrived for me to collect sand filters for our vehicles. That settled it: we were definitely bound for the cold northern areas of Europe, perhaps to support the Russians in Siberia.

Recently issued Khaki Drill uniform.
Timsbury 1941.

"I always have my hands in my pockets but if I didn't my trousers would fall down!"

Reverse.

Recently issued Khaki Drill uniform. Timsbury 1941.

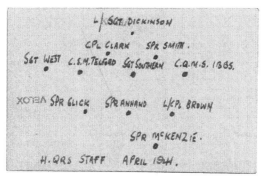

L/SGT. DICKINSON

CPL. CLARK   SPR. SMITH.

SGT. WEST   C.S.M. TELFORD   SGT. SOUTHERN   C.Q.M.S. 1385.

XOTEA SPR. GLICK   SPR. ANNAND   L/CPL. BROWN

SPR. M°KENZIE.

H.QRS. STAFF   APRIL 1941.

Reverse. Group members` names.

CHAPTER TWENTY SIX – Farewell Britain

By the beginning of March 1941 we were just about ready. Everyone had been fully equipped with both battledress and khaki drill uniforms. We had our Wild West revolvers, and the men all had brand new Lee Enfield rifles made in 1918. The Transport Section sported a full complement of vehicles which looked very smart indeed when lined up, all beautifully camouflaged in olive green and black. We had a few spares, but no tools at all. Sneakily, I was one step ahead of the Royal Ordnance Corps in this because the vehicles we handed in went back without a tool in their boxes. Very naughty, of course, but I worked on the theory that we`d be miles away in a foreign land before the complaints arrived!

It wasn`t possible to keep the departure date in mid-March secret and when the great day came and the last item was loaded aboard and only a rear party was left to lock up Timsbury Manor, the WHOLE of Timsbury was out to line the main road and wave us on our way. As the long convoy of trucks, proudly headed by the CO in his new Humber staff car, slowly moved away, tears flowed freely.

Most of the men in our Unit had formed some sort of association with a Timsbury home. Some had actually married girls they had met, while not a few would certainly have to! Everyone was genuinely sorry to leave that little village. To most of us it had been a very, very pleasant period.

Leaving Mrs Cook and the Post Office was like leaving home again. It seemed to me, and I`m sure to the dear lady watching our departure to war, that a piece of history was being repeated. I kept in touch as far as it was possible in wartime conditions, and then after the war was over and I was married, she paid us a visit. By then she was very old. Shortly after that she went to live with her daughter, Jane, for a few years before her death.

233 Brigade RE was to embark somewhere on the Clyde, aboard a ship called "The Duchess of Bedford."

There was no mistaking the Duchess. She was a very elegant liner of the "between the wars" period, painted plain battleship grey, with two funnels and high upperworks above row upon row of portholes. She rode at anchor some distance from the shore, with just a wisp of smoke drifting from one of her stacks.

The Duchess of Bedford wasn`t the only ship lying off. Various merchant vessels were anchored out there, too, mostly big powerful cargo ships, while others were loading up alongside the quays. Further up river we could see the sleek shapes of warships. It seemed that a large convoy was assembling.

We were put into a nearby school. It wasn`t comfortable and there was a lot of grumbling. I explained to my lot that the organisers of the convoy did not want the troops aboard until the last minute before sailing, otherwise half the stores would be consumed before we set off, adding that the powers controlling our sailing wouldn`t delay a minute longer than necessary, but some men still hadn`t the sense or patience to accept this.

Next day, even more ships arrived and the Duchess towered above her retinue. It was really a marvellous sight and I found it quite stirring.

Mid-morning we prepared to embark. We were told to take with us all our equipment including large back pack and kit bag. The kit bag containing all surplus clothing, marked with name, rank and number, would go deep into the hold and not be seen again until we reached our destination. The back pack had to have our KD in it, underclothes, and any day to day gear, for example polishing equipment, without which the army cannot function, together with personal possessions. We also had to carry arms and, of course, our topee. As we climbed aboard the Duchess, and again as she sailed away, we were to wave our topees like mad for the benefit of the photographers!

Perhaps the tidal rise and fall, or perhaps her size, prevented embarkation from the quayside. Instead, we had to hump our kits bags, etc., half a mile to a ferry landing, from where we were transported by barges out to the bigger ship.

It was a struggle to climb the gangway which was fixed to the side of the ship. The top was probably sixty feet above the deck of the little barge and, in full kit, carrying a heavy kit bag on the shoulder, and wrestling with that awkward topee, most of us made heavy weather of the ascent, much to the amusement of crew members who leant over the rail to watch us landlubbers.

Passing through the ship`s side was rather like entering a prison, with the studded door, the walls of thick steel plate, the foetid atmosphere, the dim lighting, the long straight corridors with doors on each side, and the massive stairways. Members of the crew scurried this way and that, and army officers consulted clipboards and thumbed through sheaves of paper. All around was the constant hum of machinery and ventilation fans. The deck underfoot trembled slightly with hidden power, held back but just waiting for release.

There's one thing we British are good at: on occasions like this we will stand in a queue and wait patiently. The head of the queue disappeared along the corridor and round a corner, while the tail trailed back down the gangway to the ferry. No-one moved, no-one pushed, everyone stood waiting to be told what to do next.

There was a sliding scale of comfort, amenities and view according to rank. The officers' accommodation was, unsurprisingly, in First Class and they were taken off to cabins on the promenade deck, as expected.

After a rather lengthy wait, which was full of interest both inside and outside the ship, albeit a little hard on the legs, a team of guides took away all the men in the Unit below the rank of Lance Sergeant. Some of the holds had been converted into troop decks where tier upon tier of wooden bunks filled the space from floor to ceiling, or deck to deck head, or whatever is the nautical term. It would be no exaggeration to say the men were packed in like sardines and I felt most unhappy about the conditions they faced. It didn't do my conscience much good when a guide led me to the cabin I was to share with another sergeant. Two bunks were fixed against the wall and there was the luxury of a washbasin on another. In addition, there was a large porthole with a seat underneath it at the end of the fairly narrow space which was to be our accommodation for nearly four months. Not sumptuous and fairly cramped, but it was vastly better than the accommodation our men were enduring.

At certain times we could open the porthole, and there were ventilators above the beds blowing hot or cold air. The washbasin was undoubtedly a blessing but, later in the voyage, we were rationed to water for a mere half an hour per day. The water we did get was not for washing any clothes, nor was it supposed to be fit to drink, although we did drink it. Across the corridor were baths and showers with unlimited hot and cold water. Unfortunately, the water was straight out of whichever sea we were in at the time!

After a wash and brush up, I went off to see the ship. Officers' quarters were completely out of bounds to all but officers and, strangely enough, Other Ranks' quarters were out of bounds to all above lance sergeants. This meant that we never saw our men or our officers other than during parade each day, for the whole of the journey. None of us had any responsibilities, being completely in the hands of the ship`s crew and its naval complement. The misfortune, as I saw it, was that because our men had no contact with us, it was well nigh impossible for them to register any complaint or have a wrong righted. It was a troop ship, it was wartime, and a large number of men had to be moved in a vessel which had not been designed to carry anything like these numbers, so there was bound to be discomfort but, sadly, the contrast between conditions for upper and lower ranks was marked. My NCOs` class would, I suppose, be Tourist or perhaps Second Class, and really I had nothing to complain about.

I discovered that we had a hairdresser, a shop, a library, reading rooms, a beautiful dining room, a vast lounge, and a large deck area around which we could take a stroll. The officers had all this plus a swimming pool, a sun lounge, a promenade deck for games, and a gymnasium. The men had absolutely nothing other than a steward`s cubby hole for a shop.

Sad though these contrasting conditions were, there was nothing anyone could do but make the best of it.

Next morning we woke up to great activity, the noise of winches and the heaving of ropes. The blue flag with the white edges was hoisted which meant we were about to sail. As directed, we lined the rails, topees at the ready for a photogenic wave. All the other ships in the convoy were also prepared to sail on a signal from the Commodore, our skipper. Flags ran up the flag staffs, sirens blew and slowly, very slowly, we began to move down river.

As the Duchess cleared her position the other ships in the convoy fell in behind. Along the river bank shipyard workers paused to raise a cheer and we responded with our topees. Cars, buses and people near enough to toot a horn or wave a hanky, sent us on our way. Excited but not without a sinking feeling, everyone aboard that great liner waved their farewells.

What a spectacular and proud departure this was, the ships emerging from the Clyde, led by the majestic Duchess of Bedford. Other merchantmen could be seen lying off, ready to join this large convoy. Further out still were some of the escort, destroyers, I guessed, from the speed at which they moved, and perhaps there were even bigger warships beyond the horizon waiting to offer us protection.

In the fairly narrow confines of the river mouth the Duchess of Bedford had to navigate at a rather sedate pace. Even so, the bow waves of the smaller ships indicated that we were moving at perhaps ten or twelve knots. It would have had to be something of this order to keep way on a ship this size. It was, therefore, quite a shock to everyone lining the rail when our great liner suddenly came to a sudden shuddering stop. Not being familiar with things nautical, our first thought was that some obstacle had been sighted and the ship quickly halted, though it didn`t take much reasoning, even for a landsman, to work out that a ship of thousands of tons cannot be stopped almost in its own length.

Flags shot up and down the poles in a series of what were obviously urgent messages. Sirens, including ours, bellowed across the water. The other ships following took rapid action. Those too near to do otherwise squeezed past and went on, while those further behind glided to a standstill. A destroyer came close and his Aldis signalling lamp flashed rapid Morse. Our Tannoy blared, "Lifeboat Stations!" and we saw the ship`s officers directing the unfastening of all the lifeboats. What a way to start a war: we were sinking! One minute we were safe and secure aboard a great liner, as big as a small town; the next it suddenly starts to tilt.

We had been shown our lifeboat stations once and there had been a desultory practice muster. With the novelty and excitement of being aboard, and the fact that we were still on the river very few, if any, of us had taken much notice of what we had been told during that first short drill. Now it was happening: we were about to abandon ship. A few wise guys reckoned the Commodore had stage-managed this as an exercise, and we had to admit that, if this was what he was doing, it was certainly realistic. It soon became clear that it was just too real to be a trick. The lifeboats were swung out and we were counted off ready to disembark ... but not quite.

The Tannoy blared again. "Stand fast!" Perhaps we`d only sprung a little leak.

The ship shuddered from stem to stern as the great engines were first put full ahead, then full astern. We`d either impaled ourselves on a submerged wreck or run aground. News that it was the latter filtered down shortly afterwards, and was quickly confirmed by one of our number, an ex-merchant seaman, who could read flag messages. We were to find several times on the voyage that he was a most useful man to have in our company.

The poor Duchess of Bedford had run aground on a sandbank. I learned much later from one of the crew that this was most peculiar because the Duchess was built with a much shallower draught than most ships of her size in order to enter the rivers of the world for the convenience of passengers, rather than lie off and have them ferried back and forth.

We weren`t sinking but there was a danger that the ship could capsize. As the tide went down the Duchess, sitting on her sandbank, might tilt one way or the other, and her towering upperworks could pull her over. Those in charge decided that we must be taken off the ship just in case. So we climbed down the gangways onto the barges that had brought us out the day before. Speed was less crucial and I was disappointed not to get a ride down the ship`s side in a lifeboat.

We were lined up on the quayside to await the next move. Needless to say, the crew and their officers were too busy wrestling with the problems of the Duchess of Bedford to bother about us passengers, so we were told to "Stand Easy and then "Sit Down."

Our rapid exit from the ship meant that we`d brought nothing with us to do and we didn`t have greatcoats. Fortunately, the weather, although overcast and not very warm, was fair. To begin with most of us were quite content to watch the activity round the ship and quayside. As the tide fell, the Duchess began to list further and further. Another few degrees, said our ex-merchant mariner, and she`ll go over. She didn`t, however, and as the tide rose again the ship levelled off safely.

Meanwhile, the rest of the convoy bypassed our liner and sailed away. The river looked empty. The instruction came for a route march along the riverside road. The order was to "March Easy;" as long as we kept in step and didn`t put hands in pockets, nothing else mattered. We marched, we sang, we waved to the populace, we laughed and joked. Eventually the column turned round and we all marched back again. King`s Regulations had come in useful. "Never allow troops to get bored. They must always be kept occupied by tidying, polishing or, if there`s nothing else, marching." King`s Regs had been satisfied.

Back at the quayside, we found the Duchess sitting very upright with her bottom firmly embedded in the sand. As the tide rose we were allowed back on board for a meal and a limited number of hours sleep, but the falling tide put the ship in danger again so, once more, we had to leave and be occupied, marching up and down the shoreline!

This routine went on for several days while tugs and the ship`s engines fought to clear her of the sand bank which had sprung the trap. At first it was all good fun, but the daily route marches in one of two directions and the boring "Stand Easy" in between were tedious. The tide times changed and our routine had to change with them, of course, which was a nuisance.

Finally, after several days, all the pushing and shoving by the tugs succeeded and the dear old Duchess moved. Only a trifle at first, but her progress increased and, to a siren chorus and our own ringing cheers, she dragged herself clear. Divers were standing by to check for damage. She was a tough old girl, thanks to British ship building, and the bottom of the Clyde must have been soft just there because news soon arrived to say that all was well. We were going back on board to stay. It almost felt like coming home.

By now the rest of the convoy had long sailed without us and it was necessary to wait for another convoy to gather before our journey could be resumed. We lay at anchor for a whole fortnight, including the grounding. Just so that we wouldn't get lazy we were still taken ashore every day for a route march. Boy oh Boy, did we grumble, this time with plenty of justification! After all, it wasn't our fault the ship had stuck on a sandbank, it wasn't our fault the convoy hadn't waited for us, etc., etc.

Only later did we discover that the convoy with which we ought to have sailed was caught and badly mangled by none other than the Bismarck. The Duchess of Bedford would, almost certainly, have been the prime target for the German battleship. Perhaps they even knew we were on our way. Fortune had smiled a wry sandy smile!

CHAPTER TWENTY SEVEN – Finally We Arrive

Conditions were rough when we reached the open sea and I took little interest in proceedings for some days as I was violently seasick.

Seasickness was absolute purgatory because we had to be at daily boat drill no matter what our physical condition. Standing in line for long periods in full battle dress, greatcoat and lifejacket, while the deck tipped, rose and fell in all directions was very, very unpleasant. Afterwards, we were supposed to attend mandatory lectures on engineering subjects but when one man, then another, and finally the lecturer himself was sick all over the place the order was changed from "compulsory" to "those who can." From that point onwards no-one turned out!

After a week or so, we entered calmer waters and things began to improve. We were probably getting our sea legs, too, and gradually troops began to emerge on deck, and the dining room filled up again.

When I finally managed to drag myself out onto our promenade deck for the purpose of looking around rather than suffering a miserable boat drill, I was most surprised at the sight of our present convoy. Unlike the grand flotilla which had collected for our original voyage, there were only two other ships with the Duchess of Bedford on the open expanse of ocean now, both fairly large merchant vessels. We understood from the crew that one was an ammunition carrier stuffed full of high explosives, and the other carried transport for the whole Brigade, plus tanks and guns for other services and branches of the force.

The Duchess was carrying troops of 69th Brigade and attached units, together with a large contingent of Royal Air Force personnel who were to establish an airfield, and some nurses of the Queen Alexandra`s Nursing Service. They were to be spotted every now and then, leaning over the rail of a sun deck well above, but that was our closest contact. Only those above Field Rank enjoyed their company: the licentious soldiery was much too unreliable for such female company.

We steamed along at a good turn of speed. The Duchess could do 22 knots though the merchantmen were not capable of that. It was comforting to know that a submarine could be easily outpaced on the surface at 22 knots should it be necessary to escape.

Our three ships were not alone, although it wasn`t always possible to see what protection we had. In close proximity was a very flashy, fast, powerful light cruiser, the "Ajax." Her sleek, grey painted lines, bristling with guns before and aft her squat single funnel, assured us that the Navy was "holding our hand." Most of the time, on the horizon, destroyers scudded to and fro at high speed. All ships zig-zagged continuously, we assumed in some pre-determined pattern. I think they took their cue from our Commodore because the siren on the Duchess always gave a sonorous snort whenever a course change was made. Thank goodness we didn't zig-zag throughout the night otherwise the hooting would have put paid to any sleep, and the heat inside the ship, with all the scuttles closed, made sleeping difficult enough as it was.

One day, an aircraft appeared on the horizon. It was a very long way off and didn't approach the convoy but merely circled it. The gun crews took station and the Ajax tracked its every move with her AA guns. I was able to get my glasses onto the plane and identify it as a Condor, a four engined, long distance aircraft the German used for shadowing convoys at sea. We knew from this that there were submarines about, probably being guided by the Condor in our direction. Everyone was told to look out for a periscope, so the ship's lookouts were supplemented with thousands of pairs of eyes. It would have been difficult for any submarine to have approached unnoticed.

The convoy cracked on at speed for days while the Condor flew round and round tirelessly.

Shortly after the first sighting of the German plane, a very strange looking ship appeared and made straight for us, which was disturbing until its shape became clearer. The vessel was a British merchantman which had been stripped of practically all its upperworks. In place of the missing superstructure was a long lattice catapult and, perched on the back end of the catapult, was a Spitfire. Should we be attacked by enemy planes, the sole pilot aboard could be launched in his fighter to beat off the enemy. Whatever the outcome of the battle, the plane would eventually have to be abandoned to crash into the sea and, hopefully, the pilot would parachute to safety and be picked up out of "the drink" by an escorting vessel. Of course, only in an absolute emergency would this action to be taken and I did feel sorry for the pilot, but it seemed someone had sent word about the Condor's presence. As long as the Condor stayed with us, so did our miniature aircraft carrier, steaming alongside us, but as no attack was ever made, the Spitfire was never launched.

One day the German was gone, and next day, so was the merchant ship and its lonely pilot with his expendable aircraft. Presumably we were now out of the German`s range.

By some rough mathematical calculations, I worked out that at a steady 20 knot average over nine days, allowing for zig-zags and course alterations, we must have steamed southwards for over 4000 miles and any time now we might be turning east to put in at Gibraltar as most convoys did.

I`d just discussed my calculations and deductions with the others in our group of senior NCOs, when the convoy did begin to change direction but, surprisingly, westward away from Spain or Gibraltar, and shortly after that we turned north at what appeared to be higher speed.

Night fell and the ship still maintained her northerly course without slackening off as she usually did during the hours of darkness. I marvelled at this feat of navigation because once darkness fell every porthole, door and open space was darkened. If any light was necessary it was only a pale blue one. It was a serious offence to smoke on deck. The ships of the convoy were, therefore, running at maximum speed, completely blacked out, with only the stars and the phosphorescence from wash and bow wave to betray their presence.

When the next day dawned we got a shock. The vast Atlantic Ocean stretched blue and placid in all directions. Apart from our two merchantmen, not another ship was to be seen anywhere. The Ajax had gone, together with the rest of our escort. We discussed and argued amongst ourselves what this could mean, hoping that a destroyer or corvette might be just below the horizon, but no wisp of smoke suggested this was the case. We were alone, and steaming west again.

For another two days our course took us north, south, east and west, but predominantly west. There didn`t seem to be any obvious reason for these frequent and sudden changes from one direction to the other. It was almost as though the Commodore was doing an elaborate square dance with his three ships, trying to confuse an invisible enemy by making him dizzy.

I really cannot remember how many days we "swanned" around in the Atlantic. The only hope of working out a very, very rough position was by means of the weather. It ranged from cold and rough to calm and hot, which enabled us to say with some confidence we were either in the North or the South Atlantic. As no land ever came into sight at any time this wasn`t the most accurate of fixing.

Eventually the Duchess and her two faithful courtiers settled down on a straight line again. Smoke appeared and on the horizon we could distinguish the shapes of ships which were obviously men-o`-war, but whose?

We needn`t have worried. Our escort was back, with friends. The Ajax took station on one side and I think it was the Exeter on the other. If it wasn`t the Exeter it was a twin funnelled cruiser of the same class. Not far off was the huge aircraft carrier Illustrious and then, on the horizon, an even bigger ship which rumour had it was the Prince of Wales or King George V. Lots of destroyers and corvettes buzzed hither and thither in the distance. It was comforting to feel safe again.

We were heading east. To confirm this, a message came over the Tannoy announcing that due to the fact that we had been at sea longer than expected, we were very short of fresh water and fuel oil, so to replenish stocks the convoy was heading for Africa. The voice was even good enough to say it would be the port of Freetown.

Land, at long last, and Africa too. The prospect was exciting. We`d been at sea a long time and everyone became quite animated when this news was given. The lethargy of weeks at sea was having an effect and the thought of putting one`s foot on solid ground again brightened us all up.

There was a tailpiece to this story which I didn`t learn until years later. Unbeknown to us, the German battleship "Bismarck" was out in the Atlantic. The Germans had a very powerful and dangerous High Seas Fleet. Although they were no match for the "heavies" of the Royal Navy, the menace these swift and deadly German warships posed to our convoys was enormous. They were carefully watched from the air and by the many brave agents in occupied countries, their movements meticulously monitored. At the same time, our enemies were no fools and they knew the havoc just one pocket battleship could do. Somehow or other, the Bismarck slipped through our sorely stretched net and reached the Atlantic. In an ocean this big, with skill and a lot of luck, a ship, even a big one, can move around unnoticed for a long time. The Bismarck did just that. Her commander was an experienced sailor and handled his ship well. He did a great deal of damage, and one day caught up with the convoy in which we ought to have sailed from the Clyde. Ships were sunk and lives were lost. The Duchess had stuck on a sandbank and we had grumbled unmercifully about it at the time, but Fate did us a good turn that day. It seemed that the warships which escorted our little replacement convoy had left us alone for a while, fought the Bismarck and sunk her.

172

It would have been nice to know it at the time: we could have given them three very rousing and sincere cheers when they reappeared.

There is one more co-incidence connected with this episode. My future wife, Kathleen, was in the WRNS during the war. Whilst we were on our way to the Clyde, she, with others in her WRNS section, had been given her medical examination, had returned from draft leave, and received her movement orders to travel to the Clyde for embarkation with the very same convoy, taking them to the Middle East. The WRNS knew where they were going. It is almost 100% certain that Kathleen would have been in the convoy caught by the Bismarck. WRNS lives were lost, but Providence moved again in a mysterious way. At the very last moment her journey to the Clyde was cancelled. No-one had ever explained why, but the girls had been bitterly disappointed.

CHAPTER TWENTY EIGHT –
First Port of Call, and On

Freetown.

As dawn broke the straight line of the horizon had changed to humps and bumps. There was land – Africa, the real Africa, David Livingstone stuff. At the moment it was too far away to make out anything in detail, even through binoculars, but every nautical mile enlarged the humps and bumps until a definite outline of hills and green lowland came into view.

After the usual boat drill we were dismissed for the day; it seemed even the officers wanted to see everything. The ship's speed dropped and, with our escorts in line astern, the Duchess entered the wide estuary of the river at Freetown. For the first time in my life I saw palm trees and, beyond a sandy fringe, the thick jungle of "Darkest Africa." Later, when the ship was at anchor, it was possible to spot monkeys in the trees. Colonial houses nestled among the greenery along the bank sides. A Union Jack flew here and there.

Our very slow passage up river was brought to a noisy halt as the anchor plunged into the turquoise green water. After weeks of throbbing vibration, the ship stilled as someone on the bridge rang down, "Finish with engines," and we could feel the silence. It was so peaceful.

Opposite the anchorage was an imposing edifice that might have been Government House, and around a square there were other buildings, all brilliantly dazzling white in the incredibly hot sun.

At last we were given the order to change into tropical kit and what a relief it was. The air aboard the ship was so hot and heavy that even the revolving fans did little to make it bearable. Outside, a still, humid atmosphere like the heat from an open oven door, made the view shimmer. We leaned on the rails in the shade of an overhanging deck and gasped for breath, reluctant to miss anything, though it was uncomfortable to move.

We had all expected to be allowed a little time ashore to see the sights, although from our observations there wasn't a lot to Freetown. Nothing happened. Small boats came and went carrying khaki uniforms with flat hats and red tabs, or white topped hats and gold braid, but no movement of the Rudyard Kipling/North West Frontier KD of the riff-raff. Presumably if this was the "White Man's Grave" only those of high rank were not in any danger and we ordinary soldiers were to be saved from a fate worse than death. A broadcast over the Tannoy announced that Freetown was alive with malarial-bearing mosquitoes and we were to keep all portholes and doors closed after dusk, just a little something else to add to our discomfort and exhaustion.

The Duchess took on water and when I looked down onto the filthy decrepit water boat alongside I had to wonder exactly what was being pumped into our tanks, knowing how many disease carrying creatures begin life under water. The fuel tender was much cleaner, being "Shell."

The wreck of an oil tanker lay in shallow water nearby. At first glance it looked perfectly sound, maybe waiting to unload its cargo. On closer inspection, however, a very large jagged hole could be spotted down by the water line where a U boat had scored a bull`s eye. Miraculously, the ship did not appear to have been on fire. Perhaps she was travelling light. We never knew the story of her destruction but the sight of that big hole in the hull was a sobering thought for those of us who still had many miles to travel on seas where the enemy lurked. A hole in the Duchess like the one in the tanker would most certainly leave us swimming.

When all was still and shimmering in the mid-day heat, an aircraft tore across the anchorage at zero feet. I happened to be on deck in the shade at the time, hoping for a waft of air. I saw the plane turn and come screaming back towards us. Astonishingly, it had Italian markings: a white cross on its tail and the Fascist bundle of sticks and a chopper on its wings. The sound of the enemy`s guns ripped the air but, although we were a big enough target, nothing seemed to hit us. By now the gunners on all the British ships had woken up and were throwing explosive at the rapidly fleeing Italian. He got away, but his sortie was a bit of a puzzle to everyone. Nobody could really work out where his base could be because the Italians didn`t have colonies on the west side of Africa, though there might have been an airfield in the southern Sahara, and there was no rumour of an Italian aircraft carrier in the vicinity even if they had one. The plane was a single seater fighter. For such an aircraft to fly a considerable distance to make two sweeps across Freetown, firing once, without destroying anything, seemed a fruitless risk and a wasted effort.

A couple of days later, just after dawn, we sailed slowly out into the Atlantic again. The Duchess of Bedford and her two ladies in waiting were guarded, it seemed, by a large number of the Home Fleet. It was a fine morning and getting hotter by the minute.

Life aboard ship had, by now, settled into a very boring routine. Lectures had fizzled out, either stifled by the heat or brought to a standstill because the list of topics was exhausted.

It was rather pleasant to stroll down to the great cream and gold dining room, there to be waited upon by the peacetime stewards of the crew. Few of us took more than fresh fruit, juice and bread and jam for breakfast, but it was vital to drink gallons of tea to stave off dehydration. By ten o`clock in the morning most of the liquid imbibed at breakfast had been sweated out. The only relief from the terrific heat inside and out was to take bath after bath and showers in between. We could fill a bath to the brim because it came directly from the sea. Although it was most pleasant to lie in, the temperature of the water was in the seventies, though cool by comparison with the surrounding air. After a bath we then had the problem of the salt on the skin. It was acceptable if we could dry ourselves quickly but allowing salt water to dry left a white crust which caused unpleasant irritations once dressed. Talcum powder might have helped but there wasn`t any. Fresh water to shower off the salt would have been the perfect answer to the problem but it wasn`t allowed, so even baths and showers were a mixed blessing.

After boat drill, which was a sweltering chore, most of us lay in any shade where there was a little breeze from the ship`s movement. Lunch was sometimes taken, sometimes not. Unfortunately, although the menu was quite varied and remarkably good, printed out on elaborate cards at each table, all too often the meal was hot, I suspected due to the influence of the army cooks. I missed my lunch on many occasions which, health-wise, wasn`t very sensible but the heat in the dining room, despite huge fans, combined with the smell of hot food, rapidly drove me back to my shady spot.

Hardly a soul moved during the baking afternoons. Even the crew weren`t in evidence, although we felt sure there must be somebody driving the ship. On all sides the deep aquamarine ocean stretched away to the horizon. The ships around us didn`t even seem to be moving. I thought of those lines from the "Ancient Mariner" – "a painted ship on a painted ocean." The circumstances were hardly the same: the high bow waves of the vessels told of their speed, the green creamy foam thrown to either side by their passage, whilst the straight line of the wakes broke the mirror calm of the south Atlantic.

I was fascinated by the warships, steaming close enough for me to look at their details through my binoculars. Sometimes guns moved in practice on the cruisers, or flags ran up and down on halliards, or a white capped sailor moved among the crowded weaponry which occupied every nook and cranny.

The aircraft carrier gave me hours of interest. Its huge bulk glided through the water, steady as a rock, vast and powerful. Seafires and Swordfish were lined up on the afterdeck, but they never took off. They might have done had danger threatened but, much to my disappointment, they never moved throughout the whole journey.

One day, one of the cruisers did catapult off a Walrus amphibian. It disappeared over the horizon and was away a long time. Eventually the plane returned, settled near its parent ship and was hoisted aboard.

As we ploughed our way for mile after mile there wasn`t much to look at other than the shipping around, but every now and then nature provided a little light relief.

For the first time in my life I saw flying fish. These swift, silvery, fairy-like creatures swam alongside our ship in large shoals. In appearance they looked very like a full grown herring, but their fins were much elongated, so much so that they really looked and acted like wings. They could not imitate the wing beat of a bird; rather did they gather speed beneath the surface of the water then plane upward and out of their natural environment to skim four or five feet above the waves, eventually gliding back down to plunge into the sea again. They sometimes followed the ship for many miles then, as suddenly as they appeared, some officer fish gave the order and they were gone. Perhaps fish followed ships for the garbage thrown overboard and, goodness knows, there must have been a tremendous amount for the Duchess to get rid of. A wartime instruction forbade the dumping of rubbish into the sea during the hours of daylight, and we were warned never to throw even a cigarette packet overboard. Quantities of food, papers, cans, etc., would be a glorious marker for a submarine or aircraft to trail a convoy. During the night when such rubbish would not be visible it would sink to the bottom and little would be left on the surface by dawn.

Some days the flying fish were replaced with a school of porpoises. They are graceful creatures, diving and surfacing in perfect unison, a troupe of aquatic ballet dancers. I also saw the occasional shark, and once a whale in the distance, a large black humped shape, spouting as it swam along parallel with the convoy.

Strangely enough, even well away from land there were always large sea birds, albatrosses and skuas. Even when land wasn`t visible, we knew by the rapid increase in the number of gulls circling above that we were near to a coast. Sea birds were amazingly aerodynamic and could glide for long distances, keeping pace with hardly any movement of the wings other than a slight tilt as they rode an air current. We amused ourselves by flicking small squares of bread at passing gulls to be caught and swallowed in flight. There was never any danger of betraying our position to an enemy submarine by means of a 1" square of bread because none ever reached the water. A hungry gull would see to that, even at the risk of a mid-air collision which happened occasionally.

Time passed slowly and the weather cooled slightly as we left the equator behind and moved south. The days were long and terribly boring but the part which sticks in my mind most was the night.

During the day we could slop around in PE slippers, shirt or no shirt, and shorts. Even underpants weren`t frowned upon. As the heat of the day slowly dropped we`d make our way to our cabins first to have another bath and then to change for dinner. The order was to be fully dressed even to boots, puttees and webbing belt, with shirt worn inside the shorts. Once suitably attired, we`d make our way down to the dining room. We all had a table to go to, four to each, and I shared mine with the Orderly Sergeant and two others from the Artillery. Dinner would be fruit juice then soup with a bun, nearly always good but never second helpings. The main course was a roast with vegetables, never a cold course with salad. Finally, we could choose a dessert of tart, fruit, ice cream or a milk pudding. Not a bad meal except that after the heat of the day and the effort of dressing in a rather uncomfortable uniform, appetite was dimmed. The only drink with the meal was water, warm, insipid and no ice. How I longed for something with a tang.

After dinner, one choice was a book to read and, fortunately, the ship did have both a bookshop and a library. I think I must have read the entire stock! The only alternative was the Lounge, opened after dinner for drinks and Housey-Housey, or Bingo by its modern name. There were pub games and a sweep on the day`s mileage. The smoky atmosphere and lack of ventilation in the Lounge didn`t attract me every night, although I did go sometimes for a change and for a drink.

I think it was here that I had my first taste of beer. It was cold and quite palatable, all bottled and gassy, and as far as I remember Ind Coope, Bass and Guinness. My efforts at bingo were a failure, as were the guesses I made to forecast the ship's mileage, but I had to do something other than read.

I found going into the Sergeants' Mess and WOs' Mess a little difficult. All my friends were down in "tourist" class, not having sergeant's rank. The sergeants of my own Unit were not exactly welcoming to someone so rapidly promoted, all were much older than me, and we had nothing in common. The Jarrow working class background, whilst not to be criticised, was poles apart from mine. These were all hardened drinkers who could dispose of pint after pint whilst I drank only to quench my thirst.

Early in the voyage I made myself stick with their company one night. Round after round came in including, I'm sure, more of mine than I should have paid for. The inevitable resulted: I was soon hopelessly and helplessly drunk. They had intended this, of course, and I knew I'd have to accept it. My last memory before being carried off unceremoniously to bed, was the leering brown teeth of my Lance Sergeant grinning down at me. He had, at long last, exacted some retribution. When I was still sober earlier in the evening I had known he'd be involved in any attempt to humiliate me. I thought, stupidly, that if he saw me accepting the challenge it might bring out some good in him and encourage a little respect. On the contrary. He was one of those who plied me with more and more drink just so that he could gloat over my demise. His success was absolute but I was determined never to fall into the trap again.

Drinking sessions were the order of every evening, together with Three Card Brag, played in deadly earnest and with large amounts of money changing hands. I never played Brag although there was a time when I thought I'd like to try. Before asking to be dealt in, it seemed only sensible to sit and watch and learn the form. That part of my education didn't take long because it is very much a game of chance rather than skill. There was one rule that definitely put me off before I ever began. The winner, when the game finally did come to an end, was under a very definite obligation to be there the next night to play again. It seemed pretty obvious that this requirement would prevent anyone from keeping a jackpot, aboard this ship anyway.

The playing of Brag went on whenever a few men could get together. Much later, in the desert before the Battle of Alamein, a Brag school was under way. I happened along just as the game finished, fairly late at night, just before the battle. The winner was counting his spoils, having scooped the pool. It ran into a couple of hundred pounds or the Egyptian equivalent. This man`s worry was pitiful. He couldn`t trust anyone with whom he could leave his money, to be collected on his safe return. On the other hand, if he was wounded with his money on him, someone would certainly pinch it from his person. What a dilemma! In the end, he took the risk and carried the £200 odd on his person. Right into the thick of the shot and the shell he was surrounded by his faithful followers who, needless to say, were not protecting his body, only what he carried. The ending was to be expected. A mortar bomb blew the owner of the money to bits, while all his "friends" were so close to him that they suffered the same fate. I never considered there was much to be said for that card game: the stakes were too high.

It was now noticeably cooler but the voyage still dragged on. We`d left Timsbury in March and it was now May. Other than our call at Freetown, all this time had been spent at sea. Fresh water was very strictly rationed to a mere trickle for half an hour in each twenty four hours. Our speed had dropped, as an economy measure, we`d heard. The beer was rationed to two bottles a night. They`d even given up the sweepstake on the miles travelled each day. For some time we must have been in the Southern Hemisphere because each night the brilliant Southern Cross stood out clearly from the myriad stars across the heavens. What a fantastic sight, making even the discomforts of the voyage tolerable.

CHAPTER TWENTY NINE – Civilisation Again, Of Sorts

Aboard ship we always knew when "something was up." The crew appeared from the bowels and began lashing or unlashing something, hosing, scrubbing, oiling, repairing or moving machinery; derricks were unfastened and hatches loosened off. The ship's officers put in an appearance, gold braid shining like new. All was activity and we stirred, too. After hours of peering at the horizon we saw a definite change in the straight line that had been there for so long. Land ahoy!

A mountain with a flat top. Any child knows from geography books that there is one famous mountain with a flat top, Table Mountain which stands behind the bay and city of Cape Town. We'd arrived in South Africa.

As the ship moved nearer, the shapes of glittering white buildings and sky scrapers appeared through the blue heat haze. The engine throbs changed and our bow wave fell as we slowed.

What an attractive harbour Cape Town has, the encircling piers surrounding a vast stretch of mirror calm water.

The pilot boat and tugs fussed around the Duchess and we were soon edging gently between the piers towards a quay over on the far side of the harbour. Cape Town will always be a busy place but in wartime it was an absolute hive of industry, seething with activity, noise, smoke, fumes and smells quite foreign to us.

The Tannoy announced that we were to leave the ship for a route march ashore soon after the ship docked. For once, this news was not greeted with the usual chorus of groans and catcalls: everyone was more than ready to stretch their legs and see the sights at the same time. Furthermore, we were British troops on our way to a war zone and surely the South Africans would be as interested to see us as we were to see them.

To set foot on terra firma after so long at sea felt most odd, almost intoxicating. For weeks we'd been making allowances for the movement of the deck at each step. Now the ground was absolutely still. To put one foot in front of the other sent shock waves through the body and, to our amusement, we had the greatest of difficult even walking in a straight line.

Going on parade to march through the streets of Cape Town meant the elaborate performance of lining up in columns of three, "dressing," and being inspected, and there had to be some rifle drill to refresh everyone's memory of all those strange movements necessary to get a rifle on and off the shoulder. I was mighty glad I had my revolver instead, even with its contra-Hague Convention bullets.

Eventually, after all the shouting and bawling which is essential to everything the army does in public, and rather more practice than had been anticipated, we were ready to move off into the city. We weren't the only ones going: the Air Force, Artillery, Infantry, Ordnance and lots of other odds and sods had been "winkled out," too. That the latter had been dragged out of their many cubby holes, much against their will, was quite obvious. There are little branches of the army which don't normally become involved in silly things like parades, for example, the admin staff, Pay Corps, Education Corps, Military Police and Intelligence Corps, and others with even more obscure titles. More often than not, this lot were too "busy" to join in the drudgery of squad drill. In some cases, their reasons might very well be genuine but, of course, the frequency of their excuses gave rise to suspicions in the minds of those of us who hadn't any excuses.

It was a very long column of British forces which set off that morning to "show the flag." Unfortunately, we had no band to help us keep in step and provide the uplift military music can give to marching troops. That, together with the fact that we hadn't walked more than a few yards for weeks, produced a very rickety performance which must have raised a few eyebrows among the populace. If our efforts at marching in step in a straight line looking militarily smart were anything to go by, the confidence of the South Africans in the British Army and Air Force must have reached an all time low that day.

Before we'd covered a mile most of us were feeling quite exhausted and many had sore shoulders where their rifles rested. Not a few men had had to fall out with cramp and they were promptly ferried back to the ship in taxis – free. Needless to say, cramp was rapidly catching!

We stopped and, just to prove the stop had nothing to do with exhaustion, did a bit of rifle drill there and then in the street. After standing easy for a while, off we went again. There were people around but, because we hadn't yet cleared the dock area, those along the pavements were workers going about their everyday tasks, menial jobs, so most workers were black men. Their fascination was more of amazement than of interest. We got the impression that they didn't know what we were doing, why we were doing it, nor even why we were there. There was certainly no demonstration of welcome displayed, not even in their expressions.

We never reached Cape Town city that day. It was quite obvious that to go on would reduce the whole column to a shambles, officers included. We were turned about and more or less dawdled back, rifles at the trail and feet shuffling.

Never was I so glad to see the dear old lady again, nestled against the quay with a lazy wisp of smoke going straight up into the hot blue sky. Anything, even the stifling heat between decks, was better than route marching. The temperature was certainly cooler than in Freetown, but the weather here was equal to one of our very best British summers. It was nice for relaxing but not for doing anything energetic.

There was terrific activity going on around the Duchess. She was being refuelled, re-watered, and re-victualled. Huge crates were being swung off the dockside and lowered inboard. It was a happy feeling to know that the austerity of the last few weeks was to be left behind and we could look forward, once again, to good food, drink, fresh fruit and some luxuries.

Despite our miserable performance on that first day we weren`t to be allowed off the hook: for the remaining four days in Cape Town we went for a route march every morning, each somewhat longer that the last. I suppose the Powers That Be were right: we had become flabby, we`d certainly become lazy, and the exercise was vital.

The crew of the ship had a chance to tidy up and sort things out while we`d all gone off on our little walk, and it probably facilitated a faster loading programme, too. We grumbled at first but, as our feet hardened and our bodies toned up, it became easier. Furthermore, we were now reaching the populated part of Cape Town and the shopping areas. The people there, all white, did take an interest, did express welcome. There was a lot of hand waving, clapping and even a cheer here and there. Spirits rose.

The first day in Cape Town was exhausting. The excitement of our arrival, the march and its farcical ending, and the bustling activity around the Duchess, all played a part. Everyone was waiting for word to say we were going to be allowed to go ashore alone. During the afternoon Company Orders were posted as usual but this time there was a rush to read them.

With the regularity of the rising sun, Company Orders appear each day for any army unit whether or not there is anything to say. For the period of time we'd been at sea, the Company Sergeant consulted the CO as usual and then typed out whatever messages he had to pass on to us in the way of instruction or interest. Seldom, if ever, had there been anything other than the same old times of Parade, Boat Drill and Lights out. These gems of literature rated little more than a glance from even the most conscientious of us but now we awaited company orders with huge anticipation.

The foolscap page arrived and was duly pinned up. From after lunch each day we were free to "go ashore," but must return to the ship by midnight. There was a reminder that we had to conduct ourselves in a manner befitting a soldier in the British Army, etc., etc., and a strict order that on no account would anyone enter the black quarter of the city – it was dangerous to any white man! Furthermore, it was pointed out that South Africa is a foreign country with different laws which must be respected. This was a reference to what we now call apartheid, and meant we were not to consort with, speak to, or be seen with a black or "coloured" person, as they were referred to in those days. Otherwise, however, we could do as we liked and the people of Cape Town were looking forward to welcoming us.

There was a sting in the tail of the Company Order for me. Now that we were tied up to the shore and the ship connected to the land by its gangplank, a guard had to be mounted at the doorway in the ship's side, and that gangplank must be watched to prevent the illegal entry of any intruder, spy or saboteur. We would be assisted in this responsible and dangerous task by an officer and NCOs of the Military Police. They would be available to make any necessary arrest or shoot down any person or persons trying to force their way aboard, if you can imagine anyone trying to do it, but we certainly couldn't. For the next twenty four hours, starting there and then, I wasn't going to enjoy the fleshpots of Cape Town. As Sergeant of the Guard, I had to change immediately into best battledress and equipment, and be fully armed, with half a dozen unfortunate drivers to help. To say I was disappointed is putting it mildly, but of course I knew who had it in for me, putting my name down as Guard Commander on the first night.

From lunchtime onward the ship began to empty as the liberty-men, dressed in their best KD or battledress, waved me "Cheerio" and merrily clumped down the gangplank on their way to town. I suppose there might have been the odd sympathetic remark but most revellers didn't even notice me standing by the ship's exit in full equipment, trousers creased, buttons and boots shining – the usual bull required for any guard duty.

By teatime only the buzzing of machinery disturbed the rather eerie quietness of the vessel. Very little moved. Hardly anyone was to be seen: only the Air Force guard, the MP contingent in the background, and those of the ship's crew who, like ourselves, were unfortunate enough to be detailed for duty. It was strange to have the vast dining room to myself, all the other NCOs being ashore. At least there was an unlimited amount of everything to eat.

The time dragged by slowly. Quite early in the evening darkness fell very suddenly and the sight which met my eyes when I looked across to Cape Town will remain vividly in my memory for the rest of my life. We'd left England in a total blackout which had been in operation for two years. Now here was Cape Town in wartime, a blaze of twinkling lights, broken here and there by great splashes of colour where neon signs advertised. It brought quite a lump to my throat, partly because it reminded me of a world so much changed by war and partly because I was confined to the hulk of the Duchess while everyone else was enjoying themselves. Chiefly it hurt, though, because at that moment I felt utterly homesick, something that had never bothered me since we'd left Britain.

Much as I hated my role here aboard ship I couldn't tear myself away from the fascinating fairyland of sparkling diamonds which spread like a vast tiara round the hillside upon which Cape Town was built. It wasn't quite black dark yet and the coloured lights of shipping reflected long fingers of red, green and white across the calm waters of the bay. Behind it all, Table Mountain provided an imposing backdrop of black against the deep purple sky. I spent quite some time drinking in this spectacular panorama and, in the circumstances, had plenty of time to stand and gaze.

Orders were that all troops would return aboard by midnight. At round about ten thirty a few rather sober types began the first trickle home.

The gangplank was a wooden construction with slats of wood across to ensure a secure foothold, and the sides were enclosed by a sort of fence. The top end of the walkway had two metal pegs underneath which slotted into loops welded to the ship's side. The gangplank fell away steeply to the quayside. For anyone sober it was not difficult to ascend the steep gradient and enter the ship through the wide iron door at the top where we were waiting to extend a hand of welcome. This extended hand was a necessity because there was a gap of about eighteen inches between the end of the gangplank and the ship`s side, designed to allow for the vessel`s rise and fall with the tide. On this particular night it was at its widest and we were told to warn each returning person of the gap.

The influx of soldiery increased around eleven o`clock and these arrivals had wined and dined rather well, rather too well by and large. A few thoughtful souls were tidily sick on the quayside before hauling themselves slowly up the gangplank. These individuals we had to warn sharply before helping them over the gap. There our responsibility ended and we hoped they eventually arrived back at the right cabin or bunk.

The next group to arrive were the real drunks. It was quite funny to see their approach. Some were weaving from side to side, mostly still clutching a bottle, others were supported by equally intoxicated friends, while a few more disgorged from taxis. All, without exception, were merry and singing at the tops of their voices. It was difficult to deal with this lot on the gangplank because, in their state, most found it difficult even to climb the steep walkway. It was considerably more of a problem to get a hopeless drunk over the eighteen inch gap with a sixty foot drop beneath.

As you might guess, the inevitable happened. One man, despite warnings, missed his footing and slipped, feet first, through the gap. There was no premeditation about my actions: I simply grabbed the only part of his body around which I could close my fingers – his hair. By the hair and with help, I managed to haul him back to safety. He never even knew of his near escape from a rather nasty "killed on active service." Being quite sober myself I was far more shaken than he. The stupid man went off to his bed singing, "Nellie Dean" or some such ditty at the top of his voice. I`ll bet he wondered why he had such a sore scalp as well as head next morning and some missing skin from his knees and elbows. Naturally, I didn`t receive any thanks for saving his life.

By midnight the flow of merrymakers had dwindled to a trickle and those arriving at that hour did so by taxi at high speed. One man was completely unconscious. We had to carry him aboard on a stretcher. The problem then arose of who was to pay the taxi? Naturally, the driver wanted his money and was quite voluble in his demands for it. The drunk was in such a stupor he was eliminated completely from the discussion. I certainly had no intention of paying: the soldier wasn`t even an Engineer. The only solution seemed to be to bring the MP officer in on the case. I found his cabin and, after considerable banging on the door, he appeared, only half in uniform, bleary eyed and obviously awakened from a deep sleep and an alcoholic one too, by the look of him. After a smart salute I explained the situation and his reply was a rather tetchy,

"Well, deal with it, Sergeant. That`s what you are there for!"

I pointed out, as carefully as I dare, because one doesn`t tangle with any military policeman if possible, much less an officer of that ilk, that I`d dealt with every difficulty up to now to the best of my ability but when it came to a demand for money – which I didn`t have – I felt that the matter required the intervention of his skilled expertise. My diplomacy was wasted on him. The alcohol swirling round his brain played havoc with his focus and there were signs that such support as his knees had given was about to let him down, quite literally. As was to be expected I suppose, he fell back on that hoary defence so beloved of a certain section of commissioned officers who, fortunately, were in a minority. Drawing himself up to his full height by means of the door fittings, and taking a deep breath which reduced him to paroxysm of coughing, he finally spluttered some phrase which was unintelligible, but the meaning was clear.

"Are you questioning my order?" or "You heard what I said," or just plain, "Do as you`re bloody well told."

With what dignity he could muster, and to me that was none, he slithered about and re-entered his cabin with a slam of the door in my face. I was not amused.

The taxi driver wasn`t at all pleased that I hadn`t returned with the money for his fare. I could only tell him that if he left his name and address, the amount of his fare would be sent to him by the War Office. He hadn`t much option other than to accept. By the time the War Office coughed up, if ever, we`d be far away.

Our stretcher case snored in his stupor all night as we continued our guard at the gangplank. In the morning, when he came to, amidst a lot of moaning from his hangover, we were to learn that his wallet, with his every penny, was missing. He swore he had it when he got into the taxi. I wonder where that money went?

I`d gone on guard duty at 18.00 hours the first night which meant that I didn`t come off until 18.00 hours the next night. It was the most boring and frustrating period of wasted time for me and I was bitterly disappointed and upset that it had to be me. I knew full well the Guard Commander had to be one the senior NCOs in the Unit, and all the other sergeants were older, with long service, and were contemporaries and buddies of the CSM. Obviously, it had been a case of, "Well, if it has to be someone it might as well be West. He doesn`t drink and he is certainly too green to object." They were dead right.

By the time I was relieved there was very little time for anything. My friends had all left long ago for the city. I walked to the gates and took a taxi to the main street. For the next few hours I just wandered around looking at the brilliantly lit and well stocked shops and enjoying as best I could, on my own, the great city of Cape Town. I was lonely but, at least, I was now free to make the best of what little time was left before we sailed again.

Altogether, our small convoy lay alongside the quay for four days. My time ashore amounted to about two and a bit days.

CHAPTER THIRTY—Cape Town

Needless to say, those who had already been ashore were full of the sights to be seen, and the overwhelming kindness and generosity shown by the people of the city. By the time we were ready to leave the ship each day, queues of cars, and even people on foot, were waiting outside the dock gates. As each serviceman appeared, he was swamped with offers of genuine hospitality. If he accepted, the lucky one would be wined, dined and entertained for the day. There was no class, rank or favour shown: every man received the same offer, no matter how high or how lowly his rank. The stories of entertainment in the beautiful homes of Cape Town were almost unbelievable. It was humbling to think that these people, many of them with British roots, of course, would do this, but I squirmed at the thought of how some men in the Unit would behave when entertained in a style never before experienced, imagining with horror how, knowing no better, they might let the side down within the first five minutes.

The morning parade on my first promised day of freedom seemed to drag on and on. When the "Dismiss" finally came I was determined to get away from the Duchess at the earliest possible moment, even to the extent of foregoing lunch. By one o`clock I was walking towards the gate in my best battledress. I'd decided on this too-warm rig rather than the cooler khaki drill because, being as embarrassingly old as it was, I felt sure it would put off any South African who knew about the Boer War! And the topee? Well!

The visit to Cape Town first introduced us to the stylish and much more acceptable drill uniform designed for and worn by the South African forces. To start with, the colour was a pale greenish khaki and much easier on the eye than the putty/buff of ours. Their shorts were shorter and cut to fit more closely to the legs, unlike the baggy clown-like long shorts or short longs we had to wear. Their knee length stockings were far more sensible than the footless "hose" which we pulled up over our army issue grey socks to the knee, followed by those stupid, frustrating puttees. Army regulations dictated that the tapes on each puttee would be tucked in, not tied. The very first time we saluted, bringing the foot down with a smart stamp as per Army Regs, the puttee on that leg invariably slithered down over the boot in a limp coil, leaving us looking like Just William caught with his socks down again.

The safari jacket designed for the South African soldier had patch pockets and a collar with lapels which lay flat, as they do on any normal jacket. It was well cut and had a belt to maintain its shape. Our jacket, made of rough "Aertex" material, had no belt because, according to Army Regulations, the jacket had to be worn either inside the shorts or outside, depending upon the position of the sun! Our collar, if it could be called that, was completely shapeless and even laundering couldn`t improve it. The two pockets in the KD jacket, one on each side at the top, fastened with small thick unmanageable buttons. There was no provision for the addition of rank badges on this antiquated uniform. Any stripes were merely lengths of ordinary white haberdashery tape. We had to judge the right length for each tape, hem the ends, bend it into a lumpy overlap to form the V, then sew it onto the stiff material. Trying to ensure that three chevrons, all home made, lay upright and parallel was incredibly difficult. Above mine, of course, I had to fix the little bomb. This meant making a hole in the material to take the pins on the back of this awkward metal part of my insignia. Due to the weight of the bomb, it always hung down or sideways or both because the material of the jacket was neither rigid nor strong enough to support it. South African badges were embroidered separately onto patches of uniform material so all insignia was custom made, neat, rather smaller, and no trouble to affix.

When I reached the gate, I was met with a great string of cars stretching away on both sides of the road, the owners standing alongside, smiling a welcome. It was embarrassing, moving and intimidating all at the same time, to be almost trapped into accepting hospitality. How could one possibly refuse and – this seemed the problem – whom did one choose?

The difficulty never arose. My hostess, a very elegant, well dressed, elderly lady, chose me. I say she was elderly but she would probably dispute that, having obviously engaged the very best beauticians to disguise the fact. She exuded charm. It was strange, being "chosen" like this, rather as a puppy must feel when it is lifted out of the pet shop window and sold to the lady who has just got out of the big car. I was ushered into the back of an enormous plush American limousine, my hostess took the wheel, and with a swish we were off.

It is difficult now after all these years to recount every place we visited on that journey but it was a lightning and comprehensive tour of Cape Town and its environs.

Two places do stick in my memory. One was a national monument which stood on a hill and, as I remember, there were many steps up to a covered wagon on a plinth. It seemed to elicit a hushed reverence from my hostess which had not been in evidence previously during her non-stop commentary as we toured around.

The other place was a stretch of coastline round a bay on the other side of Table Mountain. Mountainous waves crashed onto rocks and a howling cold gale blew. Of course, it was winter, mid-winter, in Cape Town.

I was taken only part of the way up Table Mountain because the top had its "table cloth" on – cloud – and due to the gale blowing, the cable car wasn't running. We wouldn't have seen much through the thick cloud anyway.

I was beginning to feel rather peckish and wishing I had had lunch before coming ashore when somewhere on Table Mountain we pulled in to a lay-by and my hostess produced a picnic hamper. The lady nibbled, I devoured, and we washed down a sumptuous meal with delicious and strong white wine.

The last part of the day was the return to the boat through the centre of the city. We stopped at a couple of the largest stores and I was shown around, complete with commentary about South Africa's growth from nothing, its affluence despite the war, and its determination to stand at Britain's side. She spoke to this person and that, and everyone seemed to know her.

On the way back to the ship we passed the black quarter. There were actually wooden barriers across the road saying something like "Danger: No Admittance" or "Enter at Your Own Risk." Very little was said by my guide other than some casual observation like,

"They all have to be kept together in there for their own safety," but I couldn't work out why.

What I did learn during our very short stay was that the division between black and white was a mile wide and never likely to be narrowed. I saw with my own eyes policemen beat a group of blacks with sticks without any apparent provocation. The black men were standing on a corner not doing anything as far as I could see, and I was quite near and on foot when the police approached them. Suddenly the beating started and continued until the black men ran off.

Perhaps we hadn't expected apartheid to be so rigidly enforced, being relatively uninformed about this strange law in a modern civilised society. In the shops and the main parts of town a black person was to be seen only very rarely and he would be performing some menial task. In certain areas black people were allowed to circulate but many notices left them in no doubt about what they were allowed to do or not do. In parks and public places some seats and paths were for blacks only and all the others were for whites. Toilets had their own entrances for blacks, if they were allowed in at all, and black people could travel only on the cramped outside parts of public transport.

There were notices everywhere forbidding blacks to do anything but breathe, it seemed. They even had to step off the pavement to allow free passage to a white. This seemed so strange to us, and made me feel particularly uncomfortable. We believed that the opening up of Africa and the abolition of the slave trade had made all men equal.

It had been a very full and interesting day and I`d enjoyed it immensely. We`d travelled quite a few miles and seen an awful lot. I thought I might have been left hungry but my hostess had even thought of that. The car was luxurious, smooth and comfortable and built for sightseeing. In some ways I was sorry I hadn`t been taken to her home. It must have been something special judging by the wealth displayed in the car, the elegance of her dress and the brilliance of the diamonds which flashed from her rings and necklace.

I was delivered to the dock gates just in time to enjoy evening dinner, tired and glad to be back. Saying cheerio and proffering thanks was not as difficult as I`d expected. Somehow or other my hostess made that as smooth as the running of her car.

It may have been the case that the people entertaining our troops each day made it a practice not to invite the same person a second time. That suited me because, although I`d had a wonderful tour of the city and my hostess had been more than kind, I wasn`t sure I could stand more of the same.

The third day I had lunch first just to be on the safe side. Bert hadn`t made any particular arrangements so we decided to make our way down to the dock gates together. Like me, he`d found being on his own the day before a little too much.

By the time we got there quite a few of the waiting cars had gone, but a lady and her teenage son came up to us, made their invitation and we accepted.

All private cars seemed to be powerful and comfortable so Bert and I settled ourselves in the back seats among plush cushions. As we drove into the city centre, the conversation hinged on what we had seen and done up to now. I think our present hosts were surprised at how much had been packed into one day and it left them with the dilemma of where to go now. We, of course, were in their hands. For myself, I'd have been happy to have been taken to their home. Lots of our people had been given hospitality in this way and they all extolled the virtues of the South African homes – cool, spacious, beautifully equipped and designed, and all with swimming pools, it seemed. The home invitation hadn't happened yesterday and it didn't seem as though it was going to happen today, despite one or two subtle hints from us! We were in no position to suggest a programme for the day so we could do no other than wait and see what was to happen.

The boy and his mother began a discussion in Afrikaans. Whether this was deliberate or whether they found that language more natural I don't know, but it did seem slightly odd. Eventually English came back almost without us noticing the change, and we were asked if we'd like to see a National Park and some wildlife. This did appeal to us, real wild lions and jungle life, so it was agreed.

I cannot remember how long the journey took. For hours the car purred along a road which didn't seem to have any corners. The plume of dust raised by our passage hung in the air, blotting out any view behind. No towns appeared en route. We stopped only once, at a petrol station, miles from anywhere and got out to stretch our legs, drink a bottle of pop and admire the scenery. It was just flat dry ground with stunted trees and scrub and, away in the distance, blue mountains.

Off we went again, mile after mile, the blue mountains coming nearer. To begin with there was quite a lot of chat about where we came from, our families, what we used to do in civilian life, what we did now and where we were going. Both Bert and I looked at each other on hearing these latter questions and decided upon very vague answers. It may have been perfectly innocent, but we had grown to be very security minded.

The conversation changed at some point or other and we found ourselves being given a rather hefty dose of South African propaganda, particularly the mistaken attitude of the rest of the world to the white South Africans' treatment of the black people. It amounted to South Africa being a white man's country, discovered, developed and paid for by the whites. Those of other shades would be allowed to exist there provided they kept their place in society (slave level) and never attempt to rise above it. The black man, they told us, was ignorant, dirty, dangerous and quite incapable of being anything else. He was tolerated but had to be strictly controlled, watched and, if necessary, punished. There was a place for the black person in South African life but only as a menial labourer. His pay was low because he didn't need much in life and because to give him more would only tempt him into higher ambitions for which he wasn't suited. Blacks would be housed, if they worked, but only in special areas well away from towns and white areas. Only the white South Africans understood the Black Man and his problems. The White Man was kind to him but firm, as with wayward children. Finally, nothing and no-one would change South African policy.

Both Bert and I listened to this long and forceful "talk" and tried, out of sheer politeness, not to blow up. These people really believed what they were saying and were absolutely sure they were right. We did try to argue that all men are equal in the sight of God, black or white, but it wasn't going to work. Anyway, our hosts were devout Christians, too, probably more devout than we were, at least as far as church going and hymn singing were concerned, so the God bit was a waste of breath.

It was a relief when rather more greenery appeared on either side of the road and the car suddenly skidded to a halt. For one ghastly moment I had a suspicion that they might have brought us all this way to kick us out into the wild and we'd never be heard of again. No-one knew with whom we'd left Cape Town nor where we'd gone and we'd certainly never have been looked for out here. Not that there would have been much left to find but bare bones lying around, and we could see clouds of vultures in the air above something in the distance.

We were completely misjudging the generosity and kindness of our hosts, of course. They were just being thoroughly patriotic South Africans who, despite this one failing as a nation, were loyal in their support of Britain.

We'd even misjudged the reason for the sudden stop. Rhino, white rhino. Mind you, they didn't look very white to me: they looked distinctly grubby. We spent a while watching the rhino, which were doing precisely nothing, and then away we went again. After half an hour or so, the car glided to a standstill while a herd of Thompson's Gazelle was pointed out. Thompson's, Johnson's, Robertson's gazelle? They all looked alike to us and in their amazing camouflage were very difficult indeed to spot. We marvelled at the skill of our South African friends being able to pick them out whilst driving at speed. The only other wild animals we were lucky enough to find were a few giraffe, and some baboons. Of lions there was no sign and although trumpeting elephants were audible, they weren't visible. There was, naturally, no sign of jungle!

Perhaps it is wrong to be critical but it did seem a rather expensive and time-consuming exercise to travel all this distance to see distant groups of animals in the wild.

A very sumptuous picnic was produced. Large chunks of ham, legs of chicken and salad with tasty pickles, and ice cold wine. The picnics offered by my hosts on both days' outings were, undoubtedly, the highlight of the hospitality. We had a table and chairs for this one, too, with a cloth on the table. I half expected that the smell of fried chicken, even cold, might have attracted a lion or two but nothing happened, although our hosts were continually on the look-out for baboons which they said were more dangerous than the big cats when people were having a picnic. They kept a big stick handy.

We finished our meal in peace and began the journey home. It was a long drive and a long day and we were tired though we'd done nothing. The lights of Cape Town twinkled in the darkness before we got back. I thought perhaps we could ask to be dropped off in the city and go to a restaurant or cinema but by the time we did get into Cape Town we felt too weary to bother, and were happy to be put down at the dock gates. Again, we said our profuse thank yous. I was happy to treat the day as another of the many interesting and exciting events life was presenting me: here today and gone tomorrow. No doubt the South Africans felt they'd done their duty for the war effort and they certainly had, in their own way.

I still hadn't made any particular friend among the other sergeants in our Unit. It may sound prudish or even anti-social but they were all hard drinkers and I wasn't. I didn't really like plain beer because I only took it as a thirst quencher and then only in shandy form. They were also obsessed with sex. It would be ridiculous and untrue to say that I wasn't attracted to a pretty girl, particularly one with a good figure, but the girls our lot were interested in were not the sort I wanted to know. Those girls were pretty enough and their figures were certainly eye-catching, but that was part of their stock in trade. It seemed to me that wherever we went, both at home and abroad, the girls with whom I would have wanted to be friendly kept well clear, or very soon lost interest when they recognised there were men in uniform who wanted something more than companionship and innocent fun out of life.

I still enjoyed the friendship of Bert, Robbo and a few of those fellows with whom I`d gone through quite a lot since we all joined the Territorial Army. Unfortunately, they were still drivers and I was their sergeant. Not that this made any difference to any of us in private, but in public it was very much against the army`s rules. The Military Police would certainly act against us if we were seen together and certain officers were also inclined to apply the laws over-fussily. It was not easy to be together because some entertainment was segregated for officers, sergeants and other ranks. This meant that I usually had to go alone to a dance, a cinema or event. At other times, I wore a shirt without any stripes in order to join my friends, but making sure I had my usual shirt on when leaving and returning to the ship. Sometimes, much later on when Bert and Jack were on leave in Cairo at the same time as me, I borrowed two sergeants` shirts and they wore those all the time. Few of our Unit were out and about in such a big city so it was worth the risk. Had we been stopped and asked to show our pay books we`d have been in trouble but, fortunately, that never happened.

Bert, Robbo and I managed to meet on their deck the third night and we agreed to try and have a day together in Cape Town, declining all offers of hospitality outside the gates. We knew we`d be moving on soon and probably quite suddenly when the time came. It seemed a good idea just to walk around the streets and look at things rather than fly past in a car. We didn`t get a lot of pay but, having spent nothing for so long, we wanted to buy a few presents which we might, one day, get home. Not only that, but we all wanted to sample some restaurant food of our own choice and perhaps go to a cinema afterwards. It was decided that at 1.30 pm we`d leave the ship, not together but within sight of each other until we were clear enough to join up into one party.

Taxis were not expensive so we hopped into one to be taken right into the centre of the city by the Town Hall or whatever the main public building was called. That was a fortunate move because as we got out of the taxi I noticed a dance advertised that evening, with meal included, run by some organisation offering free tickets to HM forces in transit. Without more ado we collected three of the few remaining tickets for later.

The shops in Cape Town were ultra-modern and very well stocked. It was fascinating to wander around and watch the shoppers. Everyone looked well dressed, elegant, prosperous and cool in clothing suitable for the climate. It was their winter but temperatures were still in the mid sixties during the day. There was a wind and at times the sky clouded over but it still seemed very pleasant to us.

We chose a restaurant and had a meal. I cannot remember the menu but I do recall that we enjoyed all we had to eat and drink. There was a "Palm Court" style orchestra to provide background music and everyone in the place seemed to be without a care in the world. Quite a few people stopped when passing our table, to wish us luck and a safe return, and someone even sent over a bottle of wine to supplement the one we'd bought with our meal. There is no doubt that the vast majority of the South African people were very much in sympathy with our cause.

Early in the evening we duly reported to the Town Hall Dance Hall. It was brightly lit and decorated in the most elaborate fashion. Flags, South African and British, were everywhere, as were strings of bunting, banks of glorious flowers, coloured ribbons and so on. The Mayor and all the Corporation were waiting at the door to extend a welcome. Every member of our Forces who entered had their hand thoroughly shaken and then, with typical South African attention to detail, a line of local beauties was waiting to act as partners. There was no choosing a partner; one was simply given the first girl in the queue, labelled with her name in large letters on a card pinned to her ... upper works. The phenomenon we'd already experienced, that all South African girls were good looking – poured from the same mould, in fact – was no less obvious here, so there were no moans or groans: all our lot seemed quite satisfied with their partner from the queue.

There must have been a very thorough briefing for the girls before the dance, something along the lines of, "One drink only, no slipping outside or into dark corners, keep the conversation going, be jolly and light hearted, keep off politics, Blacks, and the war, dance every dance, and make sure your partner eats his fill."

Fortunately, most of these rules suited us well. We weren't there to philander, although there were always those who tried, and they got short shrift! The band was good, the floor marvellous, and all the girls wonderful dancers, partners and hostesses, in a sort of clinical way.

We could certainly enthuse about the food. It seemed that every imaginable dish was there. Shellfish par excellence from shrimps to huge lobsters, tender undercut steaks, succulent lamb chops, pork with crackling, honey cured hams, thick ox tongue slices, sausages of every description, size and flavour, and pies with crusts that melted in the mouth. The side dishes defied description but each tasted even better than it looked, and that is saying something. Roast potatoes, boiled potatoes, creamed potatoes, fried potatoes, chipped potatoes and sweet potatoes to mention just a few, and if anyone wanted bread they had the same difficult choice to make between English crusty, German black, Swedish biscuit and French baguettes, all to be spread with a further choice of butters. We'd had quite reasonable food on the Duchess so far but nothing could compare with this, and we were determined to do justice to it, this being our last meal in this beautiful country. We all ate too much and it was a comforting thought that transport was laid on to take us back to the ship.

Feeling more than replete after two very good meals and a very pleasant day doing what we wanted to do, our taxi driver delivered us safely back at the dock gates and home to the Duchess. The Tannoy announced, shortly after our return, that the ship would sail on the morning tide. We were on the last lap to war.

APPENDIX – Dad`s Box

As children we had heard Dad`s story about losing his box when the unit was hurriedly evacuated from Bécourt before Dunkirk. It was always one of our naggings, to go back and find it.

In 1965 our family went on the adventurous holiday of a lifetime, taking the whole of the summer school holiday to drive through France and down Italy to visit his wartime friend Nando in Sicily. Our parents must have been mad: it was long before the days of mass tourism and mobile phones, air con and Airbnb, and southern Italy was untouched. All we had for backup was a list, given to my mother by her best friend, of convents whose nuns, she was sure, would be prepared to offer assistance should we need it (we did, twice).

We got to Sicily, and back to France again, nearly all in one piece, and before we caught the return boat from Calais to Dover we pestered to go and find Dad`s Box.

Reaching Albert and then Bécourt was no problem and Dad was able to recall the lanes which led to the chateau where he had been based. It was still there and Dad called at the nearby farm to ask if there was a corner where we could pitch our tent for an overnight stay, and use their outside tap to collect water. He explained, in his rudimentary French, that he had been billeted here during the war, twenty five years earlier. The young farmer, whose parents had worked this farm during the war, was very welcoming and after we had erected the tent in a field a short distance away our family of five was invited into the farmhouse for a drink and a chat. During the course of this conversation The Box was mentioned somehow and Dad asked permission from the farmer to have a poke around to see if it could be located.

Full of excitement next day we wandered down to the place Dad thought he`d buried the box. It was in what would be called a "green lane" here, a wide grassy path between high banks topped with bushes by which farmers had access to further fields. We had taken a couple of sticks and a folding camp shovel but despite encouraging Dad to close his eyes at the top of the lane and visualise how far down he had gone before burying the box, then pacing it out and scouring around, we found nothing. It was disappointing, particularly for we kids.

We were just about to give up and return to pack up when the farmer himself arrived with a pick and a heavy spade over his shoulders. He hadn`t known that any soldiery had been here in his father`s day and was keen to see if he could find any signs of activity. This had been part of the First World War zone and plenty of his neighbours were still turning up all sorts of ephemera in their fields.

Within minutes the pick and spade clashed against metal and there was frantic digging and pulling as all sorts of rotten and rusty bits and pieces appeared from below the sods. Dad was horrified to identify it all as German! Iron supports, lengths of barbed wire, unidentifiable pieces of cloth and metal were dragged out and examined. Laurence found a corrugated cylindrical gas mask case which he wanted to keep but it was foul and Mum insisted he toss it aside. Eventually something big was discovered, a good clunk on the end of the spade and obviously of considerable size. This must be it! With much care and effort the object was cleared and brought out for examination. It wasn`t square: it was circular, and flat. Dad recognised it immediately, having been a Royal Engineer. A Teller Mine! At that, the young farmer legged it back up the lane as fast as he could. Dad, however, could see that it wasn`t "primed" and after he had wiggled around with a metal rod we had found, he announced that any explosive which might have been inside had all rotted away. The farmer returned for a closer look.

The Box itself was never found but the Teller mine was scrubbed under the stack yard tap and Laurence was permitted to bring it back to the UK where it became a prized item for Show-And-Tell at school. It lived in the coal shed back home for many years along with Dad`s tin helmet.

Whilst we were in the area Dad took us to see the huge First World War mine crater nearby, and we visited some of the overgrown trenches which were abandoned in copses around the area. In one of those Laurence found a metal "thing" which he and I tossed around between us until Dad got his eye on it and suggested we just "pop it on that wall over there because we are leaving now." It was shaped like a squat tin can with a raised circular flange around the top, and a curved handle attached to one side. After we had driven away we felt Dad let his breath out as he told us it had been a German stick grenade whose wooden handle would have rotted away, and Laurence and I were playing with the remaining explosive end. No wonder we left so suddenly!

Effie Cadwallader
October 2019

Printed by Amazon Italia Logistica S.r.l.
Torrazza Piemonte (TO), Italy

15643181R00119